urrounding Countries

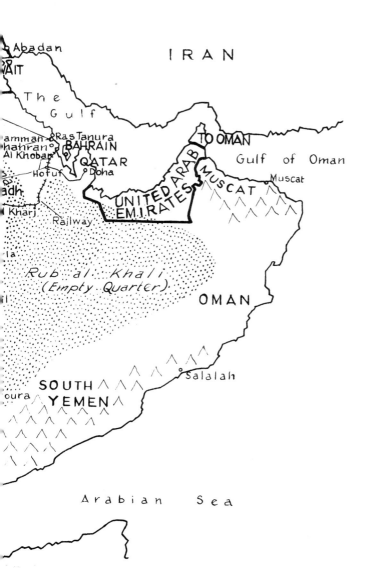

A
Doctor In Saudi Arabia

King Abdul Aziz ibn Saud in 1910, at the age of 30, when he had captured the centre and southern regions of what is now Saudi Arabia, photographed by Captain William Shakespear, and the first known likeness.

A
Doctor In Saudi Arabia

by

G. E. MOLONEY

Regency Press (London & New York) Ltd.
125 High Holborn, London WC1V 6QA

ISBN 0 7212 0780 4

Printed and bound in Great Britain by
Buckland Press Ltd., Dover, Kent.

CONTENTS

CONTENTS (continued)

PART THREE
JOURNEYS AND DIVERSIONS IN SAUDI

PART FOUR
MEDICINE IN SAUDI

List of Illustrations

ACKNOWLEDGEMENTS

I wish to thank—The Saudi Ministry of Information for the illustrations of the kings, the mosques and the King Khalid Hospital; the Department of Community Medicine in the Medical College at Riyadh at the time under Dr Zohair Sebai for three of the clinical photographs; GAMA Services for the photographs of the Riyadh Ophthalmic Hospital and the al Nawa Hospital at Yenbu; the *Sunday Express* for the picture of HRH Prince Charles censored in Saudi; the *Arab News* for the extract concerning the renegades and for the portion of an advertisement concerning cars; Mrs B. Vincett for the picture of the lake at Layla; International Distrib. Jeddah for the aerial view of Dhahran; most of the other photographs are my own indifferent work but for the best pictures I am indebted to Howard Martindale, Michael Ford and Charles Dearnley and my son, John. The various quotations from the Koran in Chapter 7 are taken from the translation by N. J. Dawood published by Penguin Books, London, 1974, and the author thanks them for their permission. For interpreting my scribbles in manuscript and typescript I am most grateful to Vickie Martindale, Rosemary Smyth, Caroline Barton and Henrietta Petersen. For reducing my prolixity and correcting my grammatical weaknesses I am particularly grateful to Mr Eric Buckley's skill with a blue pencil. And to my publisher, Mr J. Thorpe, I am equally grateful for much help in general.

PREFACE

I have set down here some of my experiences and impressions of Saudi Arabia, mixed with descriptions of the origins and changing patterns of the nation, culled both from reading and from what others, including Saudis, have told me.

Living and moving about in the country, like other expatriates was instructive in one way; being a teacher of surgery to young men and women, working intimately with Saudis of all ages and both sexes, mingling with them when they were distressed by illness, and living with them under the same roof for a time all revealed the national characteristics in a way given only to a few.

The foreigner said by King Abdul Aziz to be the one he most admired was a man named Shakespear, no poet but a soldier-diplomat with charm, intelligence, toughness, fidelity, self-possession and courage —very much the great King's own traits—who died bravely in a desert skirmish near him when both were in their salad days, and so started an enduring understanding. Subsequent allegiance with Britain in war and with the U.S.A. in the oil business resulted in the adoption of English as the second language. Mutual interests have continued though not to the exclusion of other nations who seek a share of the business of building a new Saudi to pay for their oil.

Saudi Arabia is unique in some aspects both in terrain and people, but as the nation's resources of accommodation are swamped by visitors on business affairs, the ordinary tourist cannot be housed at the moment and will have to wait until the surge of new hotels allows it. Permission to enter for business or professional reasons is not too stringent and once inside the country movement is not restricted any more than in the West, except for the Forbidden Cities of Mecca and Medina. So in the meantime, most rely on traveller's tales, of which there are many oral but remarkably few written, dealing with the people of the present day, and scarcely any which deal at the same time with the nation's history, including medical and surgical aspects.

Most people have little idea of Saudi other than about oil, veiled

PREFACE (Continued)

women, forbidden alcohol, public executions and Lawrence of Arabia. All these matters and many others are dealt with, and I have tried to bring that widely-known and controversial figure of wartime Arabia, Lawrence, into focus with a chapter devoted to assessing how many pillars of his wisdom still stand for the reason that he and his deeds are one of the common topics of discussion amongst expatriates. His book about war in Arabia is still very well worth reading. I present this work on activities in peace which "also hath her victories", as a further pillar of information on those remarkable people, the Saudis.

G.E.M.

M.R.C.P., F.R.C.S., (Eng. and Ed.).

Oxford, 1985

Part One
SETTLING INTO RIYADH

CHAPTER I

A Beginning

" 'Tis not too late to seek a newer world. "

In March 1977, at the Association of Surgeons' meeting, held that year in the College of Surgeons in London, I was talking at tea with an old friend, the late George Qvist. After a while he looked me up and down, and I later realised with intent, and asked, "When do you finish at the Radcliffe Infirmary?"

"At the end of June," I replied.

"Why don't you go to Riyadh?"

"Where's that—Outer Mongolia? What have I done?"

"It's rather warmer; in Saudi Arabia. They want someone to teach the Saudis surgery."

That conversation brought a change in my life.

He told me that the University of Riyadh were searching for a Professor of Surgery, if possible from a teaching hospital and with plenty of general surgery behind him. Younger men did not have the status they required, middle-aged men were difficult to find as they were unwilling to jeopardise their careers and practices by long leave of absence, and those already retired or on the point of it were mostly not feeling up to it or unwilling to go on for one or other reasons. I seemed to fit the bill if prepared to go, and I now realised that his earlier questions were very pointed, for George's wife, Dame Francis Gardner, was in the chair of the London-Riyadh Universities' Committee and George was lending a hand with the homework. I told him I still had plenty of private work and other work as well, but to console him said I would think it over.

That evening Dame Francis phoned. We had first met in the Radcliffe Infirmary in Oxford at the War's end. Dame Francis, a brilliant lady, dynamic and persuasive, has devoted a lot of her time both in England and Saudi Arabia to helping the University of Riyadh build up a medical school which started only in 1968.

The unusual occurrence of a woman being made head of the London-Riyadh Universities' Committee in which Saudis participated was due mostly to her own qualities but also to the Saudis having started a women's medical college in Riyadh by a Royal Decree of King Faisil, in connection with which the experience of a former Dean of The Royal Free Medical School in London would greatly help. In 1980 I heard the then Dean of the Riyadh, Dr Hassan Kamal, say on the platform of the Annual Saudi Arabian Medical Conference that as Dr H. Jezairi, the then Minister of Health and the first Dean of the Medical College, was the Father of the Riyadh Medical College, so Dame Francis Gardner is the Mother of it.

She gave me the full treatment, making it clear that they badly needed a teacher and surgeon with experience but frankly admitted that those with suitable qualifications were not falling over themselves in the queue to fill the role. What, I asked, about the language, the operating facilities, the food, the flies, and so on. Teaching is in English, I was told, and the other problems could be taken care of. She got the same dusty answer—I would think it over. Meanwhile I would get some information from others who had worked there or like her, visited. She told me I must submit a curriculum vitae and be interviewed by some Saudi doctors. It felt like starting all over again.

My informants were all helpful and even persuasive, but were kind enough to point out where the problems lay. The teaching of women students in clinical subjects was starting in the coming session, so they needed help as well. It is always pleasant to be wanted and appreciated, at any age, and there seemed to be a call where needed most, with a chance to keep scalpel and tongue in action, with some adventure, after a long spell in Oxford. I felt I would venture forth like Tennyson's Ulysses, "Come my friends 'tis not too late to seek a newer world . . . for my purpose holds to sail beyond the sunset and the baths of all the western stars until I die." My stars were to be eastern, for after an interview with Saudis and others they offered me the job. I promised them two years and doubt if I would have gone had I then realised it would run to five years.

There was a lot to do in connection with resigning and tidying up, and one felt more drained than at full steam in the ordinary way. One useful aid before leaving, I felt, might be a short attack on Arabic, and a smattering proved to be of great help, especially with greetings, taxis, and shopping after arrival. Though English and sign language usually serve in most places, anyone going to Arabia will find a few words, especially numbers one to twenty, are useful.

New arrivals in Saudi are given very differing accommodation. Some go from the airport to a modern hotel at which they conduct their business and depart, seeing and knowing little of the country and its people. Others go to a company villa which may be for one family or single men, luxurious and complete with servants, or small and shared. Others go to flats, large or small, or single rooms, and the poor of Yemen or Pakistan go to a shanty made of bits of cardboard, plywood from boxes, or flattened tin canisters. It is not greatly different from cities in other eastern countries. In 1977, most University employees were being given a housing allowance which varied according to status, while nowadays most are in pleasant flats, heated and furnished by the University. The type of experience on arrival which others and I had to endure is still possible but much less likely. Most people are given a good idea of what to expect before leaving. Ours was the result of anticipated accommodation not being completed, but improvements go on as resources improve, though it is still necessary to struggle through the glue of the bureaucracy to achieve a resting place, for as elsewhere, there must be jobs for the boys.

The British party for the University of Riyadh flew from London Airport on 19 September 1977 to a different world.

CHAPTER II

Settling In

We arrived, tired out, in the early hours of the morning, having suffered the usual delays, including a rummage at customs for booze, Bibles, and banned books. (I went in and out for five years before being relieved of a "bad book, bad book, bad book" that I did not know was not in favour.) Several considerate old-timers had turned out in those early hours to guide and help us. When all strays had been collected, men and women were separated, except for husbands and wives, and we were taken to our allotted villas by minibus, the men's being on the fringe of the city about half a kilometre from the desert, some three kilometres from the city centre. This seemed to be adequate accommodation for the few days we expected to be in it before going into flats which, we understood, would shortly be allocated to us.

Hotels are expensive, so the University provided this temporary housing in a typical villa, high-walled with a lockable, large, heavy metal door leading into a paved area with a gatekeeper's house on one side and on the other, two rather sad, young, dehydrated palm trees grew in deep rectangular pits, unprotected, and dangerous in the dark. On hot nights the old gatekeeper could be seen on his bed of sorts by the side of the house with one or two of his wives draped about him. The solid building had stone floors, some polished, and a front verandah up and down, the main door being of a type very common in Riyadh, wide with lots of brass on it.

Muslim houses usually have a small house near the gate which may be for a gatekeeper or used as a reception room, or both, for it is not the custom to receive visitors directly into a large detached villa. On passing through the gate, which may be opened by an official gatekeeper or the smallest member of the family with a charming, curious, but fearless smile, one is ushered into the reception room, removing shoes at the door. There will be a carpeted floor and cushions around the walls one sits cross-legged or lies on one's side on an elbow. Sweet tea is sent for and business proceeds after a few pleasantries.

If friendship or business develops, an invitation to the main house may follow later, where everyone will be seated on very comfortable settees and chairs mainly ranged around the walls, with occasional tables here and there, and a few *objet d'art*, especially long-necked coffee

PLATE 2

From the 'Sunday Express' *of 11.3.79—on the front page. Part of the caption reads, "Prince Charles emerged from the sea at Perth, Australia, yesterday to be grabbed and kissed by a glamorous model . . ." The picture was treated as above.*

Is there Censorship in Saudi? Sometimes a whole page of a newspaper is cut out or a column, and if left in is not blue-pencilled but black-brushed. Some books are censored or may be on sale for a time and later withdrawn and vice versa. Only one book was taken from me at customs, I being unaware that it was not acceptable.

pots. Nowadays, there will also be pictures, prints or oils, often of lakes, trees and mountains, very typically Mediterranean or European of some sort and often of a garish style not to western taste but much admired by Saudis; richer houses have better pictures. The other feature in the Muslim home of any size is a *hammam*, a lavatory and washroom by the entrance or on the way to the main room. In the West on entering a house we take off our hats, but they take off their shoes, and wash. Arabs are very concerned about personal cleanliness; it is part of their religion for them to wash before prayer and, in a land where water is in short supply they do their best to keep their bodies as clean as possible. In the desert, where water is short, sand serves for the purpose.

Our villa had basins, a bath, and a lavatory, on the way to the main reception room, which served as our communal downstairs ablution area, and upstairs there was another bathroom. Many of their toilets are of the Islamic type, a hole in the floor surrounded by a glazed sloping surface and foot-pieces, with a flusher and a small piece of hose pipe fitted into a nozzle to wash the tail end after action. Paper at this point is not part of the Muslim way of life. In a new block of flats for one of the hospitals, the small entrance lavatory was just inside the main door, but it had a problem. This very small room was fitted with a modern lavatory bowl against which the door opened a full six inches, and the problem was not only how anyone could get in but how did the little man who fitted it get out?

It was back to school with a vengeance, four to a room, and in ours, we were aged from the twenties to the sixties, and none of us was yet conditioned to the heat of an Arabian summer; two had wives and families waiting to be told to follow to a flat anytime. The unusual luxury of a telephone in the villa was a great asset, enabling phone calls to be made to the homeland, but whether these made the ensuing delays any easier to put up with or were interpreted only as palliatives from husbands thought not to be trying hard enough to get other accommodation, was hard to say. In spite of difficult times we managed to have a lot of fun, with very little dissension, though the occasional anti-social activity was treated by more than a hint.

Younger men with wives and families can miss them very badly when first so separated, but phoning home can be of uncertain benefit. For wives it is usually placatory; to others in the family it can often be disturbing. One of us in the flat who went home at Christmas said that the distress of his children after he had left them again took a long time to calm down and subsequent telephone calls brought on their agitation again. He settled for letter writing. With others, home visits did some good, and a visit by a wife and family to Saudi did even more. Most younger expatriates away for months or more have to face similar problems wherever they may be.

In our room there was a physicist, a chemist, a physician, and a general surgeon, representing experience of the Universities of Oxford, London, Essex and Otago. In other rooms were graduates of Aberdeen, Glasgow, London, Manchester, Cairo, Khartoum, Cambridge, and St. Andrew's, presenting a fair sample of the faces and accents of the present and past British world. This villa had been used during the last academic year as a hostel for lady students. On our bedroom wall were some cut-out magazine pictures of young western ladies in quiet sentimental poses, following homely pursuits, and behind the wardrobe door, rather pathetically, one of a typical Saudi man; I seldom saw a clean-shaven Saudi, and if unbearded they would almost certainly have a moustache, usually with down-curving ends. The windows had grills and the roof high walls so that one could sleep out unobserved on hot nights. Almost all roofs in Arabia are flat, with similar high walls.

Meals were our own affair and we bought supplies mainly from two small shops nearby with special items from the supermarket in the town.

For two weeks the University supplied us with a minibus and an excellent driver, Ali. After that we were on our own and dependent upon taxis, when available—though one or two bought cars and gave lifts—otherwise it was a walk of two or three kilometres to the University and even further to the hospital, the classes and hospital work starting soon after arrival.

Even getting a taxi could be a problem, phoning being fruitless from as far out as our villa, although it was easier coming back.

Unfamiliarity with the language makes things difficult, for few drivers speak more than a few words of English. We found that it helps to be able to count up to twenty in Arabic. The Riyadh taxi drivers have a habit of not keeping to any particular fare and the more helpless one appears the higher the demand. At the end of the journey the passenger, hoping that he looks like an old timer and knows what is due, can thrust anything from 5 to 20 riyals into the driver's hand with a knowing look and see if it is acceptable, but this does not always work for Europeans and more may be demanded, in which case riyals are dropped into his hand until he nods. Asking the fare first, after stating one's destination, is rightly taken as a sure sign that one doesn't know how much the fare should be. Drivers tend to double it for Europeans, anyway. Women have an additional problem in that they are not allowed to drive, and in journeying alone in taxis may suffer soliciting and unpleasantness. Occasionally men also are solicited. A comment on the standard of driving is that women are not allowed to and the men cannot.

Living so close in our community was in one way a big help, enabling information to be pooled from many sources, and we spent a long time considering the problem of cars. A couple of us hoped that we could do without a car if we got a flat near the hospital, but it soon became evident that we were having to travel long distances with taxi fares mounting very considerably; one day I paid 120 riyals (about £18) in taxi fares, and that could not go on for long. The problem with most of us was that we had no money with which to buy a car as none was supplied to us. Walking the three kilometres or so to the hospital at 7.00 a.m. on a brilliant morning was almost a pleasure, but returning in summer heat in the early afternoon, exhausted and covered in sweat, was distinctly unpleasant.

Registration at the University was a titanic effort of bureaucratic mountaineering, over both paper and the administration building—one floor up and along, one down again, up two floors, and all repeated several times, with mistakes on both sides calling for fresh starts, partly due to the language problem. We were not quite sure what we were doing most of the time but kept on seeking yet another signature in a different room, with a great deal of politeness on the part of the officials and as much mystery to us. Time was of no consequence whatever.

My own registration took eight days. This included documentation for a housing and furnishing allowance and at the end I was presented with a massive wad of riyals, 30,000 for housing and 15,000 for furnishing, some £7,000, an embarrassing amount of cash to conceal. However, the almost total absence of any risk of burglary was reassuring, and none of us lost any while awaiting its disposal after a varying number of weeks. A few banked it, but the thought of wading through more bureaucracy at the bank, and the hope of any day using it for paying for a flat, made under the bed the most popular depository. One or two, Scots especially, took it with them wherever they went. The University's own experience and response to representations made to it on these matters has eased the initial battle with bureaucracy a little, but a lot of it remains unchanged, and sometimes it is worse.

CHAPTER III

A Place of One's Own

To help us find flats we were put in the hands of the housing manager of the University, a bland, smiling Saudi who was in effect an estate agent, and not without some benefit from it all. We wanted some comfort and to be near our work if possible. The fickle landlords, as soon as they learnt that our grants from the University had been put up, automatically put up their demands to equal the grant, recognising us as babes in the wood, and the University not much better. The agents were to some extent in league with the landlords, who thought it unwise to risk black-listing by trying to cut them out. In the end we were led by the nose to where the manager more or less wanted us. It wasn't much for £5,000.

I went with the manager to see an agent in his rather sordid office and there signed the contract for my flat and paid a lump sum for one year's rental. The contract was all in Arabic, but the housing manager gave me a rough outline and promised to send me a copy (which I got out of him a year later after some pressure from very high University levels).

At last, after five weeks of a bed, bags, and bother I had my own little private world in Saudi, or so it seemed. However, there were some snags—that power house, the kitchen, having neither window nor extractor fan, could not be used for cooking, which in Saudi is mostly done by gas using a portable cylinder—very cheap, less than £1 for about three months—so the cooker had to be put in the corridor outside, beneath a window. The bathroom had a shower under which I could just make it with a stoop, a bath covered in cement (for it was the favourite mixing place for builders) with manufacturers' labels stuck on it, and a bidet and lavatory bowl both covered in cement splashes, which were also to be found all over the floors in the flat, together with a liberal sprinkling of paint. The bath, in any case, was so small that I could not fit into it. Scraping for about two weeks resulted in the whole flat looking a little tidier at least.

1. *Our allotted villa almost on the edge of the desert where 14 of all nations spent from 2-6 weeks with 3-4 to a room while awaiting flats. The bus is the type in use for schools.*

2. *At rear of this building was my badly designed flat, paint and cement splashed when I took over, and where I spent a year.*

PLATE 4   25

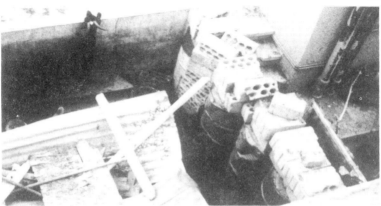

1. *Below the balcony to my bedroom at the corner of my neighbour's house were penned 3 goats, a rooster and 3 hens, the rooster starting up about 3.00 a.m. and all were noisy but made their presence most obvious in summer.*

2. *Some had it better, especially the business men and executives who frequently had a villa to themselves. Howard Martindale, an electonics engineer with Rockwell Int., gave me much hospitality at his villa's pool, one of about 10,000 similar private ones in Riyadh.*

Hot water was another problem and required the purchase of a wall electric heater, which was not a fixed fitting. We all needed one and went to a shop along the street where a boy of about twelve had been left in charge. Saudi children mature early and so are given early responsibility. This budding tycoon easily held his own with us, even getting the better of three large Britons. He calculated rapidly on his fingers with the aid of a few quickly scribbled figures, murmured a price in English, from which he would not be budged, and a smile and handshake settled it all. We had our water heaters and took them home where my younger friends kindly did the fixing while I mostly stood back to admire their skill. There were complications, but when we had mastered the main problem of the hot and cold being labelled the wrong way round we finally got all junctions sealed of leaks and the battle was won.

Life in the Saudi heat is a strain without a cooler of some sort. Nowadays air-conditioning is fitted in all the houses and public buildings, and life indoors is very different from that which the bedouin endures. None of the Saudis in the town show any natural ability to tolerate the full heat of summer and certainly have no inclination to flaunt themselves in the sun: sunbathing is for Europeans. The Saudis I met seemed to be no better than the Europeans at becoming conditioned to the heat, the imperturbable Yemenis being a race apart, though of course all dark-skinned races feel less effect of the sun's rays upon the skin.

The type of cooler is a matter of choice. The air-conditioner operates in the same way as a refrigerator, with a fan to force the cool air about the room, and the level of moisture is scarcely changed. The desert-cooler operates by blowing air across some layers of water-saturated straw and needs a source of water, the air passing from it having in consequence, a high water content. If doors or windows are not left open, rooms and contents will dampen heavily, but they have a pleasant effect upon the nose and lungs. Water stoppages are not infrequent in the city, and electricity cuts as well. Most expatriates settle for the air-conditioner but some use both, the desert-cooler being about half the price.

Acquiring a flat is one thing, getting the furniture is quite another. The University had been generous enough with its once-and-for-all furnishing allowance, if considered as providing the means to buy a cooker, fridge, chairs, bed and the like, but to some of us a car was also

PLATE 5   27

1. *Doctor's housing at a smaller privately owned medical service in Jeddah.*

2. *Technician's housing being part of an annex to a hotel near the old airport.*

3. *Blocks of 3 maisonettes for single doctors at al Nawa Hospital of about 100 beds at Yenbu.*

4. *Married quarters at al Nawa Hospital, Yenbu.*

1. *At the approach to the average village is a heap of written-off cars. Today, many go to the steel mill at Jeddah.*

This damn car consumes less than a camel. From where can I pay for my new swimming pool.

"Böse Kiste brauchen weniger als Kamell Wovon ich soll neue Swimming Pool bezahlen?"

Suzuki Carry
Steigen Sie ein wo Sie wollen: vorne, hinten oder in der Mitte. Nehmen Sie Platz. Unter Ihnen befindet sich der Motor. 4-Zylinder 4-Takt mit 800 ccm und 20 kW (37 PS). Bevor der Tank leer ist, sind Sie über alle Berge.

2. *This picture with 3 others appeared as an advertisment in a foreign newspaper for a brand of car and gave great offence to the Saudis, the Arab News saying, "it depicted the Arabs as greedy, senseless and lecherous who only deserve contempt". Profound apologies were published by the business conscious offenders, and quite right too.*

essential, with work in two hospitals some kilometres apart and in a medical school in another direction. Doctors though forced to move about every day, are no different in University eyes from engineers or historians. No money was provided either for a car or its running costs. The next year, after representations, a transport allowance was given but still no help towards buying a car. Some of the younger members, especially if staying a year only, by sharing flats, furniture and not much at that, working at one site only and able to do without a car, managed to end up with quite a lot of money in hand. An important decision for comparatively indigent young people, when going abroad for the purpose of making money, is how much to spend on home comforts. Buying lavish comfort could be a waste when it is possible to be sent home at forty-eight hours' notice, though this may happen only rarely. I decided, like some others, to spend about half my furnishing allowance on the contents of a flat and to use the other half as the equivalent of a grant-in-aid towards a car, which covered less than half the price. There was no sign of the University providing for employee professors a pool of cars with drivers as they did for visiting professors, and is done by other hospitals and many business houses. A kindly Saudi surgical friend offered to lend me the rest until I could repay when one had earned enough, and had been paid, which is not always the same thing.

Prices put really comfortable furnishing out of the question, especially with a car to think about. I had bought a few items left by a colleague who had gone back home, and finally descended on the *souk* for the poorly made furniture reminiscent of the World War Two "utility" stuff bought on coupons, though the "utility" was better. My colleague, George Beckmann, an Oxford graduate in physics, and I had a foray together, a smattering of Arabic helping somewhat as we worked through the lists of tables, chairs, beds, linen and all the rest, completing our deals just as midday *Salat* (prayer) sounded. One takes a week or two to get used to the prayer calls which come at slowly changing intervals and add another hazard to the usual problems of shopping. The shutters were rattling down around us as we settled our account.

The only delivery service from the *souk* is the "Chinese" one— arrange it yourself. The transaction having been completed, the salesman urged us to get a move on and get it all out of his shop because he would now be closing for four hours. It made a sizeable pile in the middle of the road, the last items going out through the small gap left under the rolling shutter beneath the gaze of an angry-looking Mutawa. Somehow, we made it without injury. George minded the stack while I went into the main road for a pick-up truck to take it all to our flats.

Shops must close, but loading is allowed with the advent of *Salat*, and we set to in the midday heat, perspiring freely; the hefty Saudi driver gave us a hand with the biggest items, and very good of him that was, because he did not have to. Heavily overloaded, we all climbed aboard and were away with the spoils, no Roman bringing home his loot and captives ever felt better off than we did with the thought of those empty rooms at the other end spurring us on. The driver helped us to off-load and then we sweated to get it all inside, and I took mine on upstairs. It looked pretty miserable when spread over two rooms but it was my own and a start. I collapsed on my newly-acquired bed and fell asleep.

CHAPTER IV

The Iron Camel

Cars and their needs are much the same the world over. It is their owners, real or alleged, and their drivers who differ. We all have to make our choice.

Saudis in general are much concerned with status and "face", as is the case in most of the East. The well-heeled Saudi is inclined to advertise his opulence, having claimed all his allowances, by flaunting a bevy of wives with numerous offspring in tow, with a garage or two housing a selection of custom-built Rolls Royces, Cadillacs, Buicks, and a Range Rover or Japanese equivalent for business use and the occasional jaunt. To show that a Saudi's car is brand new the shipper's crayon marks on the windows and the sheets of paper showing custom clearance must not be cleaned off, but stay indefinitely as symbols of the latest-model-status of the machine.

As well as having a main business it is becoming fashionable to own a farm, not so much of the camel, sheep or goat variety, but arable land to grow wheat and barley, for which subsidies are very high. I was told that a very rich Saudi who put on his farm twenty or more of the ½km-long sprinkler irrigating arms at about a quarter of a million riyals each, paid for the lot with his first wheat harvest. There are hopes that Saudi will be self-sufficient in wheat in five to ten years, and at the rate at which the new farms are growing there is just a chance of this. So a rush is on for suitable hectares and more Land Rover sales and more cars in the garage.

For the ordinary man, driving being for men only, what sort should his be is his problem. If he settles for a new one it is much the same as in the West—off to an agent, who arranges the deal and paperwork for him, and away he drives, licensed or not. Less than half the drivers, it is alleged, have a licence and still less are insured. If you are pranged slap in the middle while stationary by, say, a little Yemeni in a pick-up, you will almost certainly find yourselves paying for all the repairs to your own car, because he will be found to have no money. If you are struck in the rear by a Saudi, perhaps while parked, whereas in Western eyes the whole blame would be his, there is a fair chance that you will have to pay some sixty per cent of the damage to both cars. I cannot say if this is invariably so but such is the experience of several of my friends. In any accident the cars must not be moved until the summoned police arrive and settle the blame on the spot.

Buying second-hand or selling is done somewhat differently from what happens in western countries. The usual start is to put up a notice on a board in a supermarket, or a shop where it is allowed, or in a block of flats by the lift on the ground floor. It is as well to make it clear that it is a European or an American who is selling, because as such you are considered, perhaps erroneously, to be more likely to have looked after the car and to have had it serviced regularly. It is essential to ask more than you expect to get, because there is bound to be some bargaining over the price.

There are no advertisement columns for second-hand cars in the newspapers, Arabic or English, and there is some prejudice on the part of traders against advertisements. It is worth trying a car dealer in the special areas on the edge of the city where there are large pens full of new and old vehicles, with something for everyone. In Saudi, where the accident rate is high and dust percolates into every joint and tube, and where maintenance is often considered to be too costly in time and money to be indulged in, the average life of a car is three to five years. Arabs are skilled dealers and you can expect to come off worst in any bargaining, though as you buy and sell you may possibly reflect charitably on the help being given to keep him and his numerous children and unspoken number of wives alive and in comfort.

The only other way of acquiring or disposing is the Car Auction, one of the greatest sporting events in the Kingdom. When I arrived in Saudi the new and second-hand car market and the car auction were near to the football stadium well into the town but they have now been moved to an area along the Khurais Road about ten kilometres out. There is a second smaller car auction behind the industrial area. Auctions are daily, starting about 3.00 p.m. Their style is essentially Arabic and, I am told, only exist like this in the countries of the Gulf.

As I approached the site from the main road, on my first visit to one of these events, sounds as if a goal had just been scored rose incessantly from over a wide area. At first I thought this must be the local football pitch, but soon realised with all the people and cars coming and going and the tooting of horns that it was indeed the auction, and so worked my way towards the centre of the hubbub. After getting my bearings I counted about fifty small mounds on which stood or squatted what could only be the auctioneers, aged anything from sixteen to sixty, each with a hand-held electric amplifier in constant use and all of them all at once. The mounds were about twenty yards apart and disposed in an L-shape in two lines with about fifty yards between them, and a space about twenty yards long cleared before each where the owner could show off his car to those present. This was done by revving up the engine then slipping suddenly into gear and charging in the direction of the auctioneer, whose life seemed considerably at risk. The car was suddenly braked short of catastrophe, shot into reverse, and the process was to be repeated once or twice more. The bonnet might be opened before the display to show that the car really did have an engine, clutch, and brakes, but that smooth Rolls-like purr could have been achieved in a worn and rattling piece of scrap by replacing the usual engine oil with a very thick variety for the purposes of sale—something that will choke the last bit of life out of the works before the car reaches home. The few whom I know to have bought at an auction and to have got bargains have all been Arabs. Familiarity with the language and an inbred bargaining ability is essential on these occasions: a talk with the owner before the sale, accompanied by a certain amount of glowering, seemed to help too. After the "parade" the auctioning starts and a few more runs up and down may encourage any doubtfuls; after watching for a while a fair guess can be made at the likely final bid.

Putting on a reserve is all part of the game, as in Western auctions, but in this arena if the auctioneer does not sell he gets nothing and the car can be taken off to another auctioneer, and yet another, to try for the hopefully-fixed reserve. They work hard at selling, like our own best auctioneers, but they are quicker, and try good-humouredly to get the last riyal for the customer amidst the indescribable noise of fifty others with their amplifiers all doing the same thing, and the revving of the cars, and the shouting of the customers. The quick running back and forwards invariably produces occasional collisions and resentful looks but there is not a lot to be done about it except to keep out of the way as much as possible. The crowd are amused, at least.

The Arab Car Auction must be the most colourful, lively,

and seemingly chaotic, market anywhere in the world. It could not happen in the west because the Arab character is an essential ingredient for its performance. The final price seems to be common knowledge but no one appears to make any record, and they pass on to the next deal at speed. Amidst all the chaos, however, a clerk will have noted everything down and at the end of the auction money will change hands, with the auctioneer getting his, reputedly high, share.

The purchasers eventually drive off with their new weapon to show off in front of the opposition. The elder Saudis are, in general, good drivers and, allowing for their different, freer, approach are considerate and careful. The same cannot be said of the young men who, with few other hobbies, use their cars for diversion rather than necessary travel. Worse is the inconsiderateness of the Arabs of other nations. The police are very concerned about some of the wild driving, much of which has tragic consequences. The father of a boy of about fifteen admitted to hospital with a smashed leg in his fifth accident (one having caused major injury), asked the surgeon about him and was told it was serious but he would recover, saying that he understood that the car was written off. The father replied, "Oh, poor boy. I must get him another car."

The frequency of traffic offences would cause great concern in Western countries. Driving through red traffic lights was common while I was in Saudi, but I have heard this is no longer so bad. Other than the type of carelessness that leads to calamity in traffic the world over, one of the most nerve-wracking sights was to see cars halted in line at the lights suddenly and without warning switch lanes as the change to green came. That seems to be a less popular pastime now, but one car cutting across the front of all the others is still too frequently seen. Saudi authorities have done a lot recently to improve the safety of driving, and many who have known it for years say that it has improved. Double lines have been tried out and lanes are being re-drawn, but it is not in the Arab nature to stick to rigid rules unless the penalties are severe, and such is not the case. Taxis used to be driven by anyone, not so long ago—many by soldiers and National Guard off duty, with most of them trying to rid themselves of their repressions on the road. Now every taxi driver has to be over the age of thirty, and the standard has noticeably improved. From the airport a regular service has started, with set charges, and although the "yellow perils" still ply and charge what they feel they can get, they are under pressure to keep to a reasonable fare.

Few Westerners realise the great amusement that Eastern people get from watching, what are to them, our strange ways of doing things. Our antics provide them with a great deal of free comedy to be laughed at in private. Westerners often have the same attitude to the habits of other nations and there is no point in reacting violently to having a little fun poked at one's national traits. Coming my way from a hand understandably reluctant to be known in Saudi is a little document entitled *Guidelines for Drivers New to Saudi Arabia*. Some paragraphs of it are reproduced below. It describes the Saudi driving scene in caricature but a telling point is made here and there. If the author wishes to declare himself he will be given full acknowledgement, but I doubt if he will own up. Saudis are free to retaliate, of course, and it is to be hoped that they will look tolerantly on the British and American habit of mocking each other over national oddities.

An extract from "Guidelines for Drivers New to Saudi Arabia"
Written by an Unknown Warrior of the roads of Riyadh

Before you start your car in Saudi Arabia for the first time, sit in the driver's seat, hold the steering wheel, and think; I AM THE ONLY DRIVER ON THE ROAD AND MINE IS THE ONLY CAR. This may be hard to do, especially after you have seen the traffic rush hours, but thousands of Arab drivers believe it and so can you. And you had better; you will not have a chance unless you have this faith. Remember, your car is *the car;* all others are aberrations in the divine scheme.

As elsewhere, there are laws about stopping, crossings, maximum speed and so forth, but in Saudi Arabia these laws exist only as tests of character and self-esteem. Stopping at a stop sign, for example, is prima-facie evidence that the driver is an impotent cuckold; contrarily, ignoring a stop sign is proof that the driver is a Person of Consequence. This is why the Arab driver who is stopped by a policeman goes red in the face, beats his forehead with his fists, and upbraids the officer: it is not the embarrassment or the inconvenience, it is the implication that he is not quite important enough to drive the wrong way down a one-way street.

The basic rule in cities is—force your car as far as it will go in any opening in the traffic. It is the rule that produces the famous Arab Four Way Deadlock. It would appear that the Deadlock could be broken if any of the cars would reverse, but this is impossible because of the other car right behind and the car behind that. Anyway, if a driver did reverse, he would become an Object of Ridicule, for this would suggest a weakness of character.

The impossibility of reversing accounts for some of the difficulties in parking. You will find that when you stop just beyond a vacant space and try backing into it, you cannot because that other car is still right behind you, hooting away. You can give up and drive on, or you can get out and go back and try to convince him to let you park. This you do by shouting Personal Abuse into his window. One of three things will happen: (1) he may stare sullenly ahead and continue blowing his horn, (2) he may shout Personal Abuse back at you, or, (3) he may get out of his car and kill you, subsequently pleading Crime of Honour which automatically acquits him in Saudi courts.

It is important to overtake while driving, as this ensures acceptance in all social areas: moral, sexual and political. Not to overtake is to lose status, dignity and reputation. It is not where you drive to that counts, but what or whom you pass on the way. Wordsworth phrased the intention more aptly, although unknowingly, with the words: "It is better to travel hopefully than to arrive." The procedure is to floor your accelerator and leave it there until you come up on something you can pass. If the Saudi driver sees the car ahead of him slow or stop, he knows that can be but two causes: (1) the driver ahead has died at the wheel, or (2) he has suddenly become a Person of No Consequence, which is roughly the same thing. He therefore accelerates at once and passes at full speed. If the driver ahead has stopped for a gaping chasm, the passer is done for, of course.

When, not if, you are involved in an automobile collision—the Arabic word for it is *sedam*—the procedure (provided there are no serious injuries) is rigidly structured. First, all drivers and passengers spring from their cars shouting Personal Abuse. Passers-by spring from their cars. Pedestrians spring forward as eye witnesses. Stores empty as shoppers join the crowd. Invalids rise from their beds for blocks around to totter to the scene. Do not be afraid of this crowd, even if you are absolutely in the wrong. Half of them will be on your side and will defend you vociferously, shouting and gesticulating. You must make an immediate, but accurate, estimate of those with you and those against you. Based on this count you must make your decision as to whether to reimburse the other party or whether to stand out for reimbursement for yourself. Blame has nothing to do with the actions of the crashees: it is entirely a matter of status and virility. Who cares what happened? That is over, the present is what counts—the battle of dignity and manhood. You are being watched by hundreds of eyes, alert to the slightest loss of poise, the first retreat from savage indignation. But you can win; as you stand there in your wilted sport shirt, comprehending little, groggy and confused, just remember and keep telling yourself: I am a Person of Consequence. I am! I am!

CHAPTER V

A Vision of Abdul Aziz

Riyadh is a sunbaked, dusty, half-built city, not yet come to terms with time, for most of it is not as old as many of its inhabitants. It is one gigantic building site. Everywhere, amongst the concrete giants of our age, are found some areas where mud-brick, time-expired, traditional abodes have been bulldozed down, sometimes with added heaps of rubble dumped on to bring the height up to the level of the new road, the whole scene dotted with discarded debris from the hulks of motor cars and millions of empty tins of some thirst-quencher. Then there may be places where the traditional style of building remains, perhaps only one or a cluster, but they will be unpiped, unwired, and as such are mostly additional fodder for the bulldozers.

The dust descends on everything, both in and out of doors, and from the bare, part-levelled or part-worked building sites on windy days, especially where some earth-moving dinosaurs are nosing about, the dust will rise like sandstorms in the desert, blotting out the scene for minutes at a time. Also, just as in the surrounding desert, dust devils— those spiralling winds that lift sand, dust, papers and cloth—then spread their debris everywhere. In a rare, angry mood they have been known to lift whole motor cars and even houses. It is a strange sight on a dry and almost windless day to see drifting about the desert these dusty whirlygigs, gathering, playing and dying, some rising to twenty feet and some to hundreds.

Throughout the city resounds the burr of the drills, the banging of the hammers, the chatter of an engine, the shouting of the men and then, mingling with it all, come the many voices of the mosques, dotted thick as pubs in London all about the city. At every call there is the regular response of the devout and some say—including certain Saudis, those with a good business sense—of the occasional attender resenting the interruption of the climax of some business. But whatever their feelings and responses, there comes the clatter and bang of rolling shutters rattling down, scores of them in the bigger *souks*, with a sound like kettle drums. They make a staccato tattoo in the quieter minutes to follow, ending in a series of scattered single rat-tats as shopkeepers, sluggish to obey, are visited by the police, civil and religious. The khaki beret-headed civil officers are accompanied by a member of the religious police, the *mutawa*, traditionally dressed in a brown cloak, the *mishla*, with a head-cloth but no head-ring (the Prophet did not wear a head-ring), and his beard well-trimmed and thrusting forward, looking rather fierce and barking impatiently, *"salat, salat"* (prayers, prayers), and one or both of them will have a cane of size familiar to generations of schoolboys of a bygone era, with which to hit out at any object, often human, to encourage a rapid response to the end of business and the expected visit to the mosque.

Sometimes it may be unexpected; one of our chemistry lecturers, Ian, short with dark hair and eyes and sun-tanned, when shopping one day in the *souk* as prayers were called, found himself being shuffled off to the mosque by a *mutawa* threatening with his cane. His broad northern accent as he strongly protested could possibly have been mistaken for Urdu or some such non-Arabian Muslim tongue. He got out of it with some difficulty, though others similarly mistaken have been known to land up inside the mosque, a serious misdemeanour which, if intended, might have unpleasant consequences, for in Saudi, no non-Muslims may enter into a mosque, in contrast to Egypt, Jordan, and other Muslim lands.

Some years ago when all religious affairs were conducted more strictly, everything closing down and all going quiet at prayer time, a recently-arrived Briton, a very amiable man, was sitting at a table out of doors when prayer time came and a *mutawa* appeared and hit the table before him with his stick, shouting, *"salat"* (prayers). Being of an agreeable nature, the young Englishman replied to what he thought was "salaam" (peace) by lifting his glass of lemonade and saying, "Cheers." The *mutawa* hit the table harder and shouted out another *"salat"*, and the young man lifted his glass even higher, and gave his most charming smile. The *mutawa* gave up, no doubt thinking him a little mad.

The midday break is meant not only for prayer but also for the partaking of food, for rest and sleep. When the days are very hot, most people in these latitudes feel the need to sleep away the sizzling discomfort. In the evenings when the routine of business is broken by prayer, but final closing is not until nine or ten or whenever business

1. *Looking to the centre of Riyadh from the top of the darker block of flats shown on plate 8. The tallest building on the skyline is at the city's centre and was about 30 storeys high and is not going up but down several floors as it started to tilt and is 'the leaning tower of Riyadh!'*

2. *Showing the hole in the rock, Abu Makhrouq, once 3 miles from the centre of Riyadh and now surrounded by buildings far and wide.*

3. *A typical suburban street in Riyadh.*

PLATE 8   41

1. *This block of flats attached to the King Abdul Aziz Teaching Hospital were of much better quality. I had a flat here for 2 years.*

2. *A block of privately owned flats of medium quality from which the picture above was taken. I had the top-right flat for 2 years.*

3. *Some of the numerous cranes (insert).*

falls off, one sees the men of commerce who are not overwhelmed by religious feelings, standing about for fifteen to twenty minutes near their shops, with their hands upon the shutters, ready to "up" at the "all clear" and on to their concerns.

On the streets are nationals from more countries than the forum of Rome could boast; here is anything from anywhere and anyone from everywhere, with their own babble and style; the Moslem men of Egypt, Algeria, and Morocco from the west; the Jordanians, Palestinians, Syrians, Turks from the north; the Sudanese and other Africans from towards the south; the Pakistanis, Malayans and Chinese types from the east. Many, but not the Sudanese and Yemenis, wear the European form of dress, and may not be as responsive as the Saudis to the frequent call to prayer, although devout in their own way, they may be given to praying privately each day and to attending the mosques on the day of devotion for all Moslems, their "Sunday", *Yom al juma* (The Day of Gathering), and Friday in the Christian week.

Above it all loom the buildings, some mere steel skeletons, some completed and filled with occupants of business or new residents, and amongst them tower the huge cranes, some two or three adjacent, looking as if their booms will clang together as they gyrate slowly. Although all are strategically deployed in height and site, collision has been known. On the ground the charging, weaving traffic hoots and lurches into the mass of potholes, and in the *souk* small boys scrap amidst the cartons and paper cast on to the alleyways as the tolerant, good-natured people carry on making deals in their unhurried way, with a great deal of shouting to assistants, friends, and potential customers, as pressures mount.

Wood is very dear in Saudi. Tamarisk, date palm and acacia provide the only wood of any size and all are unsuitable for modern purposes, therefore nearly all wood must be imported. This makes furniture expensive, so that "Make-it-yourself" is a popular pastime with some expatriates.

I decided to chance a finger or two in the cause of economy and craftsmanship in spare moments, but at my first attempt to find the wood *souk* I lost my way and found myself instead in the car repair *souk*. This was an astonishing place that must easily beat anything in any other city for size. The most important trade of Riyadh is building and all that goes with it. Its largest business must be selling cars, the next largest the knocking out of dents after the innumerable collisions. (On the first day I took over my brand new car it suffered its first bump, while parked.) The car repair *souk*, like the car auction, has no counterpart in the western world. Like so many other trades or businesses the motor repairs are concentrated very largely in one area, which extends for about a kilometre or more, interspersed with builders' merchants' yards in which plain and cavity bricks are made, as well as concrete pipes and the like. Just behind in the open air or barely covered areas are the remains of thousands of cars, torn or crushed or otherwise unserviceable, and they stretch away into the desert, dumped in one layer instead of being piled into a hill of old vehicles as in countries where spare land is not so readily available. And having once been strewn there may soon be a gathering up again, for here lie riches in metal scrap spreading to the skyline, the greatest car dump that the world has ever seen. I drove in two directions through it, on and on, up and down through the desert hillocks, expecting the next to be the end, but it went on still further for some six kilometres until it finally petered out, and there was nothing on the desert surface but the stones that marked the plots already sold for future building, or an area cleared for the building of a villa that would fetch a goodly rental among a house-hungry population. I drove back through the repair *souk* and listened to the anvil chorus as the twists and dents were banged away.

On the road to the east to Dhahran soon after leaving the city, the sides are strewn with the wrecks of cars about every few hundred yards; cars crunched, abandoned, ransacked of all that is usable, the hulks a future source of metal, too expensive at the time to be worth collecting at some central point, each a sad, silent story of a vehicle that left Riyadh or Dhahran destined to finish a crumpled heap. In between this metal lining, this avenue of sorrow, is a rubber wall made up of punctured, burst and abandoned tyres.

One of the peoples helping to build Riyadh are the Yemeni. When you see a large refrigerator walking at a slope down the street ahead of you with no visible means of support or traction, you can be pretty sure that beneath it will be a five-foot, give or take an inch or two, slight, tough wiry man of Yemen. It is a stirring sight to see a large, well-fed, languid manager of sorts, to whom physical exertion may be nearly unknown, laying into a small uncomplaining Yemeni for failing to put a heavy burden down exactly on the right spot. The rate of pay is good, comparatively, for the Yemeni who live two to six to a room somewhere in Riyadh or on the desert, perhaps on a building site in a shanty made of flattened tins or some scrap wood and cardboard. They will make perhaps 800 to 1,200 riyals a month (about £90-£150) for their hard labour in the heat or cool, a wage well below subsistence level for a European or other expatriates, for whom it will not even pay the rent. It is the basis of a better life for the Yemeni when they return home. Their native land, around the south-west corner of the Arabian Peninsula, fairly sizzles with the heat in summer, and 110°-140° in summer in Riyadh appeals to them as a fine day in Autumn does to any Briton in his garden. They slog away through the heat with only a glisten on their foreheads, where most of us would have dropped pounds in a pool of sweat into which we would have collapsed eventually. The other people building the city are mainly Koreans, Japanese, Philippines, who are all prepared to do the heavy labour, but many of the members of the non-Saudi Muslim races, Hindus, and Christians of different races, also contribute. Europeans and Americans do much of the architectural, contracting and consultative work.

One day I sought a new route off Sittin Street, a fine 60-metre-wide thoroughfare (*sittin* means sixty in Arabic), I came upon a limestone hill topped by a natural arch beneath which is a large and shady hole, which the Arabs call Abu Makhrouq (Father Hole). Here King Abdul Aziz would sometimes take his sons on hot days to seek some shelter with a view to sit and contemplate upon the then far-off expanding capital of his domain across the desert, and talk to them of what the future should contain; and doubtless have his fun, for there was a lot of that in him.

Today the city has mushroomed far and wide in all directions right up to and beyond that hillock, but it is still a fine vantage point from which to view the great surround of Riyadh.

The city fathers have constructed here a splendid monument and amenity, for the rugged piece of limestone has been terraced in attractive, asymetrical designs with moulded stones well-matched in colour to the hillock to form small banks and terraces, some crossed by curving frames of iron to take a shade in summer. All the features slope away in interesting lines to make a place for recreation with a fine view of the city all around.

Steps at intervals about the terraces lead to the hole, also called a cave, and on this day three young Saudis were sitting talking, smoking and chewing; there are no better chatterers in the world than Arabs. Given a year or two young men like these will be back with thermos jugs of tea and cards.

Small Arab boys and girls rush about the streets and backyards like their counterparts anywhere, and are lithe, swift, released and very happy. When the girls come of age the veil descends, and with it come decorum and reserve. The little boys, in passing in the street, like to greet one and show their gift of language with a "Hello" or "Good-bye" or "Good-day", but older boys seem quieter and respectful to an older man; but with my "Hello" or *"Sabar el khair"* and a smile they open up and are friendly and generous. One day at the traffic lights I nodded to a young man in his car beside me whereupon he opened his window and offered me a chocolate on a tray.

The three within the cave offered cigarettes but they were very young and I declined and then began to climb the score of yards on the unpaved rugged surface to the top. An Arabian explorer once observed that when you most believe you are utterly alone in the vast expanses of the desert, if you then climb onto a sandhill and put a glass to your eye, scanning the skyline, there perched on some neighbouring hill you are bound to see a bedouin sitting peering towards you wondering what you are doing so far from home.

I took the last three strides of my afternoon Everest and lo! There they were, two Arab lads tucked in a hollow at the top, surveying it all like the King's sons had done, interrupting their chatter to return my greeting. The view is every bit as good as in the King's day but now there is much more of it; for many miles around sprawls out the substance of the royal insubstantial dreaming. Here East meets West in mud and concrete all blended in the summer's haze. The old adobe palaces and home are crumbling away, for nothing made of mud and straw and dung stands long against the melting rain, the driving wind and baking sun, unless expensively preserved. For some few that is intended.

Amidst the decaying clay rise the giant boxes that are the architecture of our times, and how good it is to see much of it with neo-arabesque decoration added, that suits so well the palm-lined avenues where guttraed-heads and white-robed figures mingle with the rest of the scene. These plain square concrete boxes are evidence of the urge to get them up, get them in, and take the rent. All about is evidence of one of the greatest building explosions of all time. I felt pleased to have been asked to play a minor part in the great eventful history of this country.

Early in 1978, the long-awaited refuse lorries arrived, a hundred of them, large, bright orange, shining new, and unmistakable with their stomach-like containers and huge mouths which at the touch of a lever reveal teeth and jaws whose capacity to gobble up garbage makes feeding-time at the zoo seem but a nibble at a sandwich. Their advent had news and political value for this was a genuine effort to aid the whole city by ridding it quickly, regularly, and thoroughly, of offensive and disease-breeding materials. An added bonus, all part of the scheme, was the free distribution throughout the city of large bins at regular intervals especially in the *souks* where wrappers, boxes, and tins, were discarded in profusion; there were smaller bins for households.

To proclaim this new era, a parade of the garbage corps was held along the main routes of the city, all traffic being held up as the hundred refuse lorries and some open carriers with seats for the refuse corps in suitable orange outfits and some holding implements passed through the city, looking like an army going into attack, which in fact they were—an efficient sanitary army. And mighty well they battled, transforming the streets and undeveloped areas. The mounds of tins disappeared, the *souks* were largely uncluttered at foot level, and the streets, with mechanical sweepers and a corps of orange-clothed broomstick warriors, took on a new face. Later, when the first stage was well under way, the ugly mounds of rubble from collapsed old buildings and the residue of debris from completed buildings were gathered up and the surfaces levelled by mechanical shovels, and the abandoned cars, littering the streets and lying about for months on end to the nuisance of all, were towed away.

Large notices went up about the city urging the populace not to cast empty tins onto the roads, while the media helped to spread the word to keep the city clean. Now that there was somewhere to put refuse and it was seen to be regularly removed, many people responded as good citizens will, but it was too much to hope that all bad citizens would, and the rattle of a discarded can in a stream of traffic is still a not unfamiliar sound, indicating that Allah is not being outraged by perfection of hygiene in Riyadh.

Part Two

FROM MOHAMMED TO KING FAHAD

CHAPTER VI

The Changing Saudi Lifestyle

The Arabian Peninsula together with the Arab-speaking countries at its base forms a land mass of over a million square miles. Britain would fit into one corner and France would be swallowed up in the sands of the Empty Quarter. The greater part of the axe-head-shaped peninsula is occupied by Saudi Arabia (618,000 square miles), the base of the head being formed by Syria, Jordan, Lebanon, Kuwait, and Iraq, while the cutting edge of the head and its corners are the Yemen, Oman, Muscat and the Emirates (the former Trucial States), and the small peninsula of Qatar with the nearby island of Bahrain. The southern end and sides of the Peninsula are surrounded by seas; the Red Sea, the Arabian Sea and the Arabian (Persian) Gulf. A short way inland parallel to the Red Sea is a long chain of mountains formed of granite and lava, and in the south lies the largest sandy desert in the world, the Empty Quarter or Rub' al Khali, while in the north is another not quite so large sandy desert, the Great Nafud. Both these deserts are connected towards their eastern ends by a curving bridge of sand, the Dahna, with the outer part of the curve towards the east.

The greater part of the vast central area is limestone, averaging 5,000 feet in depth, most of it formed by sea-shell creatures, mostly minute, with others like the ones we know at the seaside today, when the region was under the sea for millions of years. In consequence, the limestone is full of fossils, the search for which distracts the picnickers and fossilers in the desert today. Subterranean disturbances over millions of years have crinkled the surface in places to produce long lengths of cliffs across the country, the longest being the Jebal Tuwayq, an escarpment averaging 130-160 metres in height and about 800km long, running west of and parallel to the Dahna strip of sand—another attraction on days off to expatriates who climb selected points.

There are three great phenomena in the history of Arabia:

Mohammed—who unified most of the Arabs in religion; King Abdul Aziz—who unified the scattered powers in most of the Peninsula into Saudi Arabia; and oil—which was found in his time and enabled him to start the modern era.

The Arabs are divided into two great social groups. The first are those who have long been town dwellers, as in Damascus, Amman, Mecca, Medina, Taif, and lesser towns including Riyadh fifty years ago. On the whole their inhabitants have not sought the desert life, many having a surprisingly limited knowledge of it, their forbears never being desert people but arriving in Saudi over the centuries on the way to Haj, the great annual religious festival when Muslims who can afford it go to Mecca at least once. For many of the town dwellers, especially at such times, some business and profits are inescapable and acceptable, and at one time the whole country was financed by the fees from the Hajis. King Abdul Aziz and those who preceded him in the west before the discovery of oil were very concerned when the Haj revenues fell off in a poor year. But with the vast oil income the Saudis are now able to forgo such tributes and spend considerable resources on improving dock, airport, lodging on arrival, transport and similar facilities.

In 1962 about two million pilgrims from all over the Muslim world descended on Mecca, with profit for the businessmen who have to organise and manage the transport, food, hygiene, health and the guiding of so many who "tour" in the spirit of religion. There is nothing wrong with that. The services are immense and take a great deal of time and trouble each year from those who have to provide them. Rome, Canterbury, Jerusalem, and Lourdes, provide similar benefits to their local business communities. Many Hajis used to stay on in Arabia, settling mostly in the regions round Mecca and Medina, though today the chances of staying on after Haj are remote, because there is a very strict system of passports and visas. Many of the descendants of the former Hajis, now Saudis, have the look of Turks, Mongolians, Chinese, Tibetans and Egyptians and are usually not as high in the Saudi pecking order as those who derive from the ancient primaeval bedouin stock, who, like many of the African desert people and the Australian Aborigines and Eskimoes developed a way of life to survive in the toughest environments of the world. The Royal family are bedouin-derived. The western coastal people have long had contact with the rest of the world and have prided themselves on a high level of culture.

The second great group, the bedouin, are proud of their desert
origins, but now almost all owe their existence to some of the products
of the endeavours of the rest of the world. The old desert dwellers
existed on camels, sheep, goats and their by-products, together with
dates, figs and water from the wells. The camel and goat can live on
desert scrub and provide milk, cheese and flesh; their skins give leather
for various purposes including bags in which to carry water and milk;
their hair is used for tents and ropes. If, after several bad seasons of
drought they lost their herds, they raided their neighbours near and far
for stock, killing perhaps a few males if necessary, but being scrupulous
as a general rule in sparing women and children. In later centuries, the
Hajis provided the bedouin with a source of other benefit from tolls, or
simply from raiding their caravans. Most of the population of Arabia in
the earlier years of King Abdul Aziz up to World War One were
bedouin living entirely in the old ways.

King Abdul Aziz, after conquering the central areas of Arabia, the
Nejd, around his birthplace of Riyadh, developed ideas of unifying
Arabia and conquered in turn the south, east, north and finally the
west. He then had to hold it against marauding bands of raiders or
tribes under a powerful sheikh who tried to take over as large a region as
possible, just as King Abdul Aziz had done, a timeless pattern the world
over. Abdul Aziz had resolved on a policy of what he had he would
hold, and suppressed raiders .with severity, making an example by
crushing them during a battle or taking them captive. Later, when more
secure, he showed mercy to most of his opponents after defeat, then
married their daughters, an age-old political move with more frequent
opportunities for him as a Muslim. Later still he devised a method of
controlling his conquests using radio communication through scattered
agents in touch with roving bands of well-armed "commandos" who
would suddenly and mysteriously confront the rebels and put them
down. Local ambitious sheikhs puzzled for a long time at the wonderful
intuition of the great man who seemed to know what they were up to.
The method worked; Abdul Aziz consolidated his position and the
raiding ceased.

But every action has a reaction, not always foreseen, and these actions
now set in train unforeseen changes in the life of the bedouin. They
enjoyed few things that could ameliorate their hard existence but some
they craved, one being the permitted cup that cheers but does not raise
the level of blood alcohol. The coffee bean comes from a shrub native to

the southern end of the Arabian Peninsula, and coffee production is an ancient industry in the Yemen. They wanted it at the beginning and at the end of the day, and the older and successful wanted it frequently throughout the day. Another thing in demand was tobacco. They also needed rifles and ammunition, some rice and corn, some cooking utensils, and some cloth, and if they were to marry from one to four wives and keep an assortment of concubines, depending on success, they needed all these and either money or goods to exchange for them. But now they could no longer raid or tax the desert caravans and the demands for their services as carriers and as suppliers of camels to others fell away.

Then came the discovery of oil in the thirties. Prices rose, motor transport arrived and increased, and few wanted what the bedouin could produce from the desert. So life became increasingly hard and the drift to the towns to find work began; not hard work, for that was not in their nature, but minding a rig or driving a lorry. So started the transition from the camel to the car and from an uncertain supply of dates and well water to three square meals a day and access to a tap. The trickle of bedouin to the towns and cities, adapting for survival, had begun and was to become a full flow. The camel driver is now the taxi driver, the repairer of tents and harness is the mechanic, the tribal leader in his tent is the business manager in his office chair, and the raider is the soldier or member of the National Guard. The secluded women of the desert are now the confined and veiled women of the cities.

Other changes followed, so that now all boys and girls in towns and villages go to school—separate ones of course—and many of the girls go on to a university education, to become teachers and some to become doctors. Some of the men mix their jobs, many of the taxi drivers being members of the National Guard who exchange their uniform for the headcloth, head-ring and thobe when off duty, but now all must be over thirty years of age.

Yet, though reduced in numbers, there are bedouin still nomadic or semi-nomadic who live in tents and keep herds as they did in the past.

A disappointment in one's early visits to the desert, after spotting the low, black bedouin tents and on looking round for the family transport and milk supply, is to find none of those "ships of the desert" that we have all read about, except for perhaps a small herd of camels grazing far away; instead one sees beside the encampment a small pick-up truck

PLATE 9   53

1. *Snapshot from a moving car of a young woman, averse to being photographed, with a child on a donkey driving a herd of camels to water.*

2. *The herd crossing the road, camels being a hazard to motorists especially at night.*

3. *At the watering place—a pond filled from a deep well. Milk and meat are the objectives for breeding camels, very few in Saudi for transport.*

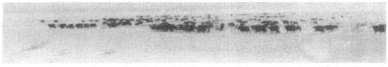

4. *A herd of sheep and goats. To distinguish them from afar—goats strut and their tails go up while sheep's tails go down.*

that was manufactured a quarter of the way around the world, which does the job much more easily in the limestone areas. There are camels in use in the old way on the sands, long distant from our region, we were told, but I saw no burdened beasts in my travels. Nearly all camels today are kept for their milk or meat and it is said that there are no longer any wild ones. The bedouin own small numbers, kept especially for milk, and they make some money from the meat, for all camel production is well subsidised, but the greater herds of a hundred and upwards are owned by the princes and rich farmers who organise a herd like a westerner his cows. Camel milking parlours are only just on trial and meanwhile the daily milk yield goes by cans to the city, to please the accustomed palates of the former desert dwellers with its slightly salty flavour. Both sheep and goats are herded in the old way, for the scattered feed must be followed where it sprouts about the desert and the animals brought to water pumped from bores or wells as they require it. But none of these activities would pay today for the coffee, rice, or tobacco, if the government were not keen to foster all resources of home grown food, so a generous subsidy from oil revenues is paid for all animals reared and the bedouins in the far-flung desert, with their little herds, rely on the flow of oil like all the rest.

CHAPTER VII

New Slaves and Old Customs

The previous habits of Saudis have, not unexpectedly, a lot to do with present attitudes. Only in 1963, when the oil was flowing freely, and just coincidentally, did the Saudis finally give up their slaves who, on release, were given citizenship. Released slaves have a way of believing that the best form of new life is that of their former masters, and with the masters in this case having in the past had most of the physical work done by slaves or their wives (a chattel, or some would say no better than a slave), their attitude is to continue to get assistance in expertise and manual labour from someone else. So today we see the Saudis, with their oil-based prosperity owing a great deal to American brain and muscle, still using both and some extra muscular aid, and building a new life-style with the help of Yemeni, Korean, Japanese, German, British nationals, and any from the rest of the world who can show they can do something that is required to the satisfaction of the owners.

In the towns and cities the Saudis are still the supervisors and managers of most activities. They still drive, nowadays, lorries or taxis or their own cars; they are still repairers, and in control in the shops doing some of the buying or selling and looking after the proceeds; in business there is always a Saudi supervising the work with a hand firmly on the cash-box, and at higher levels they are the managers in business and the professions. Only a Saudi may own land and buildings, and if the business is not in his name he has a share of it and he owns the land, the premises and has the ultimate control. King Abdul Aziz who died in 1953, ten years before the abolition of slavery in King Faisil's time, ran his country on slave labour and probably never gave a thought about it because it had always been part of his way of life; the slaves were mostly treated well and the best of them were often raised to high office, and many of the women slaves became their wives.

So, in the main, though the Saudi scene has changed a little the actors play much the same parts as before: the nomad, the farmer, the driver, the caretaker, the supervisor, the organisers, and managers with, at top level, the policy makers and executives in the ranks of power. In the professions, development has gone ahead, with engineers, scientists, architects and doctors coming from the Universities in Saudi or some educated abroad returning to take a part in Saudi life, especially as supervisors of the work of foreigners who are building the new Saudi Arabia. It all looks good while the oil demand lasts. What then? In the meantime Saudi is trying to make herself self-sufficient in food by developing agriculture with Yemeni labour. Should further new development cease who would carry out the maintenance of the present buildings and essential works? While the Saudis have the money, foreigners will continue to do it; if they ever do run out the young Saudis will have to turn to, or most of them will have to go back to the desert, and that is not at all likely. We must wait and see. Their capacity for survival in tough conditions has been well proved. At present, oil revenues pay for a different sort of slave to do a great deal of essential work for them.

They have one vast scarcely-tapped source of labour formerly much used in the desert life but now discouraged—their womenfolk, who in the tented life did the preparing, cooking, weaving, and water-carrying, and gave help with the herds. King Faisil wisely started the schools and universities for women but the only work outside the home they may do is teaching, medicine, and nursing. This huge pool of women now educated and doubtless wishing to use education could well take over a lot of the office and secretarial duties of the nation, and if employment singly is unacceptable they could form secretarial and typing pools in separate rooms, coming and going veiled like the teachers and doctors. They could also provide laboratory technical assistance, and those less gifted could be involved in food preparation and on the smaller assemblies in factories, in separate rooms supervised by older women. From my experience of the capacity of the Saudi ladies as medical students there is no doubt about their ability to undertake all such duties and to do them conscientiously and well. In a world where so much food and clothing comes ready prepared their traditional tasks have become obsolete, and until like their western sisters they start to rear their families they suffer a bad spell following school when they lack occupation. All the expatriate doctors to whom I have spoken of the Saudi ladies find them, in general, too preoccupied with minor bodily symptoms, often called neurotic, which probably results from having too little to do. Here lies a partial solution to the future of the economy of Saudi. The remedy is there; the decision is theirs.

Has all the recent contact in and out of Saudi with the people of the whole world had much effect on Saudi attitudes and basic moralities? Some certainly, for there has been no time in the history of the world when invaders have not brought about some change in an indigent population. Their customs and attitudes are based firmly on their religion, possibly more so than anywhere in the rest of the world. The Muslim religion is basically the same everywhere, but in some countries the interpretation and present practices vary as with their use of alcohol, which is freely available in Jordan, Syria and Egypt, while multiple marriage is less common in those countries. To understand these attitudes it is necessary to look for a moment at these Muslim beliefs and practices.

Islam which arose out of these desert lands and spread along with conquest is the belief of many different races and nationalities. About a seventh part of the world's population turns to Mecca when they say their prayers.

There are five pillars of Islam:
1. Belief in one God, Allah—and Mohammed is his prophet.
2. Prayer—five times daily.
3. Almsgiving.
4. Fasting—during the month of Ramadan from daybreak to sunset.
5. Pilgrimage of Haj—to Mecca at least once in a lifetime.

These call for some comment:

One God. The repeated emphasis of the first pillar is on account of the Arabs having had multiple gods like the Greeks, Romans, and the Egyptians, before Mohammed preached of one God only. When he took Mecca he went into the Holy Mosque and personally smashed the many idols in the Ka'aba in spite of protests based partly on old custom and prejudice but also coming from the merchants who made a steady income from the sale of replicas of the old gods. Mohammed had temporal power as well, so had his way, and since then the call to prayer five times a day still reminds all Muslims of this.

The words of the prayer-call are—"God is greatest" (repeated four times), "I testify that there is no God but Allah and Mohammed is his Prophet" (twice), "Up to prayer, up to salvation" (twice), "Prayer is better than sleep" (twice), "Allah is greatest" (once).

It is claimed that the call is not sung by the muezzin, but it comes very near to it, being delivered in a half-singing, half-chanting tone in a variety of styles in different districts and countries, and the words, even with a little knowledge of Arabic, are usually indistinct like the enunciation of some opera singers, though a few are very much clearer; but a Muslim knowing the words from childhood has no need for clarity. The repeated phrase of "no God but Allah" in the Arabic, *"la illaha illa llah"* is heard almost as *"la la la la"*, having the emphasis of lilt and repetition and a touch of religious obscurity in interpretation. There is a sort of Eisteddfod in Mecca for the best callers of prayer.

Of the Samaritan rituals which are older than those of Islam, Sir Harry Luke has written, "It is to be noted that each man, before praying, performs ablutions similar to the ritual ablutions of the Muslims, that he stands on a prayer-rug or cloth, and that he prostrates himself at certain parts of his services with his forehead touching the ground in precisely the same manner as does the Muslim. These practices, together with Samaritan liturgical formulae which have curiously exact counterparts in the Koran, suggest that the Samaritans have made substantial contributions to the ceremonies and devotions of Islam." And he goes on later to state that while sacrifical food is being cooked in a ground-oven the worshippers shout aloud "There is no God but one", a phrase significant as the possible prototype of the Muslim profession of faith: *"la illaha illa llah,"* "there is no God but Allah". The muezzins do not call together precisely on the dot but over a few minutes, and when the calls overlap from nearby mosques, odd tones, overtones, and beats, are heard. They no longer climb the minarets, which in the Nejd are stumpy and undecorated in the Wahabi tradition, but loudspeakers sprout from the platform above, and though the call may seem to be a recording it is, I am assured, always personally delivered. Why a call and not a bell or gong whose sound reaches further? Even had they approved, the desert people had no quantities of metals and the powerful voice of the muezzin had to serve, though mechanical aid is not scorned nowadays. I have never seen a muezzin calling from a minaret.

Prayer. The call to prayer still comes five times a day—at dawn, midday, in the afternoon, at sunset, and in the evening, but prayers may be made at other times if missed due to the need for continuity in travel or business. Many drop whatever they are doing, wherever they may be, to spread their mats and pray, frequently stopping their cars by main roads and with or without mats offer their devotions. Some of the devout will spread their mats beside their desk in an office and get on with it, though most go to some point of assembly. The frequent gathering for prayer cultivates a strong sense of oneness and the physical effect of bowing the head to the ground is not without benefit, especially in older people. Prayers may be said casually, as in other religions, God being called on for help, or lauded, and at such times beads are a common aid, this custom being passed on to us from the Muslims by the crusaders who held the Eastern Mediterranean for two hundred years, sending back to their wives, families and friends such fine cloth as muslin (Mosul), and damask (Damascus), various fruit such as lemon *(limun)*, melon, and apricot, as well as beads—including the rosary, which was taken up by the Christian world, then entirely Catholic. The rosary is in everyday use in public by great numbers of Muslims, and Saudis in the Nejd in particular, with the intended purpose of telling off the attributes or names of Allah, ninety-nine of them in all, so that the strings come in small, medium, and large sizes, of thirty-three, sixty-six or ninety-nine, and, though doubtless used at appropriate moments for their basic purpose, most seem to use them as "twitch" beads to turn over in their hands as others do with cigarettes or a pipe.

Fasting. This is a Koranic directive for the month of Ramadan (2:183) and is the hardest one of the pillars to fulfil for some Muslims. Because the months are based on the moon, with a resulting twelve months and twelve days to a solar year, the time of Ramadan comes twelve days earlier each year, so that over a period of thirty years it will come to fall in any season. The fast is from sunrise to sunset and the exact moment is defined in the Koran—"Eat and drink until you can tell a white thread from a black one in the light of the coming of dawn" (2:186).

The beginning and end is signalled in modern times by gunfire and a powerful blast is needed to be heard over a large city; so powerful that when one of my friends in Riyadh taking his family to see the gun fired and unable to get near enough watched several cars that had parked close to the gun having their windows blown in!

The fast, which is for liquids as well as solids, is a severe test in a summer Ramadan, and it is customary to prepare a special large meal to be taken shortly before sunrise. The days are spent as quietly as possible, for hunger leaves many people weak. Shops and businesses open after sunset, at which moments the restaurants, I have been told by those experiencing Ramadan in other countries, are packed full, and the ravenous can be seen with knife and fork at the ready in their hands beside their heaped up plates waiting for the gun, and from that moment it is a sight to behold. Some have told me that instead of feeling fitter and losing weight during Ramadan, as was the intention, they get so hungry that they eat more at night and put on weight.

Ramadan in summer must be a severe test for desert people, and, of course, there are those who fall by the wayside with a sip or gulp or two, though most Muslims see the trial through faithfully. Smoking in the streets and dining out during Ramadan by Europeans is unwise. All Muslim women, Saudi or not, are advised to use the veil to avoid disapproval sometimes expressed by a lash from the cane of a touchy *mutawa*.

One of the injunctions about fasting is, "Believers, fasting is decreed for you as it was decreed for those before you—but if any one of you is ill or on a journey let him fast a similar number of days later on—" (2:183).

Almsgiving. "They ask you what they should give in alms. Say, 'What you can spare'" (2:219); and one-fortieth of one's income is demanded (2½%). But with few poor to alleviate, thanks to oil, a levy is not enforced, but something is still expected from a good Muslim. "Woe to those who make show of piety and give no alms to the destitute" (107:7).

Pilgrimage. The Haj has already been described and will not be further commented on here except to mention the numbers involved. Those attending Haj in 1977 were estimated at over a million and a half, and along with them went 60,000 sheep which were slaughtered in sacrifice. This would seem to be a phenomenon of this modern age and only possible with modern transport, and a feature of the Muslim religion only. Not a bit of it. The practice of concourse in large numbers is old in the Semitic world: a Roman governor of Syria had a count made of the sacrificial lambs used in one of the Passover festivals at Jerusalem, because he wanted to give his Emperor Nero an idea of the size of the Jewish nation. The astonishing total was 236,500. Each lamb had to be free of any blemish and aged between eight and twelve months, and was to be eaten by not less than ten and not more than twenty people. On this basis at a rough estimate there were more than two and a half million people at that Passover, and as in Mecca at Haj, they packed the city and were camped near it in swarms. Christ faced some of such a multitude at His trial at the time of the Passover.

Not all Muslims strictly conform to all the pillars and it is unlikely that all ever did, since it takes all types to make a Muslim world. It is, however, a solid basis on which to build their lives; it works for them, and in their belief it was ordained by Allah.

Westerners, unfamiliar with this creed do not always appreciate that the law is in the exact words of the Koran with, in addition, another part derived from what a majority alleged that Mohammed said during his lifetime, and a third part which arises from the interpretation of the first two.

With these five pillars as a foundation of understanding, let us look at some further aspects of this house of wisdom. The word Islam means "surrender", implying a surrender to Allah, and the word Muslim is formed from *mu* (one who) and *islam* (surrenders), so a Muslim is a person who has surrendered to Allah. The word *Koran* means a recital, implying that it is a recital of the word of Allah, and the one who is reciting is Allah whose word was conveyed by the Archangel Gabriel to the Prophet Mohammed. Very occasionally the words are Gabriel's or Mohammed's own. The word *Allah* comes from the old word for God, *al lah*. To Muslims the Koran is the word of their God and his commands, both the words and the writing remaining unchanged in majestic verse since the time of Mohammed. Muslims do not worship Mohammed, they revere him but they worship Allah.

Certain of the customs of the Arabs are unchanged from days long before Mohammed; thus prayer is very ancient, and prostration before an all-powerful such as the king is well recorded in Iran before the time of Alexander; the black holy stone and the house about it, the Ka'aba, in Mecca had long been a sacred place from the time of Adam and Abraham, and Noah, in story, is said to have availed himself of the flood and sailed around it seven times in the Ark.

The circuits of the Ka'aba may well have been an ancient ritual of the religious and were certainly a part of the practice in olden times of circulating around the tomb of a king, and in the ceremony of the Holy Fire of some of the Eastern Churches circulation around the Holy Sepulchre in Jerusalem in prescribed numbers takes place.

Walking about or around something seems to be much more of a practice in religions in the East, possibly because they find it rather hard to stay still for long especially when their emotions are aroused.

Maybe we sit too long at our observances. Perhaps the East could take something from our wedding receptions and we could copy a little of their style in religious ritualism. The giving of alms was considered virtuous in ancient times and is well-recorded in the Bible, as is the virtue of fasting.

What Mohammed did in setting out the word of Allah was to discard the many gods for one and to regularize past virtuous practices, and in addition to the main five pillars to lay down a code of conduct for life and to unify the people's outlook by bringing them together both spiritually and physically.

Tolerance to other religions is commanded: "There shall be no compulsion in religion" (2:256). Jesus is accepted as a wise teacher claiming that He was another prophet and that there is only one God not three—"The Messiah, the son of Mary, was no more than an apostle; other apostles passed away before him. His mother was a saintly woman. They both ate earthly food" (5:75), and though Jesus is not regarded as the son of God, the Immaculate Conception is accepted, (3:45). "The angels said to Mary: 'Allah bids you rejoice in a Word from Him. His name is the Messiah, Jesus the son of Mary. He shall be noble in this world and in the next, and shall be favoured by Allah. He shall preach to men in his cradle and in the prime of manhood, and shall lead a righteous life.' 'Lord,' she said, 'How can I bear a child when no man has touched me?' He replied: 'Such is the will of Allah. He creates whom He will!'" Of the Resurrection there is acceptance also, "Jesus, I am about to cause you to die and lift you up to Me. I shall take you away from the unbelievers and exalt your followers above them till the Day of Resurrection" (3:55).

Taking something for your own or for your family's survival is not theft or stealing in the Muslim view, for you should not be placed in such a situation, but taking otherwise is theft and is punishable according to the magnitude of the offence or its repetition. For serious theft or repetition for the third time the Koranic command is still followed, "As for the man or woman who is guilty of theft, cut off their hands to punish them for their crimes" (5:37).

The concepts about taking or saving of life are summed up as, "—whoever killed a human being, except as a punishment for murder or other wicked crimes, should be looked upon as though he had killed all mankind: and that whoever saved a human life should be regarded as though he had saved all mankind" (5:32), but as there were no professional life-savers at the time these words were written, there is no need for doctors and nurses to get inflated ideas; the meaning for mankind in general is the same.

In the beginning of the Sura on Women the earliest injunction is, "Honour the mothers who bore you" (4:1), and many commands explain the great concern that the Muslim shows for his womenkind. Marriage counsellors will approve of "If you fear a breach between a man and his wife, appoint an arbiter from his people and another from hers. If they wish to be reconciled Allah will bring them together again" (4:35). But there are not many in the western world who would be prepared to accept, "If any of your women commit fornication, call in four witnesses from among yourselves against them; if they testify to their guilt confine them to their houses till death overtakes them or Allah finds another way of life for them" (4:13).

Men's sexual aberration is treated less harshly, "If two men among you commit indecency punish them both. If they repent and mend their ways, let them be. Allah is forgiving and merciful" (4:13). What the punishment is for such men not mending their ways I could not find in the pages of the Koran. But the whole attitude of men to women which few Western women or men would accept these days, is set out in, "Men have authority over women because Allah has made the one superior to the other, and because they spend their wealth to maintain them. Good women are obedient. They guard their unseen parts because Allah has guarded them. As for those from whom you fear disobedience, admonish them and send them to their beds apart and beat them. Then if they obey you, take no further action against them. Allah is high and supreme" (4:34).

In the Sura on Women comes the instruction on the number of wives. "Give orphans the property that belongs to them. Do not exchange their valuables for worthless things or cheat them of their possessions; for this would surely be a great sin. If you fear that you cannot treat orphans (orphan girls) with fairness, then you may marry other women who seem good to you: two, three, or four of them. But if you fear that you cannot maintain equality among them, marry one only or any slave-girls you may own. This will make it easier for you to avoid injustice. Give women their dowry as a free gift; but if they choose to make over to you a part of it, you may regard it as lawfully yours" (4:2). It would not need the word of Allah from Mohammed to reach agreement amongst all men of experience in believing, "Try as you may, you cannot treat all your wives impartially" (4:129), and, perhaps as an afterthought to the last, most would not differ from, "Impatience is the very stuff man is made of" (21:32).

The wearing of veils by Saudi women is a custom often deprecated by much of the rest of the world, especially as Muslims in other countries have, for the most part, given up the practice. The Koranic words on this are mainly in the following passages, "Enjoin believing women to turn their eyes away from temptation and to preserve their chastity; to cover their adornments (except those which are normally displayed); to draw their veils over their bosoms and not to reveal their finery except to their husbands, their fathers, their husband's fathers, their sons, their step-sons, their brothers, their brother's sons, their sister's sons, their women servants, and their slave-girls, male attendants lacking in natural vigour, and children who have no carnal knowledge of women. And let them not stamp their feet in walking so to reveal their hidden trinkets" (24:31); and again in another passage, "Prophet, enjoin your wives and daughters, and the wives of true believers to draw their veils close around them. That is more proper, so that they may be recognised and not molested" (33:55), and in the same Sura nearly those same words as to who may see their wives as set out above in 24:31. Exactly whether the face is ordered to be covered by those words is not quite clear but it would appear to be implied.

As the Saudis endeavour to follow the Koran in all respects veils go over the head and drape most of their dresses when worn in public.

Kindness and justice are commanded—"Allah loves those who deal justly" (5:42), and in 4:112, "There is no virtue in much of their counsels: only in his who enjoins charity, kindness, and peace among men. He that does this to please Allah shall be richly rewarded", while the famous, "an eye for an eye, a nose for a nose, a tooth for a tooth, a wound for a wound", continues, "But if a man charitably forebears from retaliation his remission shall atone for him. Transgressors are those who do not judge in accordance with Allah's revelations" (5:45), thus encouraging a charitable reply to injury though granting retribution in kind or cash.

There is a great deal of advice on the practical conduct of lives, the treatment of children, orphans and servants, and the disposal of property, even to the detail of, "When you contract a debt for a fixed period set it in writing" (2:282), with which all would agree, and which is one of the many reasons for the professional scribes seen in Arab countries on the streets setting out these and other bonds for the illiterate. The basis of the Muslim's (like the Biblical) disapproval of interest or usury is, "Believers do not live on usury doubling your wealth many times over" (3:126). That is still the basis of a strict Muslim's conduct in a business life and you cannot expect to make your fortune by heaping up riches in a Muslim bank. The word for bank is just that, "bank", which is a western idea. The Arabic word for a place where you get paid is *sanduq* meaning box, which is where the family wealth was kept; otherwise it was on the wife's arms and body as bracelets or coins or ornament of some sort or on the fields as camels, sheep or goats. A man's wealth was estimated as so many camels.

The Arab custom of talking at some length before a meal, up to one or two hours is common, and leaving immediately the eating is concluded, with the appearance, rather unexpected, of haste, may well arise from the injunction about entering the houses of the Prophet, "But if you are invited, enter; and when you have eaten disperse" (33:51). A Saudi told me that the saying is, 'When fed, spread.'

Amongst the vast number of frequently repeated commands only two other matters can be touched on here but they often go together: alcohol and friends. There are various passages about the use and abuse of alcohol, some seeming to approve of its use, which might account for the use of alcohol in some Muslim countries such as Egypt, Syria, and Jordan, where it is sold openly as in the West, thus in 16:63 where Allah is talking of benefits conferred, "In cattle, too, you have a worthy lesson. We give you to drink of that which is in their bellies, between their bowels and the blood-streams: pure milk, a pleasant beverage for those who drink it. We give you the fruits of the palm and of the vine, from which you derive intoxicants and wholesome food. Surely in this there is a sign for men of understanding". That does not smack of disapproval. Again in the Sura, "That which is Coming" where the rewards to the righteous on the Day of Judgement are outlined, 56:15 includes, "They shall recline on jewelled couches face to face, and there shall wait on them immortal youths with bowls and ewers and a cup of purest wine (that will neither pain their heads nor take away their reason): with fruits of their own choice and flesh of fowls that they relish. And theirs shall be the dark-eyed houris, chaste as hidden pearls: a guerdon for their deeds". What is good for heaven one might expect to be good for this world, but it would appear to call for a very special vintage. A change of tone is found in 2:219, "They ask you about drinking and gambling. Say 'There is great harm in both, although they have some benefit for men; but their harm is far greater than their benefit". Wine was consumed to a state of drunkenness in the environment of Mohammed and he condemned it as a state not appropriate for prayer, in 4:43, "Believers, do not approach your prayers when you are drunk, but wait till you can grasp the meaning of your words; nor when you are polluted—unless you are travelling the road—until you have washed yourselves. If you are ill and cannot wash yourselves; or, if you have relieved yourselves or had intercourse with women while travelling and can find no water, take some clean sand and run your faces and your hands with it. Allah is benignant and forgiving". That would appear to be a command for clarity of mind and cleanliness of body as a fit state for prayer, but not a general condemnation of drunkenness. But in 5:88, there is outright condemnation, as one has heard on occasion on the morning-after, "Believers, wine and games of chance, idols and divining arrows, are abominations devised by Satan. Avoid them, so you may prosper. Satan seeks to stir up enmity and hatred amongst you by means of wine and gambling, and to keep you from the remembrance of Allah and from your prayers. Will you not abstain from them?" These are the references to the taking of alcohol which I could find and it would appear that there is something of a choice, but there is also for consideration what Mohammed may have said in his lifetime on these matters. However, not all authorities interpret things in the same way.

Friendship with other peoples is accepted if they will accept Allah, thus in 5:66, "If the People of the Book (i.e. Christians and Jews) accept the true faith and keep from evil, we will pardon them their sins and admit them to the gardens of delight. If they observe the Torah and the Gospel and what is revealed to them by Allah, they shall be given abundance from above and from beneath", and in the next Sura, 5:67, this is reinforced as, "Believers, Jews, Sabbateans, or Christians— whoever believes in Allah and the Last Day and does what is right— shall have nothing to fear or regret". But if they do not accept Allah there is a strong injunction against friendship with them in 5:49, "Believers, take neither Jews nor Christians for your friends. They are friends with one another. Whoever seeks their friendship shall become one of their number. Allah does not guide the wrongdoers". In 5:82, the Jews and pagans are really given the stick, with the Christians coming off only a little better, "You will find that the most implacable of men in their enmity to the faithful are the Jews and pagans, and that the nearest in affection to them are those who say: 'We are Christians'. That is because there are priests and monks among them; and because they are free from pride".

Today the Jews, and pagans in the form of communists, are still held in enmity, but the Christians are accepted in tolerance and national amity, and in that spirit of tolerance very many Muslims are prepared to accept Christians as their friends in work and play in which Christians reciprocate equally. There are, of course, some very strict in their religious outlook who are prepared to work with non-believers but not to accept them into full friendship. But atheists are not acceptable, and there is no need to elaborate on their attitude to the Jews. The Saudis are the strictest of the Muslims in their adherence to the Koranic words, but there are other sects which are broader in interpretation and in practice, and, of course, all Arabs are not Muslims, with Christians in much of the Lebanon and the Post-Islamic doctrine of the Druses, as well as other doctrines.

But it is difficult to see how Muslims can live in accord with the Jews and at the same time follow the commands of the Koran. Those who framed and supported the Balfour Declaration may have been unaware of the words of the Koran, or, if they or their advisers did know, perhaps they ignored them in the stress of a national conflict going badly for the Allies at the time, when the hope was strong for life-saving support from the powerful American people and there was reason to appease their strong Zionist lobby. Whatever national and individual views may be on the rightness or otherwise of that action, the whirlwind is being reaped from the sowing of that wind and what will abate it is hard to see, unless higher priority is given to the words, "There shall be no compulsion in religion". In the end it is the thoughts and attitudes of mankind which bring harmony.

★ ★ ★

Let us look at some of the other ways in which these religious dicta bear on the lives of Muslims. Four wives are allowed, but do not imagine that every Muslim has four wives. Men and women are born in more or less equal numbers, and if all the women were allotted as one of four wives to one man, three-quarters of the men would be left without wives, and no race would stand for that. The idea of four wives is that those who can support them may have that number and no more at one time, and to do so would be a serious crime. As each wife must be properly and equally treated, a man must have some achievement behind him to provide accommodation for four and their progeny. Some men rush into polygamy ambitiously and strive hard to acquire the level of income needed to pay for the luxury of satisfying their sexual appetite in this way, a problem not unknown to men of other races and religions. A common outlook is to save up so as to be able to acquire another wife, but young men, unless indulged by rich fathers, usually cannot run to more than one wife, if that.

Many educated Saudis have only one wife, and smaller families now that the appalling infantile death rate, in bedouins being perhaps 80%, has been greatly diminished. A Muslim has an easy process of divorce by going to the mosque and saying in the presence of witnesses, "I divorce you", and after another think doing the same again; he can at this stage stop it all and take her back, but if he has made up his mind and says it a third time that is it, he cannot go back on it (2:229). Many are reluctant to divorce, as in the Western world, it usually means a split with the "ex's" family which could be carried down to distant cousins, and because of the possessions which come with a wife and must go back with her. If he can, he may settle for taking on another. On the other hand, if he has had enough of women he can get rid of the lot, but it will be expensive, since he must pay for the consequences.

He may not remarry his former wife unless she has remarried again and the new husband has divorced her (2:230). One Saudi, tired of a nagging, aging wife, and his eye falling on a succulent youngster, decided to divorce his wife but found that she insisted on taking along her sixty camels, forty sheep, and sacks of gold; so he thought he would remarry her, but in order to do so she had to remarry and be divorced. So he sought out an old family retainer, a dear old gardener, and asked him if he would assist in the matter which he kindly did. The old man and his former wife were duly married so that now, in law, he possessed not only her but her all. Unfortunately, the lady was killed in an accident a week later with the result that the dear old gardener, entitled by law to her possessions, got the lot and the greedy Saudi got none.

Women may not initiate divorce, but any woman disliking her husband for any reason can make life intolerable for him and so expect him to set about a divorce. With families very closely knit and ready to react against all the members of the other family and their relations, it pays both husband and wife to behave well or big trouble can ensue, but, if one of them is a bad spouse, divorce is expected and condoned by families. Consequently, most Saudis are very cautious about divorcing, with good reason. In many ways it works better than the free and easy system of the West.

After divorce, the woman by the Koranic law, "must wait, keeping themselves from men, three menstrual courses" (2:228), while, "widows shall wait keeping themselves apart from men for four months and ten days after their husbands' death" (2:234).

Westerners inflamed about the much-marrying Muslim should remember that there are more ways than one of skinning a goat, and, from the wives' point of view, it can be better to have your competitors in the house all giving a hand with the upbringing of the children, like the *au pair* in some instances, rather than see your man from time to time between mistresses. Wives with a lot of jealousy in their natures cannot find it an easy system, but for those with a tolerant nature and brought up to the idea it seems to work. Saudis who can afford it build separate houses for each wife.

★ ★ ★

For thousands of generations the nomad man had to fight off the raiders or do the raiding, and skirmishes could be frequent in times of drought, with little food and water and the herds dying, so the surviving man became in the urgent, acute heroic sense, the "all important" one of the pair as they saw it, and if there was more than one wife, quite a hero and competitively fussed over and made much of.

In the pioneering days of the United States, Canada, South America and the like, the hero of the Indian raids was not considered in the same light by himself or his womenfolk to the same extent. The Indians were not, principally trying to steal cattle but were concerned with eliminating men, women, and children, whom they considered were taking over their territory, and white men and their women fought together side by side. Both British and American women adopt a much more matriarchal attitude towards their menfolk, different backgrounds over the ages giving rise to different behaviour. The Arab raider left the women and children alone, and this "chivalrous" attitude was carried into their warfare. Chivalry to an enemy is Arabic and was not originally a European attitude. The Crusaders noted the Arab generosity to the conquered and distressed, and in the time of Saladin were impressed enough to copy it, which started our own age of "chivalry". Shane Leslie points out that Mark Sykes disagreed with Richard Burton's comparison of the bedouin to the Red Indians, saying that he found the Arabs courteous, humane, sober, bad shots, and bad scouts. The Red Indians were the reverse, tent-dwelling being their only characteristic in common.

The habits of the Saudi are still largely those formed for survival in the desert. They had great freedom of action and they had to rely as well on the help of an increasing family to survive against other families and then, at times, the families joined together for raiding, and so, in the end, tribes were formed. It meant you had to stick together to survive or go on your own and perish. Hence, you gave your loyalty to, and were prepared to risk your life for, your own group, large or small, just as in Scotland some two hundred years ago when the clan system was operating in this way. Some think it still goes on! In Saudi it was fully operating fifty years ago and in remote parts it might be said still to be operative in everything but the raiding. These habits were brought to the towns and like religious outlooks, inbred from early life, especially the marriage customs.

Many Muslims believe it is unwise to excite the sexual instinct even to the smallest extent, and they place little reliance on the powers of suppression in men and women. Christians and others may believe all is not lost on either side by admiration of a pretty face, figure, or leg, and suppression of feelings can be inculcated by parents or at school to an extent that allows men and women to work together without disastrous incidents being common. Both sides have their own point of view concerning these matters. Love will find a way.

Some blame the heat for the change that often comes over many cold, aloof British men and women under the thawing influence of a tropical sun and some leisure.

Egyptian nurses, though they are usually unveiled in Saudi, have told me that they believe that for Saudi women, because their men lack self-control, it is much better to be veiled. Saudi women, past the first flush of youth, when speaking to European women, say they prefer for themselves and for younger women to be veiled. That could be to avoid competition, but not entirely. Some day, when the men learn to control their sexual urges better, they believe the veils can come off. In the meantime the "women's libbers" and the men who want to have a look

at the Saudi women may feel distressed about the majority of Saudi men
and women wishing to leave things as they are.

* * *

What is under the veil? Is there much to hide? Here I am privileged
by profession and it breaks no rules to say that Saudi women are like
others the world over, some beautiful and in a minority, some average,
and some below. On the whole their complexions are paler than the
men's because of the veil keeping off the sun, though desert women
brought to hospital can be very dark. Most average complexions are
similar to those of Spanish or Italian women and their features are not
dissimilar. These dark-eyed ones seem to feel, like their counterparts
elsewhere, that their eyes are better for a surround of artificial
darkening by kohl. Lips are often tinted red or even bluish, while henna
is commonly smeared on hands and feet to produce a yellowish brown
or nearly black effect, and the hair is often tinted with it. The older,
grey-bearded men often tint the ends of their forward-thrusting beards
with it, some say to show they have been to Haj, others say to show they
have some sparks left in them still.

Gold ear-rings, occasionally nose-pieces, necklaces, bracelets from
one to dozens are almost a necessity even for little girls who, of course,
are not veiled. The women's dresses beneath the black overall which
runs from the top to the head to the knees are the usual bright colours so
often seen in hot countries. Their demeanour as I have seen it in
hospital is more reserved on the whole with some showing a lot of
charm, whatever their rank. But, on the whole, I am told by European
women who have visited them in their homes, they are unrepressed in
conversation and sociability, and when they have a women's party, the
equivalent of a stag party, they let their hair down with song and dance
and generally appear to enjoy life. *En masse* they are very virtuous, with
always the few exceptions who ask for trouble. Both men and women
are kind and indulgent to their children, who are seldom spanked, and
who are provided with plenty of affection, toys, and sweets, like
children elsewhere, perhaps even more.

* * *

Saudi men-friends have told me that ninety-nine per cent of
marriages are still arranged by the parents. No Saudi woman may marry

other than a Saudi man, though Saudi men may marry Western Christians or others, but the children must be brought up as Muslims. When a young man or woman approaches marriageable age their parents usually start talking with their circle of relatives, for first and second cousin marriages are encouraged and are still common, a matter of some medical interest and concern because congenital defects, according to my colleagues in children's diseases, seem to be frequent. Former tribal and regional alliances are encouraged still, and, I have been told are enforced at times. Fathers talk and mothers talk and, as we were once told about the selection of Conservative leaders, something emerges. Gross mistakes, and palming off the ugly duckling, are highly unlikely as fathers have studied the young man and enquired about his reputation and mothers equally study the prospective bride, probably more intently if true to form with mothers in the rest of the world, and it is very likely that tragic mismatching is less likely than when it is left entirely to youth and inexperience. These days the young man is taken to see the young lady unveiled if she is a close relative, but probably not if they are of quite separate families. If neither raises any objection and the bride-price can be met the marriage is on. But both the man and woman, though strongly encouraged to unite, have the right to refuse the parental choice, in which case another start must be made. In former times neither would ever have seen the other until the unveiling in the bedroom and this is still often the case today. A lady from another Muslim country where veiling is still practised in some parts and the old marriage customs still prevail told me that she and other women feel that the unveiling in privacy is a most wonderful moment. This is understandable, if both sets of parents have put a good effort into the groundwork. The main conclusion is that although it is a different system it is one which was used for generations in Europe at one time and may still be in some parts, and it seems to work well enough. Many Western parents may have wished that they could have followed the same practice.

Marriage has often been called a lottery and some might be prepared to draw partners out of a hat like a football contest. To young Saudis it must feel a little like that, much satisfaction being known to come from the unexpected, as happened at a double wedding in Jeddah when the father of two daughters mixed up the names of his future sons-in-law as he gave them to the marriage registrar, a moment of finality, for Muslim law says that marriage vows once taken can be severed only by divorce. The distressed father, wanting no scandal, asked his daughters to hold off until he could get things put in order. But next day the girls told their father that the wrong husbands were the right ones for them and they would not consider divorce. Love had found a way.

The bride-price is no mere formality in a country where unhurried bargaining over the price of a camel, sheep, or goat, has been brought to a high art since Adam's lapse. One alleged method, which may be still used somewhere, was for the young man's father to call at the prospective bride's house and if he finds the door shut firmly the price is not high enough; if on his next visit the small peeping hole in the main door has the shutter open he is getting near; if at his next knock the door is widely opened to him the young man can be seen about with that anticipatory smirk of joys to come.

There is a civil signing of a contract which means that the pair are wed by the law, but the key to the bed is not passed over until a religious ceremony, a white wedding, is conducted by the Iman, never more than one, in the home. No weddings take place in a mosque which, like pubs at one time, are for men only, though women pray at home and women who go on Haj enter the Great Mosque at Mecca. One can see in the streets of the town chains of electric lights about the house and across the street, and sometimes a section of the street screened off when a wedding is under way. Relatives attend, men and women sitting apart, and a reception may be held in small or large numbers, said to be a pretty dull affair with a similar separation of the sexes. One of my friends who attended one of these events said that the men sat in an ordered group for about two hours with nothing doing, after which food was supplied, while the women separated by a screen had a song and dance for their diversion. It sounded like one occasion where the men come off a bad second best, and a few cynics from the West would argue that it is about the same there. Hotels are much used for wedding receptions these days.

The groom takes his bride to his parents' home, or if he can afford it, one of their own ready prepared. After marriage the bride can see her father and mother in their home or hers, and she may unveil before any of her male relatives whom she may not marry (about the same as Christians), but not her cousins unless her husband allows it.

That is more or less the customary process for a young Saudi man and woman but it has its variations depending on power, status, and resources, the pinnacle of experience being exemplified by King Abdul

Aziz who lost count of the number of his wives, well over three hundred at the end, and when he was only thirty years old they numbered over seventy. He is said to have divorced a wife before going on his expeditions to enable him to marry another as he found expedient or felt inclined while away. At short notice he would have the recommendation of parents or assistants and could experience for himself the demeanour, the eyes and voice, and sometimes if the wedding was for a political liaison he did not bother too much to make the unveiling of the bride's face at his first approach. He would go straight into action leaving the face till later on, much later on at times. There are those who may feel that he got his priorities right, for if they did not bed well he would not even bother to look at their faces but send them back to their parents with a handsome present, while the parents and bride, far from feeling disgraced by divorce, were delighted with the chance of their daughter having a child by the king, for apart from the honour, rewards could be considerable; in consequence, rumour has it, parents, at times, but using the services of other young men, made sure that a child would be forthcoming. The king had forty-three sons by his wives and lost count of the number of daughters, and by slaves and concubines the numbers have been quoted at thousands; one of such whom I saw as a patient had a magnificent personality. Even with so many calls on his time with affairs of state and otherwise King Abdul Aziz is said to have created a happy home life, was a kindly husband and father, giving his wives separate establishments and helping to keep his rivals contented by marrying their daughters, thus producing an adroit blend of business and pleasure, as the offspring would have a chance of being a part of the ruling house. Two of his wives, he said, were his favourites, one being the mother of his succeeding son, Saud, and though he divorced her they never lost each other's affection over fifty years.

* * *

For a concern wrapped up in make-believe as is the entertainment business, love of a good story seems to have come to surpass good manners, good friendship, and good co-existence. The British Television Services provide magnificent entertainment, some good instruction, and usually impress with tact and discretion in the handling of foreign affairs, while in home affairs they usually give fairly balanced accounts and comments, though causing distress at times through dabbling and raising false hopes. In general, the world has nothing but praise for our TV and most home viewers are pretty satisfied. But when they do put their foot into it the cost may be more than we can afford, sometimes in hard cash, sometimes in moral values.

The home papers reaching us in Riyadh told of the forthcoming programme of the "Death of a Princess", a young girl and her lover condemned to die for having fallen in love with a man outside the approved family circle. The comment of the few British I spoke with about the likely outcome as we saw it from the Saudi end before the showing was more or less, "For half an hour's dubious entertainment on the box it may well mean a break with Saudi Arabia and may cost us millions when we can't afford it." Most people at home and even expatriates in Saudi did not realise that in commenting at all on this subject we were commenting on and criticising the Islamic religion.

In April 1980, "Death of a Princess" was shown on TV, with the result that the Saudi "haves" and the keepers of their religion became enraged, our new Ambassador, Sir James Craig, was sent home, and we lost millions in exports. The Saudi "have-nots" and many of the expatriates of all nations were pleased that some of the habits of the "haves" were shown up, as masses of videotape copies were quickly sold on the black market, thanks to all the publicity—a reminder of the Hollywood tycoon's comment of publicity in the entertainment field at any rate, "Bad publicity, there ain't no such thing as bad publicity."

No Saudis were horrified, because they knew quite well the penalty for the behaviour of the couple concerned. Many Saudis are distressed that such behaviour goes unpunished in the West. It is unlikely that TV has changed 1,400 years of Muslim culture and it is hoped that they will remember that in matters of religion, tact and leaving well alone keep the peace and serve the purpose best. A few achieved notoriety and perhaps made some money, while some may have rejoiced that the Saudis were discomforted. The Saudi hierarchy realised that they had overreacted and in doing so had created undue publicity, and also that they should not start dropping powerful friends. Our excellent Lord Carrington showed again his intelligence and graceful touch, while our Ambassador returned to continue to give pleasure to all Saudis and Arabs everywhere with his impeccable Arabic. Some sort of agreement seems to have been reached for the future that if we do not prick the camel's hide they will not twist the lion's tail. For all our differences in outlook we need each other in a troubled world.

Perhaps the British TV might further help to restore the situation with a presentation on the achievement of King Abdul Aziz ibn Saud, the creator of the Kingdom of Saudi Arabia and one of the greatest men of this century.

CHAPTER VIII

Public Executions

The traditional centre of Riyadh is Dira Square, the largest square in the city. Long years ago, Riyadh would have started as some tents around a grazing area, a *dira*, common to the local tribe, the village green (or brown!). After a time mud huts and later houses appeared around the *dira*, and when some permanent defence was justified, the first wall was built around the whole settlement. Eventually shops and houses formed three sides, the remaining side being the sheikh's.

In 1824, Riyadh had about 6-8,000 inhabitants when it was captured by Turki, one of the tribe of Saud who rebuilt the walls and constructed on his side of the square two buildings, one for administering his territory and the other for dispensing justice. Somewhere in them he had his home, with all of them making a sort of fortified mud palace or castle *(qasr)*, while on the west side of the square he built a mosque. Both mud palaces and mosque stood well into this century when they were replaced by modern buildings on the same sites. Around the square runs a modern road, while the centre, like so many others the world over, has become an excellent car-park, when you can get in.

The square reflects much of the passing show with the heavy flow of traffic, wheeled, footed, and hoofed, the chatter and bargaining from houses and shops on the three sides, and on Friday after midday prayers, the carpet and clothes auctioneers used to be in full spate. The fourth side portrays the majesty of government with the Emirate accommodating the Prince of Riyadh, and at times providing a place for the King to meet his sheikhs and imams (religious leaders) for debate and directives, and beside it without a break is the Palace of Justice, the law courts. That part of Dira Square immediately in front of these two gracious buildings instils in informed newcomers a sense of awe, for it is here, where at all other times the traffic rolls or parks on it, that justice is dispensed by the sword to capital offenders before a large crowd. The administration of justice and power in Saudi is not veiled; they mean what they say and they do what they mean for all to see.

Some unknown Briton has aptly dubbed this cradle of Riyadh, Chopper Square.

If a condemned man is to be executed, immediately after midday prayer he is led down the steps of the Palace of Justice, hands tied behind him. Exactly what happens then I found to be uncertain, with rumours abounding. Some said he was drugged and dragged out, some said that if the executioner does not do his job properly in one blow, the prisoner is allowed to go free, and one prisoner is reputed to have taken a cut across the shoulder-blades from a slicing stroke, risen and fled into the crowd and got away. Others said that two or more blows are often necessary. Again, others said that the head is only partly severed but the victim is made insensible by the blow and dies of haemorrhage and the head is sewn back to conform with the Muslim idea of the body being intact on the day of resurrection. Others reported that small boys play football with the head, and others said that the relatives take away the body and head. There is a report that it is customary to leave the body where it is in a pool of blood all day, and that on one occasion an American and his wife parked their car in the square not aware of what had happened a short while before and the wife tripped over the body while the husband slipped in the pool of blood! Thesiger writing in the 1940s reported the tale as told to him of an execution in Riyadh when the body lay in the square all day, and such may have been the custom in Riyadh then, but times change; think what was happening elsewhere in the world at that time with execution by torture, gas-chamber, bullets, and flattening by tank the vogue then. There are also views expressed that Saudis are cruel and enjoy such spectacles. I do not believe that the first applies to Saudis any more than to Europeans, and I wanted to form a view of my own of the second and to dispose of rumour with facts. Admittedly I had some curiosity for the centre of the spectacle, but the sight of the passing of life, quickly or slowly, has been a common enough part of my occupation and my main curiosity concerned the living.

With all this in mind, I went along one day to the Square just as the service was over and waited along with some hundreds of representatives of most nations of the earth. About a score or two had gathered near the steps of the Palace of Justice past which the traffic continued to flow, the crowd causing some hindrance. Suddenly the policeman at the top of the steps with a cane in his hand shot down into the crowd and with appropriate snarls laid about a few, which created a minor stampede to get behind the ring of parked cars. The panic subsided, the traffic surged on, the watchers dwindled and it began to look like an off day. Resignation and, surprisingly, disappointment were evident in many. The hundreds leaving the mosque had mostly gone their way, having seen it in the past and registered its message. A few of the watchers had youngish children with them and I walked away musing whether the children were being taught a stern lesson to behave or else! Saudis, I found, are particularly kind and indulgent to their children and it seemed unlikely.

I tried again another time without result, not even a caning of the crowd, but on that occasion there was one western woman in the waiting crowd. A Saudi, supported by several Europeans in a group discussing these matters, told me that in the old days of public hanging or guillotining in Europe and the United States that two-thirds of the crowds were usually composed of women. The Saudis keep their women away from executions, but for that matter I did not see one woman present at a game of football in Riyadh.

Friday, 14 April 1978, was hazy and cooler, looking a good day for a trip in the desert, but one of my patients was dangerously ill and in need of several daily visits, so I waved my friends off and stayed in the city—an uncommon cause of detention for me in Saudi. I spent two hours with the patient after breakfast and took the chance at midday before going to the hospital again to drive into the centre of town to see a sick friend. As I passed Dira Square, the mosque was emptying but there were no carpet or clothes auctioneers lined up as usual, and the movement of the people was mainly towards the centre of the Square. This looked like business of a different sort, so I parked the car and walked towards the Square, finding a police car blocking the west entrance. The battle for life in one part of the town was not so pressing that I could not spend a moment to study this ritual taking of it, and as I turned into the Square there was no doubt; here were not the hundreds I had seen before waiting patiently, but two or three thousand, a solid wall of citizens of all ages and nations, but no women in view, four or five deep around a cleared space half the size of a football pitch with one side open to the Palace of Justice and the Emirate and lined by soldiers with rifles and a few rovers with canes, and around the fringe latecomers buzzing and pushing in great excitement.

To the authorities entrusted with their duties it was a solemn moment and to many of the crowd also, while to many others it was a spectacle making a tepid thing of their weekly football game, as one of the two greatest dramas of life—its coming or going—was about to be enacted. I joined the jostling late, unsighted at the back and was heaved about, my height being an advantage though not to shorter citizens behind me. After a good elbowing in the melée I stood right back but managed to get fleeting views.

Just at that moment the prisoner was led down the steps of the Palace of Justice by two soldiers, his hands tied behind his back, walking calmly, his head-cloth bound around his head and some clothing below not visible to me. He was quietly led forward to the centre of the cleared area to a point exactly in line with the division of the Palace of Justice and the Emirate, which may have been coincidence or, perhaps, intended to emphasise the junction of the two aspects of the administration of law. Some six soldiers drew up in line behind and a figure in white stood by. The prisoner was stripped to the waist, his *guttra* tucked in around his head, and he was made to kneel with the head forward. The crowd around, except for the jostling latecomers, was silent. Some official words were said and then came the first surprise. There was a burst of hand-clapping, no jeering, no mocking, not a murmur from the crowd, save from the jabbering unsighted at the back. The time was 12.30 p.m.

The executioner emerged from the group and stood some four paces from his victim and raised his long, curving, silvery, shining sword, and slowly advanced in ceremonial style and struck hard. From the force of the blow his victim flopped forward. The head appeared to be still slightly attached and the swordsman strode to the other side and struck another blow to complete his work and drew back, then slowly advanced again to wipe the blade on the dead man's clothes, one sweep for each side. There was no great spurting visible because of the victim's immediate forward fall from the force of the blow, but the inevitable pool of blood quickly formed. My inadequate view made it impossible to see if, as is related, the victim was pricked in his chest by another sword to stiffen all his muscles, including the neck. I was told this was not done now. The officials stood about for half a minute and then quietly withdrew while the silent crowd stayed on with gaze fixed on the slumped forlorn thing in the middle. Then chattering broke out all around and some of the fringe departed. A police car, holding some officials, drove away through the crowd near to me. The corpse lay in the sun and the crowd stayed on, an example to all of the consequences of his infamy. Exactly ten minutes after the sword stroke, a police van moved to the centre, the back was opened and a stretcher pulled out and the body heaved in while a policeman picked up the head by the head-cloth and put it alongside the body and the doors were closed. As the van moved off, leaving only an irregular pool of blood to mark the site, came the next surprise. The crowd hand-clapped vigorously and briefly, and again no cheering and shouting just, what appeared to be, approval like the "aye" of a committee, that all had been done and well done according to the law.

The soldiers then received a command to break ranks and they walked quietly towards the palaces. I wondered if it would then happen. It did. The crowd broke behind the soldiers and surged about them led by small boys and youths sprinting to the centre, and soon a large crowd, many deep, formed around the pool of blood to gaze and gaze. The main crowd was slowly dispersing with the bustle and hubbub as one might hear at the end of any large event, while others moved in to the centre or away, and as I moved off after some ten minutes they were still as thick as ever about the bloody remnant.

There was no head play, and there had been by the authorities only a dignified process of a duty called for by the law. There was no undignified mocking of the victim by the crowd and the first brief applause by hand-clapping I took to be approval of the impending execution. The second hand-clapping I interpreted, and later had confirmed, as a sign of their approval of the execution and the manner of it, according to the tradition and formula laid down. The public nature of it I interpreted as showing that justice is properly dispensed, and as a warning of the consequences to any who may entertain murderous thoughts. To men and children seeing it for the first time it well may act as a deterrent, but to others it is undoubtedly just a spectacle, and I saw many older citizens amongst the crowd moving away. I gathered from general talk that some attend most executions, and, like *aficionada* at bullfights, appear to enjoy the spectacle; but there are the very many who having seen it once do not bother to go again, there being many Saudis and others among those moving away from the mosque that day who wanted no part of the spectacle.

Execution in public is an example of the Saudis' dislike of furtive dealings. The traditional way of conducting business is an approach to the chief in the presence of any others who happen to be sitting about drinking coffee and chatting to pass the time or seizing the chance of settling some business. Bargaining in trade obviously cannot be conducted entirely in public, some matters needing consideration in private by both sides before a public settlement.

The newspaper report of the execution stated that the man had been in prison for five years. The Saudis will not execute until they get a confession, which he finally had given, and he had been well and truly tried in the matter. As for it being a public performance—it is certainly a very salutary warning to others, but whether this is a good or bad way of doing things is very much a two-sided debate; this is their way. If public execution does act as a deterrent then the victim serves some useful purpose in his passing, and concerning the rushing to gaze at the pool of blood afterwards, a Saudi said simply, "Well, that is the way that has been decided on as a future warning."

As to this mode of execution as one of the many varieties practised today—the prisoner is said to be given a drug to help him, usually, in his distress. On this occasion he walked out steadily with no suggestion of being dragged. The despatch is swift and painless, and I consider it to be a better means than by shooting, hanging, electrocution or guillotine, if execution is to be used. The head is not sewn back to the body, some Saudis told me, head and body being taken away for burial by police assistants.

Muslims give little deference to the body when life is over, for it is their belief that the departed is in Paradise; in some Muslim countries and sects the graves are marked and inscribed headstones are used, but for the Wahabis of the Nejd or those who follow their practices there may be a simple rough stone without any inscription on it, or there may be nothing at all. Even the graves of the Saudi great are uninscribed and most are unknown, as is said to be the case with Kings Abdul Aziz and Faisil. But though they do not pay much heed to the body yet it must not be disturbed in its grave, for that would despoil the body for the day of resurrection, a belief held also by some of the versions of Christianity. For the same reason there are no post-mortem examinations save rarely for some medico-legal reason. In other Muslim countries post-mortems for medical information are often performed. As there are no post-mortems in Saudi there are no spare parts available for surgical transplantations which means that kidney failure can be treated by dialysis only, unless a kidney donated by a relative or another is forthcoming. Much consideration is being given to the solution to these problems in both medical and religious circles. I have been told that King Fahad has recently permitted the use of cadaver kidneys.

The punishment for treason, which means that the life of the king is threatened, may be more subtle. After conviction the offender may be put in a house and guarded for the rest of his life. He will get food and may have papers, but he may see no one and make no communication with anyone, nor they with him, and thus he passes his living death. His one hope is of an amnesty for all prisoners, as might happen at such a time as the accession of a new king, when he might rejoin his relatives and friends again as from the grave.

Most Saudi justice is quickly dispensed. If a debtor will not pay the lender may take his case to the Governor who asks the alleged debtor to wait on him, and asks if he owes the money. If "yes", he is given two days to pay; if "no", there is a quick investigation and a quick settlement is made one way or the other.

King Khalid was fearful of assassination, the great King Faisil having been brought down by a close young relative, after the seventh attempt on his life, so there is justification for a clear passage and good protection for the king. One evening, returning from a desert trip and coming to Riyadh by the Mecca road, we found the National Guard in their khaki uniforms, red head-cloths and black head-rings (fan-belts to witty Brits) lining both sides of the road into Riyadh for twenty-four kilometres out and about thirty paces between each man, their rifles with bayonets fixed. Something of the same display of strength and measure of protection greets each head of state's entry and exit from the capital, but whether international pecking order is measured in kilometres I do not know. It is not just show—they mean business. On one occasion when, from a side road, an ill-timed lorry dashed into the highway just as the motorcycles with the king's car behind came along, the motorcycles scattered, the king's car managed to swerve around the lorry, and the guards let fly in all directions with small arms.

There were about five attempted coups up to 1974, according to Laquer in *Confrontation.* They mainly involved the Air Force, and according to rumour the main participants finished up in Chopper Square.

★ ★ ★

To imagine that with peace and plenty everyone is happy with the government is to take a simplistic view. In every country there are groups who would like to lead the nation whether it be in business, professions, religion or in political power, and the extremes of poverty and prosperity especially create dissatisfactions which make strong men want more of the cake for themselves, their families and maybe for others as well, and they lust for power or just feel that their leadership would be best and their views should prevail. It happens everywhere, with Saudi Arabia no exception, and like other states Saudi needs an army, guards, police and a security corps to watch for internal or external subversive elements. Britain has all these just as much as any other state, though methods differ. Saudi has something which all the world wants materially and, as the spiritual centre of Islam, must show vigilance.

Armed Forces personnel are always likely sources of subversion of political power, trained as they are in commanding men and in the use of arms, and exercising a great deal of authority, which feeds their sense of power. This corrupting set of circumstances has fired men the world over to aim for the supreme command of a nation. In Central and South American states and parts of Africa, to cite only a few, a take over bid by yet another general has come to be the common way of a change of government. For all the satisfaction that Europe and the United States of America find in democracy a lot of the world does not want to have any of it. There is much to be said for a benign autocracy—if it can be kept benign!

At times the masses are stirred by a religious revolt that has its roots in a desire for fundamentalism and a retreat from profligacy and corruption, as in Iran today, with Iraq going to war to avoid a similar priestly political take over. The banner to unify others can be just the opposite—doing away with the old religions altogether, as with the Communists. In Saudi Arabia there has long been an agreement between the powers spiritual and temporal to run things together, like the mediaeval form of government in old Europe with castle and cathedral facing each other and balancing extremes.

In the eyes of some, every government is corrupt, no matter how well it is doing. The latest attempted coup which exploded at the very heart of Islam's institutions, beside the Ka'aba in the Holy Mosque in Mecca appears to have been confused in conception, uncertain of purpose and ill-planned in action.

The first year of the fifteenth century in the Muslim reckoning of time, dating from the Prophet's leaving Mecca to go to Medina, was, according to some, 1 Muharram 1400, which by our timetable was 20 November 1979, while others have it that the new century started on the same day of 1401, but whichever it may have been, the day itself is holy in any year. Because of its importance in Muslim eyes the King and several of the high Princes were expected by many of the masses, including these new insurgents, to be present in the Great Mosque on that day.

As the Imam of the Grand Mosque completed the dawn prayer he was pushed aside, and a young man in his late twenties from the College of Islamic Studies in Riyadh, Muhammed ibn Abdullah al Qahtani, shouted into the microphone that he was the expected Mahdi and quoted Holy Muslim Writ to justify himself, "because they are persecuted everywhere until they have no recourse but the Holy Mosque". Meanwhile, the leader of the rebels, Juhainan ibn Muhammed Utaibi, a 39-year-old, wild religious zealot and pamphleteer known to the police, seemingly always strange, as if not quite human but never appealing as divine, held back those near the microphone at gunpoint, but meeting resistance fired three shots and so despatched to Paradise a young accolyte doing more than his duty. Tumult followed this murder and desecration of the holiest house of Islam, and later in the day butchery began which was to last two weeks.

After the initial panic when none was aware whether this might be an act of religious extremism or anything from an attempted take over by a foreign power, the participants and their intentions became clearer. However, at the start news was suppressed, other than for a permitted announcement that there had been shooting in the Grand Mosque, partly for the sound reason that no one quite knew what it was all about. Later, details were announced, especially when it was all over and it had become clear that it was basically a religious protest based on a wish to clear the country of corruption and to establish a proper distribution of wealth in place of the vast fortunes accumulating to certain princes and business men, and calling for a return to the old ways of Islam while ridding the country of infidels and unholy ways, and generally putting the clock back. Here they were at it again—the fundamentalists, the Wahabis, the Ikhwan, and the various other brands of puritanism, and the alleged scapegoat—the one who had started all the rot by listening to the voice of the West was none other than King Abdul Aziz himself!

The rebels may have calculated that if they could capture the King and some of the high Princes they could achieve their purposes. But the King and his brothers had not turned out.

The leader of this curious attempt at a *coup 'de culte' d'état* in his previous behaviour and his pamphlets, *The Misconduct of Rulers* and *The Call of the Brethren,* had given a pretty strong pointer to his likely future behaviour and, though examined by the authorities at one time, he was allowed his freedom together with various other people screened at the same time. His only claim to military prowess was to have served against his will in the National Guard in which he rose to the rank of Corporal; this together with his written declaration of how he would run the world, has a very nasty familiar ring—as the second ex-corporal to try and upset the world this century. Perhaps that rank should be abolished.

The army of this new Mohammed and his new Mahdi numbered something over two hundred with a few more around the country. For the purposes of their insurrection they had smuggled into the cellars of the Mosque a stationwagon full of arms and ammunition, another packed with dates and rice, and several coffins which had been brought in by men with serious faces, not out of reverence for the dead but with respect for the automatic rifles they contained. The morning found them well-placed in minarets and other vantage points, and once the melée started they proved to be impressive shots, killing hundreds of the attacking soldiers and police. The 600-strong Special Security Forces were flown to Mecca at speed. Helicopters were used to lower men onto the courtyard, where they were shot to pieces. But gradually the insurgents were cleared from the towers and upper stories and then, shielding themselves with mattresses, they were driven underground to the site of their stores in the cellars, and here they settled with some twenty-three women and twelve or so children.

The new Mahdi had a much shorter reign than his predecessor in the Sudan about a hundred years previously, having the lower part of his face shot away early in the carnage.

To add to the Establishment's concern, rioting broke out in the eastern Hasa province amongst the Shia population who took heart from the Shia success in Iran under the formidable Ayotola Khomeini. Qatif was in the hands of a mob for a time, but after security forces had killed seventeen of the insurgents, order was regained.

Meanwhile in the Grand Mosque the hopeless position of the rebels was becoming clear even to Juhainan, and in the early hours of 5

PLATE 10   87

63 renegades executed

RIYADH, Jan 9 (SPA) — The government Wednesday executed 63 members of the misled band of armed renegades who assaulted the Holy Haram in Mecca Nov. 20.

The executions were carried out in several cities and towns of the Kingdom.

In a statement, the Ministry of the Interior explained King Khaled's order to Prince Naif, the interior minister. It said "We have acquainted ourselves with your report on the confessions of the criminals who attacked the Holy Haram on Muharram 1, 1400 H (Nov. 20, 1979) with arms and ammunition, closed its doors upon the Muslims who came for the dawn prayer, subjected them to terror, killed innocent people and compelled those present inside the Haram to declare their allegiance to one of their group claiming he was the Mehdi. Those who did not do so were threatened with weapons, as is recorded in one of the speeches delivered by one of the leaders of the sedition on the morning of their assault of the Haram.

"The ulema issued a religious ruling (fatwa) to fight against them, with an inference to God's command, which says,' Do not fight them near the Holy Mosque until they fight you in there, and if they fight you, you must kill them.' They also quoted the Holy Prophet (peace be upon him) as saying.' He who comes to you to disunite you and to sow dissension amongst you, you must behead him.'

"Further, the Board of Senior Religious Scholars, in their 15th session, issued a statement denouncing this grave crime and sinful and treacherous aggression. They held the opinion that, by their sinful actions inside the Holy Haram, this straying band had subjected themselves to God's saying that ' He who tries to spread atheism in it (the Holy Mosque) by force, We shall give him painful punishment', and further that ' They will commit an outrage who stop God's name being remembered in His mosques and try to destroy them. They shall only leave them out of fear. They shall be disgraced in the world and shall be awarded severe punishment hereinafter.'

"The Board had described the leaflets of this clique as' the seeds of dissension, error, chaos, disturbances and of staging games against the interests of the people and the country. They had warned the Muslims against the false and dubious nature of those leaflets.

"The Board's statement necessitates upon us to punish them to ward off the evil and to please our Creator. Furthermore, we have received fatwas (verbal as well as written) from a number of senior religious scholars (ulema), quoting God's commands that ' Those who fight God and His Messenger and attempt to spread corruption on earth must be either killed or crucified or their hands and feet be cut in cross direction or they be exterminated from the land. They earn disgrace in this world and await heavy punishment hereinafter'.

"Therefore, kill those whose names are appended to this statement, in order to please Allah, to defend the sanctity of the Holy Kaaba and of His worshippers and to vent the anger of the Muslims. They are those whose affirmations were noted in the records of the Mecca Court by a number of judges.

"As regards those whose crime was unlike theirs and who did not shed innocent blood near the Holy House and were not among the leaders of the dissension, but only assisted these criminals by supplying arms and ammunition or guarding the gates, they shall not be punished with death. They shall be sentenced to imprisonment and we shall intimate you the prison terms of each of them in due course of time after deciding upon the punishment according to each one's crime.

"Those women who helped this corrupt band by supplying them water, food or arms and ammunition, shall each receive a prison award of two years, during which they shall be given religious education for their reform.

"As regards minors who took part in the crime, they shall be kept in the welfare centre for their reform and education, so that they become good members in our Islamic society."

Interior ministry statement

RIYADH, Jan 9 (SPA) — Interior Minister Prince Naif Wednesday said 12 officers and 115 noncommissioned officers and soldiers obtained martyrdom during the battle to recapture the Holy Haram from the Muslim renegades.

Another 49 officers and 402 noncommissioned officers and soldiers whose names will be announced later, were hospitalized for various injuries, the minister said.

He added that 63 renegades were executed Wednesday and that 75 others were killed during the siege.

He also said that during the cleaning of the basement, 15 bodies were found taken into custody.

He added that 27 renegades had died from wounds.

The Prince said that the death sentence was reduced to imprisonment of various periods for 19 of the assailants.

He added that the renegades were accompanied by 23 women and children, and investigations couldn't prove the participation of 38 persons who were set free.

Continued on back page

ARABIA'S FIRST ENGLISH LANGUAGE DAILY

arab news

saudi research and marketing company

The summary in the 'Arab News' of 10-11 January, 1980, of the last proceedings following the insurrection in Mecca.

December, just two weeks after the murder at the microphone, the wounded and exhausted leader brought out the remnants of his followers—some 170, a goodly number still, seventy-five dead rebels being found about the Mosque. Twenty-three women and thirteen boys came to the surface as well, all having been used for deception and cover by the rebels; all were submitted to some form of corrective treatment but none was executed.

The prolonged interrogations of the insurgents which followed revealed no evidence of outside inspiration or help, practical or directional, which gave ample cause for the bolting of stable doors. However, the prisoners were rebels and had murdered and had desecrated the holiest part of Islam, and after a fair trial they were executed in the usual way. On 9 January 1980, to let the example be seen throughout the Kingdom, in the central squares of eight towns, the heads of forty-one Saudis, ten Egyptians, six S. Yemenis, three Kuwaitis, and one each from N. Yemen, Sudan and Iraq hit the dust.

CHAPTER IX

The Origin of the Dynasty of Saud

Two men fought at a postern gate, one with a sword and the other a rifle. The swordsman advanced, his weapon raised to strike; the rifleman, shielding his face with one hand, fired point-blank with the other. As his sword clattered to the ground the wounded man crawled to the small postern in the large main gate of the fortress where a henchman on the inside seized an arm to pull him through just as his legs were grabbed by his assailant outside. For a moment the wounded man, the governor, became a human rope in a tug-of-war for a dynasty, then he worked one leg loose and with a vicious kick at his opponent's groin, which made him faint, he was free. But the gate had been held open long enough for the attacker's cousin to rush it, squeeze through, and in the confusion inside overwhelm those near him with his sword while others followed to force open the main gate—to a new era of Arabian history. Had that little gate been slammed on the forty raiders within the town walls, they would have been finished off either by a counter-attack or by the town's other inhabitants.

Abdul Aziz, son of Abdul Rahman of the House of Faisil and of Saud, the man with the rifle in that fight, had been turned from the fortress gate as a boy of ten with his father, then the ruler of the region. This feuding Saud family had battled for years without success against their northern neighbours, the Rashids. Learning that the Rashid leader had ordered his Governor of Riyadh to use the old trick of inviting the Saud leaders to a meal and to massacre them at it, they accepted the invitation and at a pre-arranged signal rose as one man and slaughtered all their hosts including the Governor, who was up-ended and dropped down a well.

One of the Sauds attending that feast and watching the slaughter was Abdul Aziz, the future king. That day's work was more of a survival than a victory for the Saud leaders, as a little later, Ibn Rashid set out

1. *The large gate in the Musmak fortress in Riyadh with the small postern gate at ground level, which was stormed by Abdul Aziz and his forces in the taking of Riyadh. The embedded spearpoint is behind the Saudi and is seen in the enlarged picture to the right as a small dark dot just to the right of the post and near its centre. Mr Joe Smith of Oxford supports the other post.*

2. *Abdullah ibn Jiluwi cousin of Abdul Aziz and first through the postern gate. He and his descendants were given the Hasa as Emirs.*

3. *The fortress of Dillam where Abdul Aziz fought off al Rashid, and where we had our own skirmish. Bob Hunter and Michael Ford made up two thirds of our force.*

for revenge, arriving in force and laying waste to Riyadh, including poisoning its wells.

The townspeople had had enough and turned on the Sauds, forcing them out, complete with wives, retainers and their children in camelbags, to wander in the desert until given refuge by the ruler of Kuwait.

Abdul Aziz saw it all, receiving the toughest of childhood educations. His teenage was, as the son of an impoverished, exiled desert sheikh, a broader one than most bedouin of the Central Region; for Kuwait is a seaport with a variegated life, and even then accommodated large vessels, including warships, the signs of distant powerful nations. He grew to be strong and over six feet tall, handsome and charming. Also this poor, displaced young prince of the desert had a raging ambition to win back his birthright. His father, with the help of his patron and protector, the Sheikh of Kuwait, and with 10,000 men had tried to regain his lost domain from the now well-established Rashid who had forced him out; but the allegiance of the men of the desert, for ever shifting to the estimated winner, now backed the Rashid, and once again the Sauds were forced into further exile as the price of their defeat.

Abdul Aziz, scion of the House of Saud, had now grown to manhood and in the way of young Arabs, often only in their teens, was ready to lead a band of warriors to begin the conquest of his dreams, to win back the land of his fathers.

He was, at twenty-one, already an experienced campaigner, having formed his own raiding party amongst whom were his brother, Mohammed, and his cousin Abdullah ibn Jiluwi. At the end of the summer of 1901 they left Kuwait, each with his personal equipment of camel, rifle and ammunition, dagger, sword, flour, dates and water, moving south-west into the nearest part of the former Saud territory where they enjoyed several raids, his followers believing this to be the sole purpose of their autumn journey. Abdul Aziz, however, was hoping that renown accruing from his successful raiding would win a following of many of the tribes formerly friendly to his family; but the series of small skirmishes had little effect. The bedouin weighed carefully the chances of any aspirants to leadership and, like men of all ages, were mainly interested in winners.

He had not spoken to anyone of his ultimate plan, and it was just as well for the main purpose of these raids had not been achieved, though to his followers they seemed to be a success. A few joined him, but he was soon back to his faithful following of forty, and was now pursued by Ibn Rashid with major forces. To escape he turned east into the Hasa, the territory where the Turks had troops that also turned against him. He was a hunted outlaw now and moved further south to enter the northern edge of the great desert, the Empty Quarter, to escape his pursuers, and passed the month of Ramadan about the district of Haradh with its oases. After some months of idleness avoiding capture the little band were ready for anything.

Defeat to a bold and intelligent man is a spur to deep thought and a prod to persistence, or a change of plan. With failure at the periphery he decided on a direct thrust to the heart—he would try to capture Riyadh itself! It required some nerve on the part of a 21-year-old man to take on a town of 5,000 with a sizeable fortress garrisoned by about eighty men, while his own force numbered only forty! With youth, daring, strength, imagination, and courage, almost anything is possible, but to do quite so much is unlikely, and had he chosen to discuss his plan with a "committee" support for his venture would probably have been nil. He had sworn his men to follow him to the death, and having made up his mind, early in the year of 1902 he moved them to the wells at Abu Jifan, some 75km from Riyadh and then on to Ain Heet, 35km out, where he rested and watered before going into attack. His plan was the only one possible with his numbers—surprise, and going for the vital point of power at a stroke.

They approached Riyadh from the south, and 10km out he left twenty of his men and all his camels in a palm grove, detailing them to return to Kuwait if he did not summon them within twenty-four hours. Twenty men advanced on foot, and within sight of the town walls he left his second reserve in command of his brother, Mohammed, and went forward with six men to his destiny. The great Admiral Nelson, a hundred years earlier, when about to lead a large raiding party at Tenerife, where he lost an arm, had told his commander-in-chief that the morrow would "see his head crowned with laurel or cypress". Abdul Aziz told his brother that if by midday next they had heard nothing from him, to ride to Kuwait, for he would win or die in the attempt.

They had waited for the new moon to give some light and about midnight turned to the north-east corner of the town close to the outside cemetery and near the fortress within the walls. Placing a palm tree against the wall, they were up, over, in, and unobserved as the town slept on unguarded. They worked their way along the alleys towards the central square near to which was the main gate of the fortress with a small postern gate at its centre, admitting only one man at a time in a very bent position so that he could be clubbed or cut down if trying to force an entry. Both gates were tightly shut.

Immediately opposite, across a small square, was a house where lived the women of Ibn Rashid's governor, Ajlan, being a sort of fortified harem which was also barred. Abdul Aziz, now surcharged by danger and necessity with his plan coming to a climax, cast his mind back to his childhood, remembering that the house next door to the women's was owned by a cattle dealer with two daughters, a not unlikely recollection for Abdul Aziz even though he was only ten when he was last in the square. He was always renowned for courage and simplicity, so he just knocked on the door and awaited events; sure enough a girl's voice asked him what he wanted. The best he could concoct on the spur of the moment was to say that the Emir Ajlan wanted to buy two cows and he had to see her father. Girls know all about young men coming to their doors at night with that kind of story, and she gave him a piece of her mind about what she thought he was really after and then told him to clear off. He told her to be quiet and to fetch her father or he would tell the governor in the morning, who would slit him up. The father who so far had been letting his daughter do his duty, heard the threat, opened the door and was grabbed by Abdul Aziz who, being recognised by both daughters, silenced them without hurt and shut them in the cellar. To add to the raid's uncertainties, the father escaped in the fracas.

The governor's house could not be reached except by breaking into another house beside it where a man and wife in bed had to be bound in their bedclothes. At that moment Abdul Aziz sent two men for all his reserves outside the town. The remaining four scaled up to the roof of Ajlan's house on each other's shoulders, forced open the roof door, caught the sleeping slaves one by one, and burst into the main bedroom to find Ajlan's wife and sister in bed, but no Ajlan. A gun held persuasively produced the information that there were eighty men in the fortress and that Ajlan would not come out till after sunrise.

All the household were secured, the remainder of the storming party were brought in through a hole punched in the mud wall and they settled down to wait, think, plan, consume the governor's dates and coffee, and snatch a little sleep, then pray—but not to contemplate a retreat. The die had been cast long before, and they were now experiencing the long vigil before attack.

It was thought that in the morning Ajlan would come from the fortress to the house, knock, and expect the door to be opened by one of the women as usual. In anticipation, one of the men was dressed in the clothes of the customary door-opener. Things did not quite go according to expectations. After the prayer-call, to which the attackers responded with their own prayers, they watched at an upper window with rifles ready. Action began with the large gate opening and some of the governor's horses being brought out. The sight of the open gate caused Abdul Aziz to change his plan on the spur of the moment. He decided to charge the gate, shouting to his men to cover him with rifle-fire as he bolted down the stairs and out into the square. The governor came out with several attendants just as Abdul Aziz rushed out of the house, and at the sight of him the main gate was rapidly closed, while the men ran through the postern gate like a lot of rabbits into a burrow, leaving Ajlan alone to face Abdul Aziz. Their brief fight, already described, resulted in that door being held open for victory and the march of progress in Arabia. Abdul Aziz's cousin, Abdullah ibn Jiluwi, was the first through the postern, the defenders mistaking him for one of their own in the confusion as they poured back into the fortress. His lethal sword-play allowed others to rush in and to open the main gate for all the forty men to follow. They killed nearly half of the eighty defenders, including the governor who fell to Jiluwi's sword. Abdul Aziz's green flag flew over the fort as his followers announced to the townspeople that the young master was home again.

This time he had done something that set the tribes chuckling over the coffee cups at the audacity and ability of the man, and many of them were ready to side with him now that he had given them the story of a raid not bettered in the folklore of a land of connoisseurs.

He had arrived not to revel but to rule, knowing that Ibn Rashid was not just tough and tyrannical but capable as well, and would come again. The Saud's had tried his and his father's capacity and had come off worse. So Abdul Aziz set about preparing for the inevitable by sending for the Saud family, parents, wives, children, brothers and sisters, being now able to give them a homeland and in so doing declaring his intention to stay. He rebuilt the town wall and other defences then left his father, an old campaigner, in command of the town and its defences while he moved into the desert, probably to avoid being beseiged, a fate the town had suffered in the past. He moved south towards the Empty Quarter where he expected to add to his forces by old and new allies who, far from the Rashid centre in the north, had never felt bound to his enemy. There was time to gather a small army and to bring them under his domination, though training in the ordinary sense there was none, the two main ploys being a wild charge or a line of fire and every man for himself, with the commander urging them on to keep at it one way or the other and not to stop for plunder nor to run away.

At the time of the capture of Riyadh, his enemy was about to encircle Kuwait, the news reaching him at the onset of the warm weather with no time to withdraw his army and march to attack Abdul Aziz. In Europe, in winter, Caesar and later conquerors stopped campaigning and went into winter quarters to try to keep warm and dry, while in the desert fighting stopped during the hot months because of the excessive heat and lack of water at the wells. More than six months passed before Ibn Rashid set out with a large force after the young upstart. He passed by Riyadh, for scouts told him that the bird was not at home but resting in the south.

Abdul Aziz had chosen his ground well, not the open desert but behind the walls of the village of Dillam, some 50km south of Riyadh, with palm trees all about, ordering his men not to move but to fire on the enemy as they came into the oasis. The Rashid were effectively checked by the volleys which met their advance, and though trying on and off all day they made no headway, being confronted by a novel method of fighting—no rushing about on camels or horses, no manoeuvring, just a solid fusillade when they came near. Ibn Rashid retreated, and next day, instead of the expected renewed attack, the defenders saw the whole army move off northwards, which they interpreted as an impending attack on Riyadh. But no; with his force defeated by such a barrage in this southern outpost, and being very low in ammunition, Ibn Rashid felt he might suffer a similar setback there and exhaust his supplies. As it was Abdul Aziz had exhausted his but his enemy did not know that and had given up too soon. Good generalship, courage, and bluff had won again.

Ibn Rashid then did a strange thing, taking himself off to renew his seige of Kuwait whose sheikh, as the Saud benefactor, called on the now-successful and powerful young Saud to help him. At this new threat, Ibn Rashid moved off and pretended to go home, but turned instead and marched to Riyadh, whereupon Abdul Aziz instead of rushing to defend his new home, whose defenders under his father could look after themselves safely, again showed his shrewdness as a leader by marching on Ibn Rashid's own territory, raiding the villages, collecting the spoils and moving off as Ibn Rashid abandoned the siege of Riyadh to defend his own lands. The moves went on for the next twenty years before Abdul Aziz finally conquered the Rashids and annexed this extensive province.

* * *

Who were the Sauds? They were no desert upstarts, for they were established in the central region of Arabia for generations as rulers in the town of Dir'iyah which lay in the Wadi Hanifa, one of the extensive "dry rivers" which, 10km down its course passed close to the little town of Riyadh. Dir'iyah was founded over five hundred years ago by a man called Mani on a piece of land owned by one named Dir, who took this name from that of a former village near the east coast. About three hundred years later one of his direct descendants, Mohammed ibn Saud, became the Emir of Dir'iyah. All these towns in the central region were quite independent, feuds and fights being frequent, and the remnants of ancient towers still tell the story of the constant watch for raiders. This Mohammed ibn Saud, the founder of the present ruling House of Saud, fathered more than a goodly family. He, amongst others, had become intolerant of the lax way of life of many of the Arabs and had shown favour to a religious leader and sheikh, Mohammed ibn Wahab, from the nearby town of Uyaynah, who was preaching a return to the old ways, of the need to conduct one's life strictly according to the way set out in the Koran by the Prophet Mohammed, as the word of Allah. His followers subsequently became known as Wahabis. In Arabia also, prophets appear to be not without honour save in their own country for Mohammed Wahab, had not found favour in his own little town with his preaching of the return to the strict life; he had been pushed out of his village and had gone to join his friend and neighbour Mohammed Saud in 1744. The two Mohammeds found mutual respects and interests as the powers temporal and spiritual of this very strict religious sect, and so successful did this combination prove that, fifty years later, at the end of the eighteenth centry, their followers were in spiritual and material command of the greater part of the Arabian

Peninsula and had created what is now called the first Saudi State, with Dir'iyah as its prosperous capital, becoming a place for pilgrims from all over Arabia.

Then came the reaction. An even greater power temporal, though rather less spiritual (if not in his own estimation), was disturbed by this spread of influence from Dir'iyah with its extending tentacles. In Constantinople (Istanbul), the Sultan was experiencing some unhappy nights, no doubt affected by thoughts of what had happened following the teachings of another Mohammed, the prophet of Allah, and founder of Islam, who had himself united much of Arabia, both temporally and spiritually, and whose followers went on to conquer and spread the Word as far as Spain and lower France. He must have feared that the followers of this new Mohammed might well reach Turkey itself, and he could see his soft, luxurious life-style being threatened, and even his Ottoman Empire itself being overwhelmed by this new force arising from the desert; for the soldiers of the new Saudi state had penetrated as far as Damascus and to Karbala, the holy city in Iraq. It was time to stop the rot, so he ordered his Viceroy in Egypt, Mohammed Ali, to send an army into Arabia to crush the Arab forces and to recover the territory. The Egyptians were defeated in the west but they resumed the offensive under the Viceroy's son, Ibrahim Pasha, this time with artillery and better fire power generally. Having succeeded in the west, they moved on to Dir'iyah in 1818, where the Sauds and their followers withstood a siege of six months until artillery fire finally overcame their citadel, over twenty princely Sauds being killed along with thirteen hundred others. They had fought a courageous battle against very large Egyptian forces who were estimated to have lost ten thousand men. The Ottoman Emperor, the Sultan, ordered the total destruction of the town, and all palm trees to be cut down by the townsfolk themselves under the eyes of the Turkish soldiers. The Saud Emir at the time of the battle, Abdullah, had bargained successfully for the lives of his family and soldiers, but he and the leaders were taken to Cairo. Then he alone was sent to Constantinople where the Sultan with his followers in the main square enjoyed the sight of his head being cut off. Taking no chances, the Sultan also ordered the head to be crushed in a mortar.

* * *

The Sauds are not easily put down, and within three years they had started to rebuild; but the commander of the Turkish occupying force

1. *What remains of the citadel in the old fortress of Dir'iyah which was bombarded by the Turks and Egyptians 150 years ago. Much of the old town remains in ruins about it, and a few of the ruins are still inhabited.*

2. *A very large stone-lined well at Dir'iyah, now quite dry.*

3. *Looking down the well to its dry bottom 50ft below.*

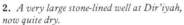

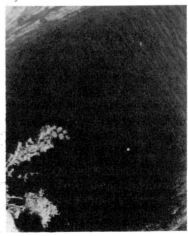

ordered its further destruction and only fifty years later did this Phoenix-town rise again.

Today, Dir'iyah is a satellite of Riyadh and not far off from being a suburb. On one bank of the Wadi Hanifa can be seen the old ruined adobe town as it was left by the Turks a hundred and fifty years ago, while from the Wadi rises the new town spreading on its banks. About two kilometres away, just opposite the site of the great battle of the Sauds, rises the new great 800-bed King Khalid University Hospital and Medical School, which proclaims that the Sauds have come a long way, that they are still strong and successful leaders of their people, and have not forgotten the site of their origins.

The palaces of the present ruler, King Fahad, and of his predecessors, the late King Khalid and King Faisil, are on the road to Dir'iyah on the edge of Riyadh, about halfway from the city centre and the old Saud stronghold of Dir'iyah. It may well be that in siting their residences, the family origins were not forgotten.

What were the beginnings in this palm-covered territory which has become the capital of this great country? For more than two thousand years a large area of palm trees arising from the Wadi Hanifa and spreading up and over its left bank for perhaps a square kilometre, had been an oasis for desert dwellers and, in time, small villages formed in these. Little is known of them till one near the junction of the Wadi Hanifa and the Wadi Batha was favoured as a refuge over two hundred years ago by Dahham, son of Dawwas, whose family had been chased out of another nearby village, Manfouha, for the common major reason of killing a few of the tribe. The leaders of this new village that Dahham had settled into were in conflict with each other and he found little difficulty in taking it over, then building a wall and a fort to keep out his enemies, the Manfouhians, and others with unfriendly intentions. The village blossomed to a town and because it all lay in such a garden—that is, the bedouin idea of a garden—the territory came to be called Riyadh, which means "garden".

Dahham quickly asserted himself as Emir, and was soon at odds with the Emir of Dir'iyah, Mohammed ibn Saud, and his son (an earlier Abdul Aziz), and not without cause, for the Sauds had fostered the spread of Wahabism which was not the life-style of Dahham. During almost the next twenty years the two sides fought some thirty-five times in raids, skirmishes, ambushes and small battles, the largest of these costing sixty lives. Dahham broke two armistices, lost two sons in battle, saw his cause was lost and moved some seventy kilometres to Al Kharj, a well-watered oasis. In 1773, the Sauds took Riyadh as their own and have had Emirs there ever since, with the exception of those ten years when they were forced out by the townspeople; their spectacular return through the efforts of young Abdul Aziz has been described. At first Riyadh was just one of the many towns in the Saud's huge domain but with the fall of the first Saudi State in 1818, when they were not just turned out but kept out of Dir'iyah by the Turko-Egyptian forces, the Saud leader, Turki, decided on an attack on Riyadh where the Egyptian forces had established their garrison. The Emir of Riyadh had gone over to the Turks and had even fought against the Emir of Dir'iyah to whom he had some allegiance. Turki decided on a seige which went on for months, forcing a surrender and an agreement that the Egyptian forces would leave the Nejd entirely. Riyadh has remained the Saud capital ever since.

★ ★ ★

This is by no means the whole story of the rise to power and independence of the Sauds. Their territory in the Nejd, that central region of the Arabian Peninsula, was subject to the Turks who had been for four hundred years overlords of all Arabia, which formed part of their Ottoman empire. The Sultan in Constantinople, now Istanbul, had made himself head of all the Muslim world in both spiritual and temporal affairs, but in the nineteenth century this Turkish rule weakened, was challenged and was to be overthrown firstly in the Balkan States, then by the Nationalist movement of the young Turks inside Turkey itself.

In the furthest parts of this Turkish Empire, the deserts of the Arabian Peninsula, their power was largely nominal, for the Turks were not a desert people and any profit from the area would not sustain even the Sultan's harem for long. They had a garrison in the Hasa, the Eastern Province of Arabia running to the Arabian Gulf; it was a weak force controlling a valuable territory, since they could charge duty on any goods entering that coast from the east. The central deserts were almost free of Turks, but the northern areas where Ibn Rashid was in control was in their pay, and in the west they kept a firm control over the Sherif of Mecca. The Yemen, on the southern side of the great desert, the Rub' al Khali, was in their control but offered no challenge to the centre, since not even a platoon was capable of crossing the sands. By 1904 Abdul Aziz ibn Saud had taken Riyadh and the surrounding territory and he had designs for removing the Turkish power in the territory to his east, the Hasa reckoning that once removed the Turks would have great difficulty in lodging a footing there again, and he was prepared to take that risk.

The whole coastline of the Gulf, both on the Arabian and on the Persian side had been ruled for two hundred years by the British Navy, who had undertaken its patrol to put down pirates and others damaging the sheikhs' interests, to guard their own routes to India and later to stop slaves being passed from West Africa, while still later they had a strong interest in protecting the oil developments of the Gulf. Abdul Aziz reckoned that if he could remove the Turks without calling on British aid, which would have amounted to Britain supporting an attack on the Turkish Empire, he would probably find that the British would leave him alone because there was little they could do about it; he calculated well, as usual. His first attack on the Turks in 1914 in which he was wounded, ended in what was virtually a draw.

Eventually Abdul Aziz did take the Eastern Province and the Northern Province and the remnants of the south. What he did not then possess was the Western Province, though he had designs to bring the whole of the Arabian Peninsula under Arab control once again; but there he was not alone, for over in the west there was another man with similar ambitions.

CHAPTER X

War in the West

In the Western Province, the Hejaz, lived the grand Sherif of Mecca, Hussein, holder of the highest office in the Muslim world, the guardian of the holy cities of Mecca and Medina and ruler of the Hejaz. Sherif Hussein had been brought up in Turkish circles in Constantinople and was well educated by their standards, certainly well-mannered and dignified but at times rather stupid, obstinate and tortuous in his dealings. He, too, wished to be ruler of all the Arabian Peninsula and beyond, and at one stage reached the position of calling himself King of the Arabs. He was the man, together with his sons, Abdullah, Faisil and Ali with whom the British had to deal. Many of the Arabs were tired of the Turks, wanting to be rid of them and to run their own country, while many others, knowing no other masters over several generations, just accepted their presence as inevitable. So some sheikhs were for the Turks and some against, and some for any nation who would get rid of them, and some not, while others were prepared to be loyal to whichever side paid them the better.

Because for hundreds of years large numbers of travellers visited Arabia especially as pilgrims to Mecca, the inhabitants of the west, especially in the port of Jeddah, were known to the peoples of the outside world, who kept them in touch with new ideas and materials. Some pilgrims, of course, had made the trek overland across the Arabian Peninsula from eastern ports and others again, similarly on the ancient darbs or tracks from Kuwait and Iraq and more westerly parts such as Jordan and Egypt, but very little was known of the tribes of the interior.

Britain and France, in 1914, at war with Germany and Turkey, saw a way of isolating the Turkish military forces in Mecca and Medina and the whole of Western Arabia by encouraging this movement for an Arab revolt, backing their aspirations and urging them on to use this as a means for self-determination. There is no indication that any of the great powers had any strong feelings about Arabia for the Arabs; they wanted help against the Turks to safeguard the oil supplies from Iran, Iraq, and Kuwait, and to keep the land-passage open to India. They decided to support the Sherif in his ambitions.

★ ★ ★

Abdul Aziz having by this time taken into his power the central and eastern parts of the Arabian Peninsula, and driven out the Turk's token forces, presented no problem there for the Allies. Access to him then was extremely difficult and the Allies were not concerned with the changing fortunes of what to them, at the time, were minor Arab sheikhs. They focused their attentions on the realities of existing Turkish forces all the way from Turkey to Medina maintained by the Hejas railway built by the Turks with German help in 1900-08 and running down the western side of the country with a terminus at Medina, while in addition the Turks maintained a garrison in Mecca supplied overland from Medina, a rail extension being planned to Mecca but never started.

The British plan was to isolate the Turks by destroying as much of the railway line and rolling stock as possible, action being started long before Lawrence came on the scene, and though the interruption of this railway was a nuisance to the Turks, who had amassed a large store of rails and rolling stock at Medina, they always managed to repair it after both the earlier efforts and Lawrence's and it was not until Colonel Dawnay was given the job in April 1918 that a large section of the line was demolished beyond the remaining resources of the Turks. The twisted rails and abandoned engines can still be viewed about Medina and Medain Saleh today. The Turks had used wood to fuel the engines, mainly desert acacia trees, but had reached the stage of pulling down houses in Medina for fuel. This railway is still in use from Turkey down as far as the southern part of Jordan, and there have been surveys made of the track in Saudi Arabia with a view to its possible reconstruction. It would be a great help in the ever-increasing Medina and Mecca traffic at Haj at the very least. When flying from Jeddah to Amman I had a magnificent view of much of the track and some of the debris of the rolling stock, with the line disappearing here and there into a tunnel.

1. *Colonel T. E. Lawrence (of Arabia).*

2. *Field Marshal Viscount Allenby, Commander-in-Chief of the British Forces, Middle East.*

3. *Sherif Hussein, descendant of the Prophet Mohammed, and father of Faisil and Abdullah.*

4. *Emir Faisil, Commander of the Arab Forces and later King of Iraq.*

Lawrence and the Hejaz railway have become almost synonymous in British minds and he has become a part of British folklore in spite of informed and even more uninformed and intolerant criticism of him. He and many others did a good intelligence job with small resources by containing a Turkish force of many thousands in the Arabian Peninsula, which might well have been used effectively against the Allies. The numbers were trivial compared to other fronts, and had the result of the main conflict in Europe with its slaughtered millions gone the other way, the Arabs would not have had a ghost of a chance of independence from the Turks, and Abdul Aziz and Hussein would have swung high with many others for their anti-Turkish activities. Though Arab independence came as a result of the Allies' need to conquer Turkey as one of the central powers, and though some of the Arab countries were not completely independent for another thirty years, they were granted it, when it came, by arrangement and goodwill for the most part and not by conquest, in contrast to the preceding four hundred years of Turkish rule. Lawrence, by a fluke, got much more than his fair share of glory, but that can happen in wartime, and when someone novel in form and style is treated as a hero, and praise is showered upon them, there are many that are resentful and indignant. Lawrence had become for many the main source of knowledge of Arabia, and an attempt is made later to bring the controversy and the man into some sort of perspective.

★ ★ ★

Meantime, Abdul Aziz ibn Saud was letting the war pass over him. He could contribute nothing positive in his central position and he probably helped the Allies best it would seem, in the long view, by not taking sides, though he was prepared to take a large subsidy of gold from Britain to encourage him to do so.

General Allenby, GOC of the British Forces with his base in Cairo, finally advanced when the time was right, using British, Australian, New Zealand and Indian forces from the Egyptian bases, sweeping the Turks from the whole of the Arabian parts of the Middle East, through and beyond Damascus and Mesopotamia (Iraq). The Arabs under Hussein's sons had come on the right flank, advancing through the peninsula with a force lacking the fire power and concerted endeavour of their European allies, but nonetheless they played their part. They have been criticised for playing the part of raiders, which they were traditionally fitted for, rather than being solid effectual takers of cities, in which role their record had been an ineffectual one; but they had, in addition, another objective—to dash to the main cities of the north as soon as the Turks had retreated from them, for there had been some sort of "agreement" to the effect that "what they took they would hold", as an encouragement to fight. What the entrance of a few scattered Arab patrols, at the same time as the European forces who had borne the brunt of the fighting, amounted to in terms of occupancy, was to be long debated.

What was the value of the Arab revolt to the Allies of World War One? Kirk, a well-balanced historian, quotes the view of Lord Wavell, British commander at one time in the Middle East in World War Two, "Its value to the British commander was great, since it diverted considerable Turkish reinforcements and supplies to the Hejaz and protected the right flank of the British Armies in their advance through Palestine. Further, it put an end to the German propaganda in South Western Arabia and removed any danger of the establishment of a German submarine base on the Red Sea. These were important services, and worth the subsidies of gold and munitions expended on the Arab forces." That view from a man who reached the heights in military and administrative achievement writing over thirty years after the dust of controversy had settled must be as near to the truth of the matter as we will get.

After all the conferences which followed the hostilities with various decisions resulting that were not satisfactory to the Arabs, they were at the very least freed from Turkish domination after four hundred years. The French insisted on having Syria as a mandate, and though they helped with the country's development between the wars, their occupancy was noted for a series of devastating revolts. British protection was given to Jordan, Kuwait, the Emirates, and Iraq, where there is no doubt that the ensuing development of those countries, including their oil industries along with other improvements during a time when they had not reached the stage of being able to manage complicated machinery and engineering technicalities, was of benefit to both sides. Though there was to be no massive state, nevertheless a very handsome contribution by Britain to a compromise resulted in Hussein's sons becoming kings, Faisil in Iraq and Abdullah in Jordan.

Only after World War Two did these countries become free agents and even though they can, should they wish, fuse themselves into a United States of Araby, there is no strong movement for conjunction, and they appear to prefer to run their own show in their own way, but will act in combination as a United Arab League for political or other benefits as the occasion arises. A total fusion of all these states into one great union under one ruler and with a common religion might have been a good thing, but there are many reasons for thinking that it is probably better for them to have remained as individual small states, coming together for certain mutual interests, including defence.

Whatever the future holds, the people and states of the Arabian Peninsula and their huge territories are as divided today as they were after World War One, though there may have been some changes in the style of rulers.

Saudi Arabia is still a kingdom with the same borders and the same ruling family as when King Abdul Aziz died. Today in the old castle in the heart of Riyadh captured by Abdul Aziz, at that postern gate, can still be seen, to the right of the doorpost, the broken end of a steel spear hurled at those speeding in retreat when set upon by the maker of the nation and his followers.

CHAPTER XI

An Eighth Pillar of Wisdom

The Western province of Saudi Arabia, the Hejaz, has long been the best known, for here lies Jeddah, the port for trade and for pilgrims to Mecca and Medina, the Holy and Forbidden Cities. The early travellers explored and wrote chiefly of the Hejaz, the most noted and still widely read book being the war epic of T. E. Lawrence of Arabia, who has been a hero to so many young and old, though a fraud to some and an enigma to others. His book has provided much of what many know of Arabia and the Arabs, other than of oil, and in recent times attempts have been made to debunk him. Both at home and abroad he provides an interesting topic of conversation, and opinion of him is often ill-informed and biased, depending on what book comes to hand. As he looms so large in the affairs of the Hejaz, and in British eyes as the "liberator" of the Arabs, an attempt is made here to survey the evidence and to bring his achievements into focus.

Whilst still in Oxford I began to read some of the works of the travellers in Arabia, being profoundly ignorant about most of them. Local interest prompted me to search out how many of the great ones had been to the city's seat of learning, and I found that Palgrave, Burton, Lawrence and Thesiger had been up. Palgrave, orthodox and rather pompous "did well" at Oxford. Burton, magnificently unrestrained and prolific was, like Shelley, sent down, possibly to avoid being hustled into the Church, where he might have been a Bishop or a hoot. Thesiger, lucid, balanced and modest, got a boxing blue. Lawrence, an enigma, got a first class degree. Cambridge had taken on Burckhardt, a Swiss, a splendid professional; also St John Philby, thorough, determined, verbose and cussed. Doughty, one of the best of them all, deep, thorough, imperturbable and very readable, went to both, first to Cambridge for Science (Geology) and then to Oxford for Literature (Medieval and Elizabethan poets).

There had been plenty of other travellers from different nations and various backgrounds but it is to be expected that those with natural ambition, physical capacity, intelligence, ability to write and interest stimulated by reading or contact with others who knew and taught about these territories, should figure prominently in the lists of those who had not just travelled and explored but also had left a record of their travels.

The works of these various writers have, as well as interest, different styles reflecting to a degree their characters. Of all these writers Lawrence was the only one who had been to school in the city and who is impressively commemorated in his old college, Jesus, and like that other odd man out, Burton, stimulated the most extensive literature about his activities and personality. As his *Seven Pillars of Wisdom* is still widely read and many people still base their concept both of Arabia and of the man on that book, I decided to have a closer look at him to see what to make of the widely divided views that had grown up about him over the last sixty years, making a start with the local relics.

The former family house of the Lawrences is still there, at 2 Polstead Road, including the small shack in the garden built for him to live and study in splendid isolation. He did not care to live either in the family house because of rows, or in college for distaste for college life.

In the hall of Jesus College is his portrait in Arab dress by Augustus John, challenging alongside him another graduate of Jesus, Sir Harold Wilson, former PM; I noticed Lawrence has a hand not far off his dagger. Also there is a good bust of him in the antechapel, just inside the door to the quad, perhaps an indication of a little doubt lingering in the minds of the College ecclesiastical powers because of his long contact with Muslims and frequent adoption of their dress. In the main gateway of the College a bronze plaque presented by later undergraduates bears the rather touching words in Latin, translated as

1907-1910

Here Thomas Edward Lawrence fearless champion of
Arabia spent three years. To prevent his name passing to
obscurity the youth of Jesus College set up this plaque
"Wisdom built herself a house
She hewed out seven pillars."

The last is a quotation from the scriptures, Proverbs (IX,1), and, as he acknowledged, the source of the title of his book *The Seven Pillars of Wisdom.*

Finally, there is a collection of some of his letters, kindly shown to me, one to Bernard Shaw discussing the *Seven Pillars* and its title, and Shaw's reply. Mainly, the letters are to his friend and banker, Robin Buxton, and in one of 1925, says that he first used the title for a book on seven cities (Jerusalem, Baghdad, Damascus and others) and judging it so immature, in 1914, he burnt the manuscript but liking the title gave it to his later book without adding any further explanation.

Any aptness appears to be that his book is intended as a house of wisdom and about wartime Semitic (Arabian branch) affairs, with the number seven being regarded in many religions as mystical, symbolic or sacred. Thus, the creation was in seven days, the Egyptians had seven years of plenty and seven of famine, the Passover Feast of the Tabernacles each lasted seven days, the Seven Churches of Asia, the seven sacraments of the Roman Church. Seven is significant in Hinduism and Buddhism, and there is a host of other sevens.

One other view, and a very likely one, is that he had planned to write seven books or chapters in his *Seven Pillars* but it ran on and finished with ten, and indeed he calls Chapter 10, "The House of Perfected". So he must have felt his house needed propping up a bit with some extra pillars, though he seems to have thought seven were enough for the title. He was decidedly odd at times and one wonders how his book would have read without the benefit of Mr and Mrs Bernard Shaw's help with grammar and construction. Burton also was a strange writer having, in places, more footnotes than text.

My own researches in the depths of Bodley's library and those of Dr Tom Parker of University College, a learned ecclesiastic, could shed no further useful light, other than ideas of the architecture of the house of wisdom which was never given more than seven pillars—a pity. The title, book, and man, are all curious, and I thought to delve into the extensive and controversial literature on Lawrence, and find out also the views of various Arabs on this dominant figure in our Arabian folklore to see how many pillars are still standing. A little background is essential to understand how Britain became involved in the Arabian Peninsula.

Due to the remoteness and seclusion of the central parts of the Arabian Peninsula, most of the world until recent times had very little idea of life there and most people are still as vague as I once was about it. Bible stories have left a general impression of an utterly different scattered people living in hot, small towns or oases, or just wandering in the sands, riding about on camels or donkeys, living on dates, figs, and camel's milk, with a few wicked merchants and rich rulers who lopped off heads or hands at a whim, hurled coins to crowds covered in sores and grovelling about for alms. The land seemed to be full of plague and leprosy, powerful sheikhs, holy men and prophets, all dressed in a sort of nightshirt or swimming towel with the sheikhs creeping into tents and singing songs, beguiling innocent young lady visitors, all compounded in a mixture of *The Desert Song* and *The Tales of a Thousand and One Nights.* Then came a young English hero who galloped all over the desert on camels and freed the Arabs from the wicked Turks and finally little more was heard of the whole place until a thick layer of oil came to gloss it all over, together with gold, glamour and Rolls Royces. There is a lot more to it than that.

The Arabs are a people who have adapted to existence in an extreme climate in a harsh land with their own language and culture, an accumulated wisdom of a way of life to survive there, and of the possible ways open to them for diversion and enjoyment. The Eskimos adapted similarly in their own way in a different environment. Our lives are given and ruled by sunlight, and there is much of it in Arabia.

Like other nations, the Arabs have conquered and have been conquered, and for about four hundred years, up to the beginning of the present century, they had been, as explained earlier, under the dominance of the Turks who had created the great Ottoman Empire. In the Arabian Peninsula the Turks had forces stationed, strongest in the west, the Hejaz, that mountainous part containing the port of Jeddah, the nearby cooler mountain town of Taif, so suitable for retreat in the heat of summer, and the holy cities of Mecca and Medina. Turkey's forces were also in that profitable eastern coastal area, the Hasa, where they could collect dues from any goods imported all along the entire coast, and in the southern coastal area of the peninsula, the Yemen, beyond the deserts, in the mountains and beyond where lived the little, tough, dark-skinned race, many of whom are now helping to build the modern Saudi Arabia. But in the arid, dry centre, only a token Turkish force existed for the Turks are not a desert people, and found survival there difficult and profitless.

For two hundred years, the British Navy had patrolled the Arabian (or Persian) Gulf, to protect the sheikhs' interests, and to try to prevent piracy; later, to prevent the passage of slaves; and much later, to guard the British oil interests at the head of the Gulf, and equally less altruistically, to keep a constant watch over the approaches to India.

From the central area, the Nejd, in the middle of the eighteenth century, arose the Sauds and the stern religious leader, Wahab, with their followers, to spread the power both spiritual and temporal over the whole peninsula, until suppressed by the Turks using Egyptian forces at the beginning of the nineteenth century. A hundred years later came the start of the rise to power of another Saud, Abdul Aziz ibn Saud, who was to oust the Turks first in the centre, then the north, the east, the south-west, and finally he took over the west with its holy cities, though only after the Turkish forces had been defeated by the Allies including the Arabs. But he may not have made this last conquest, had not the Turks, entering the war with Germany, lost that war, and in so doing lost all Arabia. The conquerors, Britain and France, took over as mandates the northern states (Syria, Jordan, Iraq), but left the great deserts of the peninsula to look after themselves, seeing little benefit or harm to themselves from this large, dry territory and its inhabitants.

Into this Arabian theatre of World War One came the English with, later, Lawrence, to compile stories of his own exploits to rival Sinbad and Aladdin, and there are some who allege that they are as fictional as those "Thousand-and-one-Nights". Let us now look at this prodigy, who still dominates the minds of millions as the saviour of Arabia, and one of the great Englishmen.

Lawrence was born in Wales in 1888, from where his parents moved when he was a year old. His father was an Anglo-Irish baronet (succeeding only in 1914), Sir Thomas Chapman, who, after fathering four girls in Ireland, cut loose with a children's nurse who was said to have atoned for her sins by trying to make her sons strongly religious. The father changed his name from Chapman to Lawrence, producing five boys, the second of whom was Thomas Edward, our hero. After the family had wandered in various parts of Britain and France, they settled in Oxford for educational reasons, where Thomas Edward with his brothers went to school, and then, exercising his birthright of Wales, entered and won an exhibition scholarship for Welsh-born students to Jesus College, in Oxford. He graduated with a first class degree in history, and produced a thesis on "Crusader Castles", following his travels in the Middle East for that purpose, and later he joined an archaeological dig there and then went on to travel in and map the Sinai Peninsula.

His Arabic language was passable, to improve later, as did his written Arabic, and in the best British tradition of speaking foreign languages his accent appears to have been pretty awful, though not as bad as Churchill speaking French. In his own way Lawrence was always true to form, being in the first class also of British eccentrics. Almost every available detail of his young days has been sifted and stored in an extensive literature. Lawrence, for all the glamour with which he and others coloured his exploits, and in spite of his detractors, was, without any doubt, a very gifted, able man in many ways. He wrote that remarkable piece of literature, *The Seven Pillars of Wisdom,* an autobiography of his war experiences, as he saw it, though others have interpreted much of what he said of himself and his deeds in a very different way. Latterly he has been called, and shown to the satisfaction of some, to be a liar and cheat, ruthlessly ambitious, self-centred and irresponsible, a poseur and a charlatan, and a rather ineffective soldier with some notable military failures, and what at times, he built up as great victories but were, in fact, very small skirmishes compared to the scale of warfare and slaughter in other theatres of war.

His whole war career is better understood if one realises he was really an intelligence and political agent of the British and at times a spy, rather than a soldier, though, of course, later these roles became intertwined. He claimed great knowledge of warfare from his reading, but he never did go through proper training as a soldier. Because of his earlier experiences of Middle Eastern archaeology in which as a student, and later in digs with men of experience, he had acquired a fairly good knowledge of parts of the Middle East. All the evidence points to his having developed a strong affection for the Arabs from personal encounters, and an equal dislike of the Turks. Also, a young man's dream had been fostered by his reading, together with his "Crusader Castles" experience—to be a crusader himself to free the Arab people from Turkish domination.

At the start of World War Two Lawrence was in England in Oxford, and is recorded as being willing but unable to enlist for various, odd, ascribed reasons of uncertain authenticity, as is so frequent with him—one being that at 5ft 3in he was rejected as below the standard height required, then at 5ft 8in a genuine reason at that time; another that he tried to join the OTC, but again was rejected because there were too many recruits; and that he did not try to enlist, but worked on a book and map for the War Office on recent Sinai Peninsula adventures.

Finally, he wrote requesting a job in Army Intelligence, approaching the head of the geographical section of the War Office and was given a job there, putting in some hard work, and in October 1914 being made a Temporary Second Lieutenant-Interpreter, an odd start in view of later events. It was pretty clear that he wanted to use his mental gifts and experience in intelligence work, and did not wish to be just another ranker. The choice was open to him.

He had a piece of luck when Turkey declared war on the Allies, for the Government decided to increase their intelligence staff in the Middle East, based in Cairo, because, amongst several reasons, the British were very concerned lest Turkey should try to take the Suez Canal and block the route to India. Lawrence, for the reasons mentioned, was considered to be very suitable for this sort of work, and with several others, mainly his superiors, was sent out to Cairo in December 1914, to become part of what became eventually, in February 1916, the Arab Bureau. He was promoted in December of that year to Staff Captain—a rocket promotion within two months. He wrote in *The Seven Pillars of Wisdom* that he wanted to be a general and knighted at the age of thirty, and he was now well on the way. It cannot be said of him that as a young man he was unambitious.

For the next two years he was mainly desk-bound in Cairo on intelligence and maps and was reported as doing his work competently, resourcefully, and enthusiastically, with a stimulating effect on others, and thus he remained for about two years, taking no active part in fighting, and writing to an old patron that he had no training as a field officer, which was the case. During his time with the Arab Bureau, he must have gained considerable experience, not just of geography, but of strategy and political moves throughout the Middle East theatre of war including a very useful knowledge of the problems arising in the Hejaz part of the Arabian Peninsula where a movement had begun by Sherif Hussein, the Arab leader of the Hejaz, towards a revolt from Turkish rule, encouraged by British support. (Sir) Ronald Storrs of the Arab Bureau, who was the leading thinker and activist on the British side encouraging this revolt, spoke of these matters frequently to Lawrence, without realising how far his young protegé would come to take an active part in subsequent events.

The notion of an Arab revolt against the Turks was far from new, Abdul Aziz ibn Saud having discussed this with Captain Shakespear at a meeting in the desert in 1911. Shakespear's report aroused little

British interest, since, until war came, there was no wish to agitate Turkish turbans.

The first event to shake Lawrence out of his Cairo routine appears to have resulted from his demeanour in the Bureau, whose members found him conceited and supercilious; suggestions from a junior officer as to how to run and win the war were not taken well. They grew tired of his attitudes and poses, and decided to get some respite from him by sending him away as a junior member of a three-man mission to negotiate with the Turks over a beseiged British army in the Gulf Front.

He later claimed to have behaved thus intentionally in order to be pushed out and so get away to start a "crusade" on his own to free the Arabs. Well, perhaps. But there was no call for him to behave similarly on this mission, in a way that won him no marks with his colleagues or the British soldiers in Basra. They would not tolerate his insolence and airs, and snubbed him, and as a result he developed a strong aversion to most regular army officers.

Though his ability in handling his own countrymen appears at times to have sunk to a low ebb his attitude towards handling Arabs was of the highest order; he had made a close study of them from the time of his earliest contacts, and after much experience and deep thought set out guidelines for others in what he called, "Twenty-seven Articles", which are quoted in detail by Liddell Hart, where those interested can read them.

In May 1916, Ronald Storrs went on a mission to the Hejaz, to negotiate with Sherif Hussein about putting an Arab revolt into action, and to arrange practical support by way of British arms and gold. The official war history dates the start of the revolt as June 1916, and there was an immediate quick result, with the Arab forces taking Mecca and then, with help from a British warship, Jeddah succumbed also. But they failed throughout the period of the war to take Medina. Lawrence asked Storrs, on his return, to take him on his next visit to Jeddah, in October 1916, when Lawrence had a "period of leave", and Storrs took him along as an unofficial observer. On his way back from Jeddah to Cairo by ship, Storrs dropped Lawrence off at the port of Rabegh, where Lawrence met Sherif Ali, a rather weak, consumptive son of Sherif Hussein, and was taken overland, some hundred miles inland, by camel in disguise, in Arab dress, to meet Faisil, the oldest, most intelligent, hardy and ablest of Hussein's sons. After some four

meetings, discussing Arab needs and future policy, they parted in what
Lawrence described as a very friendly manner, and he then went on to
the port of Yenbo for subsequent enshipment to Cairo in November.
All of this journey is described, with some flourishes, in *The Seven
Pillars of Wisdom.*

On return to Cairo, where his information and advice were of real
value, Lawrence was told by the head of the Arab Bureau, Sir Gilbert
Clayton, that he must return again to Faisil. He later admitted that, at
the time of his visit with Storrs, he had been on "leave", because the
staff in Cairo wanted to see the back of him, and he had, in effect been
fired as a nuisance. This time he went as a liaison officer to help the
Arab Army of Faisil, and his day-dreams would change to reality and
nightmares. His return to Yenbo came at a moment when the British
and French decided to take the remaining ports on the Red Sea of Wejd
and Akaba, for there was a danger of German submarines working from
those ports, and he arrived just as Faisil's forces retreated en masse
under attack by the Turks, when in the next few days, the Arabs
crowded into Yenbo. However, five ships of the Royal Navy with the
capacity to shell the Turks had been summoned; these now appeared,
and flashed their searchlights about to such an effect that the Turks, as
they later admitted, were intimidated, turning back from their attack,
and thus the situation was saved.

From now on, Lawrence was to be much on his own, and was to take
an active part in the Arab rebellion, giving his own account of the
subsequent events in *The Seven Pillars of Wisdom.*

The whole Lawrence of Arabia legend cannot be properly
appreciated without the knowledge that this clever, gifted, tough and
brave young man—with the natural desire of so many like him for fame
and a measure of fortune, with his ambition to be a general and
knighted by the age of thirty—had a secret in his background which
made him feel socially different, and not quite acceptable to his fellows,
thus twisting his nature. He knew he was illegitimate; a blot in those
days, smudging a social conscience, particularly in the class with whom
he had been brought up. He often said that amongst the Arabs he felt
comfortable, and this may well have been partly because of their
attitude towards illegitimacy, which though occurring amongst
Muslims, is much less common, and the illegitimate person carried no
slur in their society. They rightly consider that he is not to blame, any
odium being attributed to the parents, especially the woman, the

illegitimate being freely accepted. They take a kinder view than the Western world which, at the time of Lawrence, displayed a sad, censorious, ostracising outlook towards those born out of wedlock as well as towards the child's mother, while taking a much more tolerant view of the father. Lawrence, it was clear, wanted fame, but it was also clear that, because of his origins, he was divided in his feelings, for fame meant so often an investigation into origins, and he was concerned for himself and his brothers so that he could never quite revel in acclaim.

He undoubtedly did a good war-job, both at the desk and in the field, and in one of those very unusual settings which war can produce, while at the same time wishing for fame, he cultivated his achievements, stretching the turn of events to his best benefit. He would not be the first to win medals, prizes, achievements and fortunes in this way. We admire the deeds and will forgive the publicity if the truth outweighs it, though when the publicity is greater than the reason for it, we feel distaste. However, it is not widely appreciated that at the end of the war he was unknown save to a very restricted circle. Within a year to millions of the British and American people he was a hero, a military genius and the most glamorous figure to emerge from the struggle. How was it possible? Very little of it was his own doing. He happened to fit into a scheme of things, being chosen for messianic treatment by two apostles, the Americans, Lowell Thomas and Harry Chase.

Mr Lowell Thomas, a teacher at Princeton University, asked Washington for some military job, at a time when the USA had not entered the war, and a task suitable for him was considered to be that of bringing publicity to the American people of the much overlooked part Britain was contributing to the war. He was given an open brief to get going where he could find suitable stories of British endeavour and to return home and tell it to the people by lecturing, with the deeper purpose of raising the interest and sympathies of an American people mostly uninformed and largely disinterested in what to so many was, at that stage, a further struggle of distant European states.

Thomas was a highly skilled publicist, as events proved, and he quickly saw that a report on the horrors of trench warfare in Europe, with its blood-bath of millions dying in the mud, was a less attractive theme with which to stir up American interest and sympathy than something nearer to the cowboys or cavalry-versus-the-Indians type of skirmish on horseback, with rifles and pistols cracking and plumes waving, so familiar to Americans and much more their idea of warfare at that time, and dear to their hearts. He was shrewd and right in his estimation of the situation, and he set out to find a suitable cause to champion.

He was given an introduction to General Allenby, in command of the British Middle East warfare, and chanced to see, in the bazaar in Jerusalem, a blue-eyed "bedouin" in splendid Arabian white array with a curved gold dagger at his waist. His enquiries led to an introduction by Ronald Storrs to the wearer, Lawrence. The two university men hit it off immediately. Colonel Lawrence had built enough reputation already for Storrs to have described him to Thomas as the "Uncrowned King of the Arabs". Thomas realised that he was on to just what he wanted and had achieved his scoop. Lawrence helped the reporter to overcome General Allenby's desire for reticence and no reporters for military reasons, and at a luncheon, later, with General Allenby and the Duke of Connaught, Thomas received permission to go as a war correspondent with the Sherif Hussein's army and to report on the part the Arabs were playing towards winning the war.

After delays, he and Chase reached Akaba, some nine months after the port had been taken in July 1917. They thereupon busied themselves with much reporting and photography including many pictures of Lawrence, travelling inland some hundred miles to Ma'an and on to Petra. Their photography was admirable, and the reports of the theatre of war were first rate, but the action in that territory was very largely over, so that details of it came second-hand from officers and others, including Lawrence.

Lowell Thomas, after some four to five months' investigation, had to leave when the armistice came, to go to Germany to report subsequent events there, and then returned to America where, in March 1919 in New York, he gave five different lectures on the war. He soon found his audience had had enough of trench warfare, but were interested in shows "full of sweeping cavalry, Arabs, camels, veiled women, holy cities", which attracted great crowds. They were also enthralled by the beautiful photography of Chase, both stills and movies, as well as by Thomas's own considerable ability as a lecturer and reporter. He had been right from the start in his choice, and he laid it on thick.

He has admitted that Lawrence helped him a lot with his lectures, and he mentions that in spite of Lawrence's having spent a whole afternoon in going over details and helping him in endless ways with the story, he did not want Thomas to reveal his part in so doing.

Thomas also consulted some of the sheikhs taking part and members of the Arab Bureau. He did his allotted job superbly as a publicist, and undoubtedly did a great deal to inform both the American and British people about one part of the British wartime activity, and the part played by the Arabs.

When the show was brought to London, it ran to packed houses for six months, and was attended by Allenby and Faisil, Lloyd George, the wartime Prime Minister, and most of the Cabinet, many members of the Lords and Commons, various generals, as well as members of the Arab Bureau. The success in America and Australia was the same, and on one occasion quoted by Aldington, "down under", members of the audience went on the platform at the end to congratulate the speaker, one fighting general's enthusiasm outrunning his caution at the platform's edge to such an extent that he fell into the orchestra-well and broke a leg; whether this led to an addition to his pension was not disclosed. Lowell Thomas gave this glamour-packed lecture over 2,000 times. It had to have a hero, and the little Briton who lived a life alone amongst the hordes of Arabs, urging them on, tearing over the desert on his camel at their head, got the star award. Lawrence was now "made" far beyond his wildest, earliest, dreams, and had become a household name, with a build-up that went far beyond the facts in a way now common in many fictional portrayals of historical characters in films. Movies were then only just getting underway, and the full treatment of this story by the movie moguls, by then somewhat toned down, had to wait for half a century.

In his own time he sat the performance through as a spectator several times, coyly concealing himself in the audience. David Garnett who knew him well said of him, "He had a genius for backing into the limelight." He had been lifted to a mountain top of publicity out of range of the sniping that any critics might attempt, for not only was he the hero of a great show, but the whole razamataz had the strongest approval from a Government keen to see the British war exploits favourably publicised, especially those in the Middle East where vast expenditure of men and money had been heavily criticised, including the failure at Gallipoli and some of its other Middle East policies.

How much of this was ballyhoo, how much the truth? Clearly, Lowell Thomas had the strongest desire to make a great show, and he did not mind stretching and embellishing the basis of facts. The British impressario, Percy Burton, who had heard Thomas's lecture in New

York brought him to England and staged the lectures in Covent Garden in August 1919. Any British audience would, in these days, be suspicious about a lecture purporting to be an accurate presentation of facts which started off as described by Aldington: "With his subtle devices he had filled the theatre with the finest first-night audience seen in London since before the war. And Mr Thomas did not fail his hero and (secret) collaborator. From Sir Percy Beauchamp he had borrowed an opera set, the Moonlight-on-the-Nile scene from 'Joseph and His Brethren', and hired the band of the Welsh Guards to provide a half-hour of atmospheric music to get the audience in the right mood." Then there was a prologue, which, most fittingly, included the "Dance of the Seven Veils". Even this was not considered sufficient psychological preparation, so Mrs Thomas, who was a musician, composed a musical setting for the Muhammadan call to prayer, which was sung off-stage by an Irish tenor. What an experience it must have been!

Thomas, whatever else he had done, had provided the people, the Government, and Press, with a hero, and had taken the facts about a small corner of war history and turned them into something quite extraordinary, with a blaze of publicity and popular journalism. More was to follow. Thomas was encouraged by many, including Lloyd George, to write a book to expand his lectures and his *With Lawrence in Arabia*, which appeared in 1924, poured more oil on to the blaze.

Subsequent to the Thomas lectures, but before the appearance of Thomas's book, Lawrence was given the opportunity of writing about the Arab revolt at All Souls College, Oxford, his home town, during 1919 and 1920, though later he fled to an attic room in London for peaceful isolation. The task must have presented great difficulty, for he had to rely only on some of his reports and a limited number of his own notes, and a great deal of memory, because the kind of life he had led had made it impossible to keep a proper diary of his eventful days with the Arabs, at least for part of the time. In the interval between the actual events and the end of Thomas's lectures and the associated publicity, it is highly likely that he had come to be influenced by, and even to accept, the portrait of himself that would often be presented, and what had been said about him, rather than what had actually happened at times. Memory can be very fickle. However, proofs were checked and suggestions concerning the writing and construction of his text were made by friends, especially by Mr and Mrs Bernard Shaw.

Lawrence, generally, gives great credit in his preface to his many superiors and associates whom, he says, "could each tell a like tale", and to the many "un-named rank and file who miss their share of credit, as they must do, until they can write the despatches". His introductory chapter says, "My proper share was a minor one, but because of a fluent pen, a free speech, and a certain adroitness of brain, I took upon myself, as I describe it, a mock primacy. In reality I never had any office amongst the Arabs: was never in charge of the British mission with them." In this introductory chapter he sets out his case, his convictions, and his purpose in array which seems to me to be perfectly sincere; this should be re-read after finishing the book, and after reading writings that demean him. His was a freely flowing style, far removed from cold reporting, and so much the better for the liveliness and drama of the story he has to tell.

At the end of the war he was called to Versailles with the British peace delegations to act as an aide to Faisil, and, later, was especially selected by (Sir) Winston Churchill, the then Colonial Secretary and Chairman, as a member of a Commission on Near Eastern Affairs. Lawrence did his utmost for Arab unity and the independence he had long advocated and may well have promised during the pressures of war when he had no powers to grant it, then or later. He used every extreme to make known his feelings about the treatment of the Arabs, refusing his medal for the Order of the Bath at the moment of its presentation by King George V, which did not go down well with many of his supporters, and attaching his Croix de Guerre to the collar of his friend Hogarth's dog, setting it loose to run around Oxford to display his disgust with the French claims to Syria. Churchill and Lawrence, in their wisdom, both did a great deal to redeem promises and to help put the Arabs on their way to independence.

In the aftermath he suffered a reaction, clearly having a mild nervous breakdown with depression, and shrank from it all, refusing to play any further part in public affairs, refusing a good post offered to him by Churchill who greatly admired his abilities. At one time he spoke of becoming a lighthouse keeper, for soothing solitude might modify or mend his state of exhaustion and depression. He had all the classical signs of a very tired man, as seen in their hundreds by doctors. His exhaustion was greatly aggravated by losing the earliest manuscript of his book whilst changing trains at Reading, which meant that he had to rewrite it: that was the lowest point for him.

Liddell Hart wrote: "That awareness of his overstrain he confirmed to me later, saying, that he was 'nearly dotty' at the time of his enlistment. And his service in India was, I thought, a hindrance to the process of recovery which only became marked some time after his return." For that is how he was and that is what he did, feeling that he might recover some of that comradeship he had enjoyed with the Arabs by joining the ranks. This led to him being accused by some of seeking more notoriety, which was nonsense, for, had he wished, he could have achieved that in easier ways than by enlisting as the lowest ranker.

He was not basically the type to become a British commander of men, but a scholar who had started the war in map-making and intelligence, had dreams of greatness, and at one stage cultivated his opportunities. But with real greatness achieved he turned against it, tired and sickened at the outcome of his efforts for the Arabs at which he had worked at for an ideal and not just as a duty imposed on him by the war. He went in head first when his chance came, and none can deny that he carried out what was required of him conscientiously, through many trials of flesh and spirit. Millions of others, of course, did the same in that great conflict and many had much worse torments to face, often of a more familiar and drabber kind, such as came from being shelled for weeks on end in mud and cold, with exhaustion, agony and death all about, and with bodies and nervous systems unequal to the strain, leaving them shattered for the rest of their days. They too have had their chroniclers, and none deny their efforts and their pains. Lawrence's were of a different variety, and when first brought to light through the activities of Thomas and Chase they made more sensational news. Their accounts were enough to arouse demeaning thoughts in the minds of some who had endured the mud and shells, and Lawrence's own accounts made matters worse.

The incident at Deraa has never ceased to stimulate both controversy and doubt. Venturing into the town on a spying mission he was by chance apprehended by a Turkish sergeant, evidently on the look-out for any Arab youth who might be suitable for the homosexual attentions of the Bey, the military governor. Unrecognized for what he was, and unwilling to submit to the Bey, he was flogged by the guards and subjected to other humiliations which presumably included sodomy. He managed to escape at dawn to rejoin his men scarred in body and soul for the rest of his life. Years later in writing of the event, he could not do much more than hint at the full nature of his degradation, while the details went with him to the grave. Because of reticence he has been accused of lies and even total fabrications, but perhaps he was reticent for the same reason that other victims of sexual degradation find it difficult to speak or write of the details of their humiliations. Raped women often have this difficulty, and a man sexually repressed like Lawrence would certainly not find it easy.

There can have been few, if any, commanders, certainly in modern times, who have suffered torture, flogging, and degradation, and have returned to take command of his forces again to face the same enemy. It has been remarked upon that after this incident his attitude hardened, and no wonder, but to his credit he fought within the accepted customs of warfare in subsequent skirmishes and battles until that time he and his troop came upon the horrifying massacre perpetrated at the village of Tafas, the home of Talal, one of the Arab leaders who accompanied him, in which the Turks killed all the women and children. To make matters worse for Lawrence, he had received the news that the Turkish force responsible, with whom they soon caught up, included some of the soldiers who had tortured him at Deraa.

Talal, broken with grief, charged the mass of Turks single-handed and was at once shot down. The other Arab leaders had seen the results of the massacre and their friend's uncontrollable sacrifice, and the whole body of Arabs, equally overwhelmed with the instinct for revenge, charged the enemy, wiping them out to a man. The lone Briton, amongst them for so long, felt their calamity as his own and any thread of pity and control snapped in him also. Lawrence, in a superb description of the emotions and horrors of war, confesses, as the only British witness, "By my order we took no prisoners, for the only time in our war." The record, the only one giving details, is his own and he does not gloss over his own part in this retaliatory massacre. The style fits what Nutting, in an excellent and fair analysis of him, describes as his "compulsive acts of bravado by which he sought to prove himself to himself and to his Arab comrades."

Although he loathed the Turks, he has included words of praise for part of the enemy—the Germans, "Exceptions were the German detachment; and here, for the first time, I grew proud of the enemy who had killed my brothers (two in France)—When they attacked they halted, took position, fired to order. There was no haste, no crying, no hesitation. They were glorious." They could have caught them but they let them go to concentrate on the hated Turk. To be quite fair to Lawrence he does not try to make himself out to be a hero all the time, and his sense of truth and of humour impelled him to cite his own ineptness in shooting his own camel through the head at the height of a glorious charge he was leading at Abu el Lissal, coming a terrific cropper and regaining consciousness only when the action was over.

He went through an agony of indecision before seeking an RAF recruiting station where he was initially turned down on the suspicion of being a discharged convict because of the scars left by his flogging. He used the influence of powers at the very top to get in at the very bottom as Aircraftsman Ross, a name he said he took out of a telephone book, but he was let down by an RAF officer who recognised him and told the Press. The ensuing hordes of reporters made life too disturbing for the other ranks who served with him and high officers alike, and he had to go.

He agreed to do a year in the Army in the Tank Corps, again putting aside the name of Lawrence which he disliked because of its falsity and associations with his father's real name of Chapman, and, in a further attempt at anonymity, chose to be known as T. E. Shaw, again he said, from that wide selection offered by the phone service. Because of Mr and Mrs Bernard Shaw's interest in him and their help with his book, he was suspected of something else that had the makings of a good story—of being their illegitimate son. He was not; he was someone else's. But he may well have used the name from his affection for both of them. 338171 Aircraftsman Shaw wrote to his friend, Noel Coward, praising in high terms his serious play *Post Mortem*, which was published but not performed, and Coward, in reply, began his letter with "Dear 338171, or may I call you 338".

The Tank Corps did not suit him and he wanted the Air Force again, using high influence up to the Prime Minister, Baldwin, and the threat of suicide, so that the PM, in order to avoid the publicity that a refusal might have caused, told the Chief of the Air Force, Trenchard, to transfer the lowly Army private to a post at the lowest rung of the ladder of the Air Force. Lawrence's aspirations and methods were not always devoid of comedy. He was transferred to India at his own request, where the Greek-like tragi-comedy continued when he was posted near the Afghan border, with the result that some members of the American press, whose stories were taken up by the Soviets, suspected him of being a spy, which he was not. Questions in Parliament followed and he had to go home, where he was posted as far from London as possible, to the West Country on Plymouth Sound where he did first-rate work with fast speed-boats for air-sea rescue which helped to ensure that Britain had this service ready and in a position to save many lives, when war came. But even in this far-off part of Britain he was not safe from the politicians, for, while helping to organise the Schneider Trophy air race in 1929, some VIPs recognised him and chatted for a time, including not just distinguished foreigners but also members of HM Opposition, and so he was forbidden such contacts by HM Government. This gave him a chance to withdraw for a time to complete a translation of the Odyssey, till political tempers cooled and memories had faded.

At no time did he show any interest in younger women whom he might have courted and married; in fact, he shunned or snubbed them on social occasions: the only women with whom he had any dealings were older ones who gave him motherly and intellectual treatment. This strong aversion to younger women may even have resulted from his determination when quite young, after his discovery of his illegitimacy, to put aside in shame any ideas of marriage, a conclusion aggravated by the severe conflicts in the Lawrence family home life. Such reasons for bachelorhood were common when more account was taken of the effects of social stigma.

In consequence of his aloofness to marriageable or unmarried women, attempts to denigrate him have almost inevitably stereotyped him as homosexual. But as Nutting points out, "no one has ever produced any evidence to prove this assertion", and those who knew him well were definite in saying he was not a homosexual, and there was no shred of evidence of this while he was in the Services. That he was probably the victim of sodomy after his flogging is a reason for charity and not condemnation; his sexual frigidity was of the mind. Many men and women have put aside the promptings of the flesh in their various forms, and it is probable that Lawrence was one of those who early in life became, in the old phrase, a "confirmed bachelor", for the reasons stated, having at times a better command of the body than of his mental mechanisms. His physique was tough and well tested in his summer desert activities, while St John Philby, that great man of the desert, who worked with him for a time and admired him, wrote in his *Arabian Days*, "He was as hard as steel", and describes two of his reactions to cold in a severe winter when both of them were exposed, Lawrence more than the frozen Philby, who commented, "he seemed to be all right", and who could judge better.

In contrast to this complimentary testimony from a man who did not hand out unnecessary bouquets, Philby thought Lawrence's Arabic "rather poor stuff of a very mixed breed, and his accent not good, though of course he spoke fluently enough. Everything he did was fluent." Where Lawrence wobbled was in his attitudes, which ranged from petulance, querulousness, posturing, and vanity, to inspiring courage with calm authority.

In his spiritual outlook he might even, during his isolation and trials in the desert, have felt himself, as Nutting so aptly puts it, to be "some kind of new Messiah sent to save the world from tyranny and oppression". Many young men go through that phase. It did not last, as with almost all the others.

He completed his RAF service and retired to his cottage in Dorset to continue his writings, but nemesis was round a bend. He always enjoyed fast riding with camels, cars, motor boats, and latterly motor cycles, and on a Dorset road in 1935, whilst travelling at high speed on his Brough Superior motor cycle he tried to avoid two boys on bicycles and crashed, sustaining severe head injuries from which he died six days later. Amongst his old friends who were present to see him go to his rest in Dorset was Winston Churchill.

If we were to take away, to placate his severest critics, and there is little reason to do so, half the deeds he claimed and those attributed to him by others, he would still remain no minion, but a man of great intellect and capacity, thrust by fortune into some eminence, who was the author of a book that has enthralled millions and has been a main contributor to their ideas of Arabia and its people, and who, for most Britons, remains a scholar hero, personally an enigma, and at all times his own man.

In commending a man and his abilities it is customary to call for references. Firstly, how true was his account? *The Seven Pillars of Wisdom* was shown in its original form to at least six of his superiors in the desert campaign and none of them disputed the details or quarrelled with it. What did his general commanding officer think of his work as a soldier? Lord Allenby, commanding officer in the Middle East, later wrote, "Lawrence was under my command, but, after acquainting him with my strategic plan, I gave him a free hand. His co-operation was marked with the utmost loyalty and I never had anything but praise for his work, which indeed was valuable throughout the campaign."

What is the place in literature of his book? One of our greatest writers on war, and a Nobel Prize winner for Literature, none other than Winston Churchill, wrote, "An epic, a prodigy, a tale of torment, and in the heart of it—a Man."

Finally, what do present-day Saudis think of Lawrence and his efforts in Arabia?

I have asked Saudis in various occupations and ages, including a few historians, about him. Some younger ones smiled, paused, and said that the film seen on a visit to Britain was entertaining, and added little more. When pressed, all said that his part in the war was slight and that he finally let the Arabs down, having promised a lot, though they admit that they know little about him. Some historians have told me that he helped a little with the fighting but was really a British agent and a spy who promised a lot for Arab unity but let the Arabs down badly in the end. None felt that he was a hero of the Arab revolt, which was largely an Arab affair, while acknowledging that to succeed it had to have the help of the British and French to overwhelm the Turks in the whole Arabian Peninsula including Jordan, Syria, and Iraq.

Britain and France had backed the Arab powers in the west under Sherif Hussein of Mecca, which at the time seemed the right decision, while in the end the power who won over all of Saudi Arabia was Ibn Saud, of the central regions, who was, during the war, paid a handsome retainer by the British to stay on their side. Saudi views are naturally slanted towards their own achievements, while acknowledging the help they received from those nations without whose aid they would not have had a chance of succeeding. But Lawrence appears to them to be not much more than one who gave some help but did not fulfil his promises. On Lawrence's side it is only fair to recall that he was distressed by the failure of the British and French alike to grant to the people of the Arabian Peninsula and the northern lands a unified Arab state, but he was not much more than a cipher after the battles, when the politicians, as ever, made the decisions.

CHAPTER XII

Oil in the Gulf

The Americans, though playing a large and effective part in Europe in World War One, had no share in the expulsion of the Turks from the Arabian Peninsula nor in the Middle East at any point. The French effort in the Middle East was trivial, though they suffered appallingly on their own soil. The British had to handle both Abdul Aziz and Sherif Hussein, their design being to keep Abdul Aziz's sword sheathed and certainly not drawn in favour of the Turks, while at the same time paying large sums, some £100,000 a month it is said, to Sherif Hussein, to run a revolt against the Turks. Abdul Aziz was wooed by being made a Knight (Commander of the Indian Empire) while in Kuwait, and in Basra was given a handsome ceremonial sword, as evidence of British military and aerial power paraded before him—and he was given demonstrations of British medical witchcraft, including an X-ray of his own hand. But to a ruler with an anaemic treasury the transfusion of £60,000 a year and a further supply of arms proved an overwhelming inducement to spurn the Turk and stay on the side of the British. Events proved the money to have been well spent.

After the war, in-fighting continued between Abdul Aziz and the Rashid in the north and Hussein in the west, while the foreigners began their own sparring for oil already known to exist in the Gulf. The British had been first on the scene, striking oil in the south of Iran in 1908, 130 miles from the coast. That bare fact makes it sound as if one or two men with picks and shovels at a site where an ooze of oil was seen produced a payable flow like miners finding nuggets in a river. It was nothing like that. A party of Britons led by an Englishman, William d'Arcy who had made a fortune in the Australian goldfields, obtained a concession from the Shah to search for and then sell oil in his domains for 60 years. They had to haul their apparatus long distances by camel and mule; combatting Turkish officialdom at its most obstructive, facing with the inadequate medicines of those days the full battery of tropical diseases. After three years they still had nothing to show for their trouble and money was running out. Their most unlikely rescuer was the British Navy, whose chiefs were anxious to find an oil supply nearer at hand than Burma and Borneo where Britain had found oil a short time before. Burma's Scottish oil entrepreneurs, now doing nicely, were prepared to nibble at these newer but unproved fields. It took another three years and a lot of good Scots money before the pay-off came. On 26 May 1908, everything and everyone was drenched in the gush of the oily birth-waters of the baby Anglo-Persian. They piped their black gold to Abadan and built the Middle East's first refinery there, and the Navy got its new fuel supply.

British oilmen descended on the ancient oil seepages in Iraq in the Mosul region and with Germans (pre-war) taking a smaller share, and an Armenian one Gulbenkian (a name later to conjure up visions of billions) having his own smaller slice, what was eventually to become the Iraq Petroleum Company was born.

Because of Britain's treaties with the various Gulf States, other nations could not get in on the bonanza. Britain made use of these oil supplies during World War One and development went on first with the coming of peace, so that she was fully committed when a New Zealander, Major Holmes, tried to sell the rights he had acquired in Bahrain. British Companies were not interested, but the American company, Socal (Standard Oil Company of California), which was on the hunt everywhere, due to the heavy drain on the USA's own supplies, took up the concession. The first Bahrain oil flowed in 1932, and that well, now dry, is a national monument.

Holmes rightly divined that the coastal land opposite Bahrain also contained oil, as later events substantially proved, but he was not able to sell to the British the concession he had obtained from Abdul Aziz for £2000 a year! We now know that this land contains the largest oilfield in the world: but no one knew it at that time, and the British, with so much on their hands at the top of the Gulf, were mainly at that time interested only in keeping out other competitors.

The Americans, finding that Holmes was putting off making a deal with them, because he very genuinely wanted Britain to have the concession, arranged a meeting with Philby with a view to using him as a contact with Abdul Aziz, since they wanted to try their own hand at getting a concession. To be fair to Philby, he also tried to persuade the

British, his own people, in spite of all that has been said against him, to take up the concession—but the British again refused. They even got a third chance. Abdul Aziz passed the American prospectors' report to London, feeling morally bound to do so, but the government was not interested. Three chances are a lot. Still, it was a gamble and only with hindsight can British reticence be called folly, because no one knew with any certainty if oil was there, and the Americans nearly reached despair before striking oil at the Dome of Dhahran only with their seventh test bore hole.

The World War Two put a stop to the burgeoning oil production at Dhahran and Ras Tannurah but it was now known that a very large field existed in the eastern region.

In 1945 it was becoming clear to the Allies that they would win the war and a time had come for the leaders to meet to discuss final military strategy and the division of conquered territories. Churchill, Roosevelt and Stalin met at Yalta, a southerly Soviet resort on the south coast of the Crimean Peninsula. Roosevelt decided to meet Abdul Aziz on his way back to the States, no doubt with oil first on the agenda, and his staff organised a rendezvous on board an American warship on the Great Bitter Lake in Egypt to which Abdul Aziz was brought, via the Red Sea by a US warship, and there they held their talks.

Abdul Aziz had used a stick for years to aid him in walking as his arthritis advanced but he was now severely crippled and used a wheel-chair. He was very interested in Roosevelt's wheel-chair for his polio legs, and there and then Roosevelt, in the style of Arab hospitality, gave Abdul Aziz his spare chair which he always took with him.

Britain had been sweetening Abdul Aziz all through the war, and when the President told Churchill the day before his departure that he was going to meet Abdul Aziz on the way home Churchill gave Roosevelt a piece of his mind in strong Churchillian phraseology. The Prime Minister wanted there to be no special concessions for Roosevelt and so arranged to meet Abdul Aziz three days later in a hotel about fifty miles south of Cairo where they talked, Churchill smoking his cigars and drinking his alcohol in the presence of the King, saying he did not mind if the King did not join him, but little appears to have come out of the meeting—except that it was an historic moment when two of the world's greatest men of the twentieth century came face to face, and the same could be said of the meeting three days earlier.

There was a splendid anticlimax, one of the better pieces of

Churchilliana. Abdul Aziz dispensed the usual lavish gifts in the traditional Arabian way—jewels, gold, weapons, and the like. Churchill could reply at the time only with a box of scent, but assured the King he would send him a Rolls Royce—the best car in the world—as he put it. Because of the war, with none being produced one had to be found and a throne made in it. When the King received it a year later, he took one look at it and immediately passed it on to a younger brother. The British right-hand drive would have forced the King to sit on the driver's left, which would never do. He was put out by this thoughtlessness and by the smoking and drinking of the British leader.

Roosevelt was to die very soon after but he had arranged the loan of a DC-3 and crew for a year in which the King and his family went hopping about the country. The Saudia Airline arose out of that, and Britain had lost out once again.

As Abdul Aziz's health declined his mind turned to the spiritual welfare of his people, and he ordered the enlargement of and repairs to the Great Mosques of Mecca and Medina. He also ordered a search, which was successful, by American drillers for water from boreholes throughout the centre of the Peninsula with a view to the future of agriculture.

His eldest son, Turki, had died in the great influenza epidemic which followed World War One. His second son, Saud, by the same mother (Wadhba bint Hazzam) had been made Crown Prince in 1933 by the King himself, there being no confirmation of the King's choice by either the family or the ulema. Saud was always a great success as a tribal chief, with a regal demeanour and a good measure of arrogance, but he had neither the intelligence nor the interest to improve himself in foreign affairs like his half-brother, Faisil, who had travelled extensively and paid much attention to foreign visitors, and as well was the more intelligent of the brothers.

To members of the family there seemed these two as possible successors, but there was a fear that without the King's personality the Kingdom might split into three states, the Hejaz under Faisil, the Nejd under Saud, and the Hasa under Saud ibn Jiluwi; but nothing came of it. Saud exerted himself as the old King's strength ebbed away, and Abdul Aziz, now taken to Taif in the hope of improvement, spoke to Saud and Faisil about the succession, telling them to avoid any disunity and asking Faisil to accept Saud as his successor and that Faisil should be Crown Prince and should succeed Saud in turn. Much later Faisil was urged several times to take over from Saud but he would not do so until many years later events forced him to act.

The old King's heart was gradually fading. At first he bemoaned his loss of sexual power which with prayer had been his principal pleasure. Then gradually the end came at Taif on 9 November 1953, where he died in the presence of many of his family, his body being flown to Riyadh where he was buried in the limestone in the al Oud (incense) cemetery on the outskirts of Riyadh. No headstone or inscription marks the spot and at the time just a few loose stones were put about to indicate the recent mound; but some faith or superstition prevailed, for he was placed amongst several remnants of those whose company he had enjoyed in life, including his favourite sister, Nura. Saud, Faisil and Khalid were also given their last home there.

In Taif, the princes had filed past Saud with Faisil standing near, each swearing, "we give allegiance to you on the book of Allah and in the tradition of Allah's messenger."

In this brief account of the origins of the modern state of Saudi Arabia and how it is seen by the traveller today no attempt has been made to relate in detail the political ups and downs of the reigns of the subsequent Saudi rulers, but to give some continuity a brief accout of the principal events of the reigns of the three successive kings—Saud, Faisil and Khalid, follows, and an outline of the earlier career of the new King Fahad is added.

CHAPTER XIII

Brief Biographies of the Succeeding Saud Kings

King Saud

King Saud was born in 1902 at Kuwait, his mother being Wadhba bint Hazzam. He was the second son of both his father and mother, their first, Turki, being a victim of the great influenza epidemic, and though only nineteen he had wasted no time, for he sired three daughters, and a son born posthumously. These births were in Kuwait, which was the base for the Sauds at that time though it was not to be for much longer, for the day of Saud's birth was the very day that Abdul Aziz reclaimed his birthright by taking the Musmak fortress in Riyadh.

Saud in his time was to sire more sons (52), and daughters, and untold numbers unofficially, than his father, his ability in bed proving to be his best quality. He grew up without schooling of the classroom which was not part of the education of the Arabs of those regions at that time, but he played the games of the Arab boys and learnt riding, hunting, and the use of arms, growing as tall as his 6ft 4in father but having the misfortune of poor eyesight, in later life being operated on for cataracts, so that he wore thick lenses which did not help his appearance, nor did his flat-footed gait.

He had come into a vast inheritance won by his father, but he lacked his father's ambition and energy, preferring to dissipate rather than accumulate, and in the end, had he been unchecked, would have given away, in the most lavish display of extravagance, his entire birthright, and even undone much of the unifying work by his father of the lands of the Peninsula.

He was brave enough and showed his courage on an occasion in the Great Mosque at Mecca in 1936 when two Yemeni made an attempt on the King's life and Saud threw himself before his father to take the intended fatal blow. But bravery by itself is not enough and he had not the experience by travel nor the intelligence of his father or of his younger brother Faisil. Abdul Aziz had kept his oldest living son at

1. *(centre) King Abdul Aziz who founded the Saudi State.*
2. *(top left) King Saud, the second son, his older brother, Turki, died of influenza, aged 20.*
3. *(top right) King Faisil, the third son.*
4. *(lower left) King Khalid, the fifth son, his older brother Mohammed did not wish to reign.*
5. *(lower right) King Fahad, the eleventh son, and present ruler.*

home and sent Faisil as his representative. Perhaps he thought that Saud might have had less success. Again, as a warrior he played his part bravely but without the strategic sense, the flair, and the dash of Faisil.

His forte was the distribution of largesse accumulated by his father and of the increasing revenues from the oil industry which were regarded as the King's own. In Riyadh, at the start of the suburb of Nasaria can still be seen the arch with traffic flowing around it, called by many British expatriates "Marble Arch", which was the entrance to a vast complex of palaces, mosques, barracks, royal schools, hospital, harems and the rest, surrounded by a high wall said to be about seven miles in all, some remnants of which remain identifiable by their pinkish tint. But that was only part of the extravaganza which included some ten palaces about the country, the furnishings and decorations being the most lavish that the world could supply.

Saud had travelled little compared to his brother Faisil during their father's reign but once King there was no stopping him. In the spring of 1954 he went to Egypt and formed some sort of pact with Nasser to keep the West from using Arab nations in their plan of defence against the communists in particular. In 1957 he visited the USA at President Eisenhower's invitation, starting at New York, taking with him a large assortment of high officials and retainers. He received a nasty surprise shared no doubt by Eisenhower—New York gave him the cold shoulder, the very large Jewish population ignoring him and the Jewish mayor of the time refusing to receive him.

Nasser of Egypt had ambitious plans for uniting all the Arab lands with, of course, himself as the director-in-chief and he was glad to accept Soviet assistance in combating the Western powers who had so long dominated Egypt. The United States, however, were anxious about two things in the Middle East, their continued oil supply from Saudi Arabia including the protection of that supply from foreign intervention or destruction, and so, secondly, they wanted airfields for general protection against the Soviets and specifically against any attack at Dhahran. The President and his staff made an offer to Saud of vast military supplies of arms, tanks, fighter aircraft, training facilities and a substantial loan of $250 million.

In return the President sought the use of Dhahran airfield and services for the USA aircraft for five years. Saud, already feeling the pinch, liked it. The two men were purring as Saud flew away from the States in the President's own aeroplane to Europe where he first visited

Madrid and was conducted to the outstanding Moorish monuments in the different parts of Spain.

He went on to meet the King of Morocco in Rabat, then on to Tunis, then Libya, and so to a meeting in Cairo with Nasser, King Hussein of Jordan, and the President of Syria. Bonhomie at this meeting was douched by the Egyptian and Syrian bosses who would have nothing of Saud's American agreement, Nasser saying that there was no cause to fear Russia, the Russians were their friends; but he would accept one part of the agreement—the bit about the money from the Americans provided they could spend it as they liked! Nasser wanted a dole not a deal. The Kings of Iraq and Jordan were prepared to accept the plan but the dictator of Egypt and the President of Syria now well under Soviet influence, were adamant in refusal. Not only did they turn it down they also set about a plan to destroy the kingdoms and the established governments of the Arab world.

Not long after this meeting an attempt was made by revolutionary Egypt to overthrow King Hussein, whose own great personal courage and prompt action together with an army of bedouin sent on request by Saud saved the day for Hussein. The appearance of the Sixth US Fleet at the eastern end of the Mediterranean and the dropping of large numbers of British paratroopers in Jordan might also have had some influence as something more than a strong hint to Egyptian and Syrian pinkish zealots! Nasser's first attempt at smashing a kingdom and bringing another Arab state into the communist fold had failed. There was much gnashing of handsome teeth.

Early the next year the foiled Egyptian dictator tried again using different tactics. In a speech in Damascus he made allegations of a plot by Saudi Arabia, with King Saud himself at the head of it, to disrupt the Egyptian-Syrian axis by having Nasser either blown up in one of his aeroplanes or burnt up in a motorcar petrol fire. At the same time a Damascus newspaper printed, with suitable modifications, the USA-Saudi agreement concerning the use of Dhahran airfield by US aircraft.

The Saudi Princes were uncertain what to believe, being divided in their views as to whether the use of Dhahran by the States and the associated financial benefits was a good thing, or whether Nasser had the right idea. This book is about past and present life in Saudi Arabia and how it has all evolved and no attempt has been made to set out and weigh the politics of the Middle East, the author being one of those best suited to leave that well alone, but it has been necessary to make this small venture into wider Arab politics to help to explain the next event of great importance in the affairs of the Saudi state.

The uncertainty of the Princes gave rise to a feeling that King Saud was leading the country into political dangers as well as ruining it financially. The banks and merchants were owed over $100 million and there was no end to Saud's personal spending. There were those who had doubted the wisdom and even the "legality", according to the ancient Arab traditions of the selection of Saud as Crown Prince by Abdul Aziz in 1933, for Saud was unproved and the King was in excellent health. According to ancient Arab custom the rule of primogeniture as in Europe did not apply, the leadership going to the most able in the opinion of the chiefs and with the approval of the whole family, be he brother or son, though certainly not a minor who could not possibly rule. Saud when twenty-six years old had been made Viceroy of the Nejd, and at thirty-one he was declared Crown Prince, with twenty years of Abdul Aziz's life to run. There had been much tutting, and tugging of beards but none would face the King to contest his actions.

Now had come the big moment of the "I told you so brigade", but no matter what their earlier thoughts may have been, those with the nation's salvation at heart, knowing their duty, had to act, and act they did. Soundings amongst the Princes had begun and the need for a change was clear. Saud had isolated himself in his pink walls, having little taste for politics and little success in his forays into it. He preferred his women and the company of bedouins and their chiefs and, like his father, to behave in the style of an Arab desert chieftain, and he was good at that.

Faisil was approached with a view to Saud abdicating and his taking over. He knew well that his brother had emptied the coffers with his extravagance, but he remembered his promise to his father and would not listen to talk of his becoming King or even to any reduction in the King's powers. However, in the end, after hearing the opinions of so many and under strong persuasion he gave way.

The King was sitting with Faisil and Abdulla ibn Abdul Rahman who had done so much work behind the scenes when twelve princes entered the room. They were very serious and told the King that at first they had decided to ask for his abdication but had settled for his remaining King though he must hand over his powers to Faisil. It was clearly his only chance of remaining King and much could happen in the future. So he promptly agreed, deeds were immediately drawn up, and the nation was informed on the radio of the change.

Faisil took over and in his unostentatious way went on living in his ordinary house, drove his car himself, and conducted the daily meetings with the hundred and one Saudis and foreigners who have always been given direct access to a Saudi leader. He stopped the import of luxury goods and of cars for the time being, and consequently was immediately hated by the many who had been reaping huge profits from them, and he cancelled the posts of many drawing vast government monies for no efforts. He did not care that many did not like him in consequence; Saud would have been upset if he was not popular with one and all.

He calmed affairs with Egypt, but, in Syria, communists, Nasser's followers and army officers joined forces to wipe out the royal family almost to a man. All communists held in prison in Syria were released that night. The Saudi government had cause for concern and looked to its defences.

Faisil twice went to Switzerland for treatment. In 1957 he had had his gallbladder removed in the USA and two months later an encore before he left the States for a benign (leiomyoma) tumor of the stomach with an ulcered surface causing chronic anaemia, said to have been overlooked at the first procedure.

Saud made one of his European safaris with an entourage of about half the Saudi population in 1959, hunting, it is said, a cure for his declining sexual powers, and leaving a trail of bottles behind him. On his return, Faisil went for medical treatment in Switzerland and Saud took over the management of the Supreme Council, but on Faisil's return Saud was again ill and went off to German, Italian and Austrian spas, and the next year had another dose of spa waters, and, too often, something stronger. It must be said, and all Saudi Arabians and those interested in the country have mostly heard it already, that Saud, the son of a line of abstemious desert sheikhs had become an advanced alcoholic. Even when he isolated himself to try to break the habit there were always the sycophants who would smuggle it in to him. His unlimited authority was self-destructive; his own power was his worst enemy.

One night in 1962 after a disruptive meeting Saud collapsed with abdominal pains and was taken to the Aramco Hospital in Dhahran where he was diagnosed as having had a severe internal bleed due to alcoholism. With cronies smuggling in bottles of the stuff it was impossible to treat him in Saudi Arabia and he was transferred to Boston where he had an operation on his stomach, and at that time also had his cataracts removed. He had taken along the usual swarms of hangers-on and the total bill was reported as $3.5 million, probably the most expensive operation the world had known and is likely still to stand as a record.

Faisil, during his periods of full power increased the King's own Guard, now called the National Guard, to about 30,000 from its former strength of less that 2,000, the regular army staying at about 40,000. In 1962 he again had to take over full powers owing to the state of Saud's health, and he had to rally the country when the Egyptians attacked the Yemen, Saudi Arabia's south-western neighbour, a task he was well fitted to do in view of his experiences of war in the Asir and Yemen in the 1930s. Egypt was to lose that war and it marked the start of the downfall of Nasser. Saud attended a conference in Cairo when, in spite of Nasser's attack on the Yemen and bombing of Khamis Mushait and Abha in Saudi Arabia, he seemed to come under the spell of Nasser and give him some support.

This proved too much for the Saudi Princes when on top of it came a demand from Saud to have his full powers restored. This smacked of possible prompting by Nasser. The Princes would take no more. In a way Nasser had done the people of Saudi Arabia a service but they had no need to send him a bouquet.

The Princes met several times with about a hundred present and sixty-five of the Ulema—from all over the country. At no time did Faisil press for himself to replace Saud. He remembered and respected his promises. The meeting decided to send messages to Faisil and the King that Saud must go. Gerald de Gaury in his book *Faisil* relates how Faisil was approached at a moment as the afternoon prayer was called and Faisil replied, "Let us leave the answer until after the evening prayer." When the time came and they again pressed him for an answer, he replied, "It is my right to ask you how you proposed to carry out this decision." "By proclaiming you King," they answered. "What about the reigning King?" At this they were silent, and Faisil went on: "In the house of Abdul Aziz we do not depose the King except after all attempts have failed. Have you exhausted all means of persuasion?" Members of the delegation, obviously moved, replied: "Truly, you are King."

The delegation went to Saud and told him of their decision and of

Faisil's attitude, telling him also that he must abdicate in any way he preferred, and he would have his grants still. He could stay in the country or live abroad as he chose. Saud spurned any suggestions of going voluntarily. More meetings followed and Faisil went to see his brother and spoke of his affection for him, but such a decision by the Princes and the Ulema was binding as they were prepared to withdraw their allegiance to him. Saud and his sons stayed and talked in his palace in Riyadh but in the end they could see that there was no way out, for they had no support in the Councils nor from the tribes. On 4 November the National Guard swore allegiance to Faisil. Saud decided to leave the country and was soon gone.

The exiled Saud went to Greece for some time, stayed in Cairo on two occasions, and was in London in 1968 for medical treatment. He died in Athens on 23 February 1969, the exact cause being disputed amongst my medical Saudi friends. Heart failure was one diagnosis and another cancer of the stomach. Perhaps in the circumstances liver failure, as I have seen in others troubled as Saud was, might have been the answer.

His body was flown to Riyadh to be buried in al Oud cemetery near the remains of his father. Faisil had read from the Koran over the body of his late brother, but this official piety was followed by orders to strike the name of Saud from the records, and this was carried out after a fashion. However, Faisil's other wish to disinherit Saud's sons who had followed their father in dissipation met such opposition from the whole family, who were against acting in any spirit of vengeance, that Faisil did not persist in trying to visit his wrath on the next generation. Faisil had been true to the promise of his beloved father and had held back his feelings for too long as he saw the feckless dispersion of a heritage; not just the fruit of their father's struggles over many years, but also a heritage which would probably be his in the fullness of time if any of it remained. Perhaps the fault was partly his in that he should have given way to earlier persuasions to assume full control. Hindsight is always easier than foresight.

When the author arrived in Saudi Arabia in 1977, the name of Saud was taboo and none would explain to me why. There were smiles and evasions. In all public buildings and most offices there were and still are three pictures of familiar faces on the wall—King Abdul Aziz, King Faisil, and King Khalid, and sometimes a fourth, Prince Fahad, now the King. Saud, the unspeakable, was also the unmentionable. This had evidently been the state of affairs for some years, and looked like sticking. About 1981, newspaper reports again began to include in descriptions of the events of past years the name of King Saud. One very high official gave a speech on the need to remember that King Saud was one of the Saudi Kings and that during his time he had set in motion several fine public works and had especially encouraged education and hospitals for the people. Many schools had been started by him and the University in Riyadh was founded in 1957 in his reign. At the official celebrations of the twenty-fifth anniversary of the founding of the University which were held coincidently with the opening of the 860-bed King Khalid Hospital, in the presence of King Khalid at the ceremony at Dir'iyah, it was announced that henceforth the Riyadh University would be known as the King Saud University. King Khalid was a kindly, good-natured man by repute, and no doubt he remembered that his brother Saud had once saved his father's life, had been a very popular man with the tribes, and had played his part in matters of welfare, showing, if to great excess, that much admired quality of the Arabs—generosity, and with it good fellowship. He had, as well, the greatest of virtues—courage. King Khalid suffered illness himself, and this had brought him the realisation that his brother Saud had what we have now come to accept as a form of illness. Perfection is with Allah alone, but charity we can achieve, and understanding, and forgiveness. King Saud is now reinstated and we can speak of him again, and let us hope—freely.

★ ★ ★

King Faisil

King Faisil was born in 1905, the third son of his 25-year-old father. His mother was Tarfa bint Abdulla, her father being descended from Mohammed Wahab who, together with Mohammed Saud, started the Wahabi movement which spread all over the Arabian Peninsula. He arrived in the Musmak Fortress in Riyadh which Abdul Aziz had captured just three years previously.

As he grew up he learnt to ride well, to hunt, to climb palm trees, to use arms, and to pass the daring test of a boy of jumping down a 30-foot well and being hauled up in a bucket. His mother died when he was young, producing no further children, and he was brought up by his grandmother and grandfather who later greatly influenced his education in both religious and secular matters, while later he was to learn much from outings with his father in political affairs and the handling of men. Like his brothers he was made to rise long before dawn, to walk barefoot and to ride bareback and to eat sparingly, becoming tough and wiry and capable of performing all the feats expected by Abdul Aziz of his sons, but he remained the quietest and most thoughtful of them all.

When only thirteen years old he was fighting in the struggle between the forces of Abdul Aziz and Sherif Hussein at Taraffa, and he learnt sorrow during the great influenza epidemic in 1918 when he lost his closest companion, his brother, Fahad, and his half brother, Abdul Aziz's oldest son, Turki, aged nineteen and already the father of a son and three girls, and the youngest brother of five, Sa'd. He saw the sorrow also of his father who lost as well his favourite wife, Jauhaira.

In 1919, Abdul Aziz was invited for discussions in London but felt he could not leave his territories and sent as his deputy his second son, Faisil, aged fourteen, and to act as adviser and protector, a wise and experienced French-speaking member of the Saud family, Ahmed al Thunaiyan. St John Philby met the party in England and helped considerably with their tour but was not responsible for the bungling of the arrangements for hospitality which aroused the concern of King George V, who, together with Queen Mary, subsequently received the guests in the throne room of Buckingham Palace.

Faisil was taken on tours of the Houses of Parliament in session, the Bank of England, a film studio, a captured submarine, Greenwich Observatory, Cambridge, Cardiff and a Welsh steel works, and on to Ireland where they were received at the Vice-Regal Lodge, then on to Trinity College, and to horse riding and some studs. In Belfast he saw ship-building and mills, then on returning to Wales to walk on Snowdon, a snowstorm nearly finished him off. Visits to arms and motorcar factories were followed by visits to the *Mikado* and *Patience*, then to the impressiveness of Windsor Castle. From there he went to France to visit many of the recent battlefields where the ravaged land and ruined cities and even remnants of the dead were still to be seen. The tour finished with visits to various French cities including, of course, Paris. Even the cantankerous Philby conceded that it was a great success in spite of a few setbacks.

Abdul Aziz considered that his son's education of the larger world was, for the time being, completed, and that he was now ready for military education giving Faisil command of troops to fight, in the Asir, some of the tribes who were originally under Turkish forces and after the Allies' victory were supported by "King" Hussein; they were opposing other tribes supporting Abdul Aziz. Faisil's forces settled the dispute, but three years later one of the tribes rebelled and Faisil was sent at the head of an army of 5,000 to make an end to it. He returned to Riyadh to a Roman triumph—Arabic style. At the age of eighteen he was a man of much experience compared to his contemporaries leaving school in the West. In 1930 this Asir territory was incorporated into the Saudi domains.

In 1934 Faisil was again to command an army which passed through the Asir to the Yemen along the coastal route, the Tihama, while his brother Saud was in command of another army marching on Najran. Again the Saud were highly successful, Faisil proving once more his abilities in the fighting and the negotiations, the result being that the provinces of Najran and Tihama became part of the Saudi territory.

In the capture of the Hejaz, Faisil was given command of the seige of Jeddah and ordered by his father to keep casualties to a minimum, the city eventually being taken without looting and with few casualties. At the age of twenty-one Faisil was made Viceroy of the Hejaz and Secretary of State, living in Mecca and holding these offices for thirty years until called to the throne. But his foreign journeys continued. In the summer of 1926 he made another tour of Europe, and in 1932 he visited Paris, London, Poland, Turkey, Russia, and returned to London again in 1939.

Faisil married three times, firstly, Sultana bint Ahmed al Sudairi, by whom he had one son; secondly, Haya bint Abdul Rahman by whom he had two sons; thirdly, and a real love-match, Iffat bint Ahmed bin Abdulla al Saud who presented him with five sons. The family was balanced by the usual complimentary number of daughters. His father, Abdul Aziz had married Hassa bint Ahmed al Sudairi by whom he had several sons all in high posts today, including governerships, and some twenty-five of Abdul Aziz's descendants have married Sudairi women. With Abdul Aziz's mother a Sudairi, this family is one of the most influential in the kingdom. His second wife, Haya, was a member of that powerful branch of the Saud tribe, the Jiluwi, Abdul Aziz's cousin, Abdulla Jiluwi, fighting with him at the taking of Riyadh and in most of Abdul Aziz's subsequent battles. Iffat, the third and last wife, was a niece of Ahmed al Thunaiyan who accompanied the 14-year-old Faisil to England. All Faisil's sons went to a variety of schools and universities

including Princeton, Oxford, Cambridge, and the military sons to
Sandhurst and Cranwell, while the daughters were all educated in
Europe, mostly in Switzerland.

Faisil was in his time to give much encouragement to education,
starting the programme of schooling for girls, evidently pleased with
the results of the schooling of his own daughters. During his reign the
medical schools in Riyadh, Jeddah and Dammam were started and, as
well, Saud women were trained as schoolteachers, and the women's
medical colleges in the same cities were started. He was clearly a
believer in the old Arab saying that a country with its women
uneducated is like a bird with one wing. His own life-style remained
simple, almost austere by Arab standards.

During World War Two, King Abdul Aziz received an invitation to
visit the United States as did his son, Saud, and any other son. The
King decided he could not leave himself, nor did he wish to send Saud,
but instead he again chose Faisil, now aged thirty-seven, for this foreign
mission, and, as well, his brother Khalid (later King), then aged thirty,
completing the party with two experienced Sheikhs and a bodyguard for
each son. The Americans were impressed by their Saudi dress and fine
manners and the calm demeanour customary to the Saudis.

The handsome present of a jewel and gold decorated sword from the
King to President Roosevelt was followed by a lavish dinner for the
Princes in Washington with all leaders in politics and the military on a
three-line whip. Then followed the usual sort of tour of the
States—New York and the top of the Empire State Building, and some
night-life, San Francisco, Los Angeles with Hollywood, then especially
for their practical interests, oil refineries and irrigation of desert land.

The two brothers flew to London as they were very anxious to see
wartime England, staying at the Dorchester, perhaps giving it such
distinction in Arab eyes that it has since become Arab owned. In
London they got the full treatment including air-raids, fog, a tour of the
bombed areas, a visit to meet young airmen about to take off on
bombing raids, reception at 10 Downing Street, and finally the accolade
of being received by King George VI at Buckingham Palace. Before
long Faisil was to tour the Far East. He had now met many of the
influential personages of the world and in his time was to come to know
five American Presidents. Back in Saudi Arabia he continued his work
in the Hejaz but in 1949 was back in the US at the United Nations
Organisation in New York speaking on behalf of his nation and on the

Palestine problem, being considered a fine speaker and a noted leader of the Arab people.

In 1953, with the weakening and then the waning of the life of King Abdul Aziz there came to be a big overlap in the concerns of the King and his two eldest sons, and this has been set out in the description of the life of King Saud, once being enough. Faisil held his promise to his father to support Saud as King, and Saud made Faisil his Crown Prince who acted for him when the state of his health would not permit him to rule and in the end took over from him when the Princes would suffer Saud no longer.

On becoming King, Faisil settled with ease into the leadership, having acted as "locum" for his brother for long periods. In the course of his reign his travels took him once again to all the Arab countries, to Europe and to the States. His natural sagacity, patience, and, in the end, his capacity to take positive action based on his unswerving principles which were founded on his strong religious belief, kept him on a clear path. Oil revenues were creating riches which brought more responsibilities, but, amidst the turmoil and greed which this wealth created at home and abroad, he kept his head above oil. He was never a soft and pliant settler for the easy way, but he was thorough and just. He had a row with Britain and the Emirates over the territory of Buraimi; he avoided Nasser and would not attend his funeral; he had stern words for the USA and especially Kissinger, but he never ceased his efforts for Islamic solidarity and against Zionism and Bolshevism. To his brothers he had to distribute the various offices of State and he was disapproving of those with weaknesses for the glass and gambling, but he tolerated them and forgave most of them, especially the reformed and those with brains who could help him in his task of government. To their taking a percentage as "commission" in business and contracts he probably seldom if ever gave a thought because this has always been a way of life in the Arab world, and it still goes on.

One thing he would not forgive was the behaviour of his late brother Saud and of his children who appeared to have absorbed some of their father's less fortunate ways. But for the rest he continued to foster all aspects of healthy national development, especially in the fields of health, social welfare and education.

He grew more inflexible but his rigidity was predictable because, like his father, he based his actions on the Koran and Sharia law which remained his control and corrective against the corrupting influence of autocracy. His principal weakness as a king was his inability to delegate responsibilities sufficiently often, and, with the nation growing bigger, to limit the incessant stream of subjects and foreigners who wished to speak to him personally in the traditional Arab way, as in his father's time. In consequence, access to him was easy and he scorned the use of the type of heavy bodyguard so familiar to many Kings and Presidents. It proved to be his undoing.

On 25 March 1975, the anniversary of the birth of the Prophet Mohammed, one of the Ministers being received by King Faisil was Kasami, the Oil Minister from Kuwait who was being presented to the King by Sheikh Yamani, the Saudi Oil Minister. The King's nephew, Prince Faisil bin Musaid, had entered the building. Although the King would ordinarily give an audience to any member of the royal family, he would not have been keen to do so to this 28-year-old nephew, for the Prince had been involved in using and selling drugs when at the University of Colorado some five years previously and was known to be still taking drugs. The Prince waited outside the closed doors into the King's audience chamber when he saw and embraced the Kuwaiti Minister, his friend of the Colorado Campus. The Chief of Protocol was on his way to the King to consult him about seeing his nephew when the doors were opened unexpectedly and the well-nourished Minister strode towards the King. The Prince fell in behind him, being hidden from the King. At the moment of presentation, the Prince stepped out and let fly three shots from a pistol of 0.308 calibre. Two shots as good as missed, but the first bullet that had been fired hit the King in the throat. It is rumoured that the young Prince had spent time practising throat shots at a model he had made of the King. Perhaps his hand was shaky from drugs or fear, or he had not practised enough, but one shot in the right place was all that was needed.

The Chief of Protocol thought that the Kuwaiti Minister had fired the shots and courageously hurled himself at the Minister, to find the Prince behind him with gun in hand, on whom he turned and flung down as guards rushed to secure him. The King was rushed to the Central (Shameisi) Hospital but all the usual efforts with transfusions, massage of the heart, and stimulants, could not bring him back to life.

The news was broadcast just after 11 a.m. that morning and immediately the senior Princes and the Ulema gave their decision— Khalid was to succeed and Fahad was to be Crown Prince, this decision was made and broadcast just over three hours after the assassination.

Foreign heads of state, certainly from all the Muslim world, and many of other religions, came pouring in immediately, though Gaddafi of Libya stayed at home, while the Indonesian could not meet the time schedule and consequently caused offence by his absence. Idi Amin spectacularly represented Uganda as a Field-Marshal from the waist up and kilted below, with a son to match.

The burial was slightly late by Muslim rule, just over the twenty-four hours after death, and after the chief mourners and about 100,000 of the populace had gathered at the mosque near the al Oud cemetery, Faisil was placed in a grave near to his father, Abdul Aziz and, like all the others, the grave was unmarked but the approximate site is known.

Idi Amin overdid it again and embarrassed everyone present by flinging himself on the grave, giving a dramatic series of convulsions of despair. Perhaps he wore the kilt to make it easier. It was an ill-timed touch of farce at the solemn rites of a great man.

The United States had had their assassination a few years earlier with the despatch of John Kennedy, the catching of the killer and the prolonged hue and cry for causes still unsettled. And now Saudi had her own tragedy. Why should Faisil's own nephew and namesake want to kill him? What has already been written on the subject, and my conversations with Saudis, cover just about all possibilities. They do bring out some reasons for hate, but more than hate alone is called for to kill—especially your uncle King.

Prince Faisil bin Musaid, a taker and seller of drugs, had been found out and reprimanded by the King and told to keep at home. One of the Prince's brothers would not obey an order from King Faisil and was shot, the father, and so the family, laying the blame on the King. Prince Mussaid's family had always been close, the children especially in their feelings and in the proximity of their palaces to the prodigal Saud's in Nasariyah, and the Prince's mother had come from the Al Rashid tribe who had for so long been enemies of Abdul Aziz. King Faisil had been a great leader for Arab unity and it was inevitable that Zionists should be thought to be concerned, one theory being that Zionists of the CIA induced a Jewish girl friend to induct the Prince into anti-Muslim ideas and anti-Faisil feelings, and to be associated with him in drugs. A further period of drugs and debauchery in the Lebanon had done him no good and he was reported from there as saying he was out to kill the King. Complicated assertions have been made that the Egyptians, Israelis, and Soviets were really responsible. After hearing and reading all this, my own opinion is now as uncertain as it is of the reasons behind the killing of John Kennedy. A precipitating factor in a highly unstable young man could have been his impending marriage to a daughter of King Saud. It was unbelievable for him to have thought that he could shoot the King in his audience chambers then marry his niece in the next week or two, but I was told by more than one that he fully expected to be acclaimed for getting rid of a tyrant and was sure that he would be made King for doing it.

His state of mind looks very much like that of someone under the influence of drugs, and doctors in Beirut said that he was being treated for drugs and alcoholism at the time, while some doctors might see signs of GPI as a result of his sexual aberrations. The Prince did not know at first that he had killed the King, the news being kept from him, and he continued in custody to rage and scream that he had rejected the Muslim faith and that nothing would stop him, in the end, from killing the King. When he was told and then shown photos of the King's death he calmed down and resigned himself to his fate, being then judged as not insane, which would have saved his life, but guilty of wilful and premeditated murder, to which he confessed and so sealed his fate.

In Chopper Square, in Riyadh, three months after the murder, he was beheaded in the presence of some 20,000 spectators. The Saudi authorities, after much investigation, were content to report in the media that no external motive had been brought to light. So be it.

* * *

King Khalid

King Khalid was born in Riyadh in 1912, half brother of Faisil, his mother being Jauhaira bint Musaid (also the mother of Prince Mohammed), and he married Sitta and had several sons by her.

Very soon after Faisil became King the question of naming a Crown Prince arose. The next in line was Prince Mohammed, born in 1910, who had shown little interest in holding any official posts, though it is rumoured that he showed some interest when it came to the succession. Mohammed had undoubted courage and had helped the family in some of the crises created by Saud, but his reputedly extreme hot temper was too often unleashed, reaching epic heights in a dispute with Saud when in the later stages of dissipation he faced him and threatened to put daylight through him with his sword if he did not behave. The family weighed matters very carefully and concluded that the best combination to suit the country would be Khalid for King and Fahad for his Crown Prince at the departure of Faisil from the scene. Some say that Faisil offered it to Mohammed but he refused it. In March 1965, six months after the accession of Faisil, Khalid was named as Crown Prince, exactly ten years before he was called to the throne on the assassination of Faisil.

As King Faisil grew older the matter of the succession was talked about in the family, it is rumoured, and they evidently saw no cause to wish to change the order of their original decision; but there were some doubts, largely on account of his health. He had a successful operation for arthritis of the hip in England, which afterwards gave no cause for concern in respect of the succession but his heart had given a lot of trouble with anginal pain, and in 1972 he had a coronary by-pass operation, in the USA to improve the circulation of blood in the heart muscle. Both operations proved highly successful and, as well as the direct benefit they gave King Khalid himself, they have been an example to all the Saudi population of the help that modern medicine and surgery can give, and his example in the way he faced up to two major operations so courageously was an inspiration to all his subjects. But against this health risk was the fact that Khalid was so popular with the family and the people, embodying all the traits beloved of the Arab people. He was generous, kind, and hospitable and loved to travel round and meet the tribes and their leaders. Together with his brothers, Mohammed, the older, and Abdulla, the younger, they spent a lot of time travelling the country and relieving their brother King Faisil of much of this essential part of Arabic chieftainship. These two desert companions had a strong say in the choice of Crown Prince, for with Fahad playing up at the time they had no doubts in their mind.

Khalid's education had been the Palace and the desert with his father and brothers, and his foreign travel. He had made a trip to Europe in 1938 when he dined with Hitler, and had accompanied Faisil in the trip to the United States, and to Britain in wartime, and as well to the various Arab states. He had always had a fine presence and in spite of the opportunities and encouragement to accumulate arrogance, it was not in his nature. He was reported to like his fun and a joke, and on his incessant official duties kept a group of smiling people around him with his pleasantries. The author of this book was very close to him, as were many other doctors, in the new hospital bearing his name. When he was sitting in the main hall in front of a splendid portrait of himself in bluish marble mosaic, taking his pills doled out by his personal physician while he was being told the disposition of the hospital units, at one point a speaker said, "and now we come to the obstetric wards". One heard the King's reply, confirmed by Saudi friends, "Now that is really important. My heart surgeon was an obstetrician before he took up heart surgery, so it must be an important subject." He could have been solemn about obstetrics but chose the light touch and all within earshot had a laugh, especially as they knew that the speaker's own practice was obstetrics.

The hoped-for scheme of leadership was Khalid to be King—with a fine presence he looked the part and with his kind disposition would spend much of his time with the chiefs and the Ulema and greeting foreign dignitaries—while Fahad's genuine ability and intelligence would be used especially in the country's administration. This, after all, is the great secret of successful leadership, the choosing of good lieutenants and letting them get on with it while keeping a supervisory eye on results. The combination ran, as far as those of us on the edge of things could see, better than ever hoped for. Both did their work splendidly.

King Khalid was said to have been a religious man and careful like his father in his observance of the form and the rules, and as well, deeply sincere in feeling. Near the end of his days, around the age of seventy, he spent much time on his farm about fifty kilometres from Riyadh to the north-west where he had a runway made to take the planes of his arriving guests. He always went to Riyadh once a week to meet the Ulema and Ministers. During the winter he enjoyed "hunting" for several weeks, taking with him a huge entourage, said to number in the region of 2,000, to set up and maintain a great tented concourse from which he, with perhaps a hundred special guests, let loose their falcons. He spent much of his time in the desert when he was growing up, and that is where he liked to be. With his generosity, and honesty, and liking his fun, it is easy to see why he was held in so much affection by his people.

King Khalid kept the Premier's post to himself with his brother Prince Fahad as Crown Prince and First Deputy Premier, while his brother Prince Abdulla was Second Deputy and, to hold a balance of power, Commander of the National Guard.

Under this powerful triumvirate the country went from strength to strength along the lines initiated by their father, and advanced by their wise and far-seeing brother, Faisil.

The King was in his summer resort at Taif when a further heart attack on 13 June 1982 proved fatal, the news being announced the same morning on the radio. It was believed that some agreement between the family and the imams about the succession had been achieved already, and the expected result was confirmed at a meeting of the family heads and the imams held almost immediately to avoid any possible disruptions that might arise during a long delay. The Crown Prince, Fahad, was declared as King, and Prince Abdulla confirmed as Crown Prince, the nation being informed immediately by the radio.

The late King's body was flown to Riyadh where the subsequent events were depicted on television. When a Muslim dies in the morning he is buried that day; if in the afternoon then the next day, but in any case within twenty-four hours of death.

The arrival at Riyadh's airport was shown on television with the passage through crowded streets to the Great Mosque in the centre of Riyadh where the highest in the land were assembling and greeting each other with the customary kiss on each cheek, with a special individual greeting by many of the new King Fahad. The late King's body covered by a cloth and tied to a mattress was carried in bundling fashion along one side of the crowded mosque to the central point facing Mecca and laid on a ledge, then brief prayers were said; there is never a long elaborate verbal ritual as a Muslim service, though the many bowings and the obeisances are always made. The mattress with the body atop was quickly lifted and almost rushed from the Mosque to a hearse in the style of an American ambulance and driven to the cemetery of al Oud where the body was buried in the stony ground in the same area as his father and brothers—no flowers, no headstone, and so no inscription to mark the spot. That is the Wahabi way.

No period of mourning followed but, as after a soldier's burial in the Christian world when the band plays a cheerful march on the return, life goes on under the new regime.

* * *

King Fahad

King Fahad is the eleventh son of King Abdul Aziz, being born in Riyadh in 1921 to Hassa bint Ahmed al Sudairi, and so in 1982 was sixty-two years of age. He has a fine family of sons and daughters.

His early upbringing followed the pattern of his older brothers, already outlined, but he became outstanding amongst them all for his intelligence and independence, and also for choosing his own companions who, unlike Saud's and Khalid's, were not amongst the tribal leaders, nor even the royal family with few exceptions. His frequent absences from meetings of the family and his many long trips abroad created a feeling of his being "not quite one of us", amongst the rigid orthodox fraternity.

His visits to the United States introduced him to the immense power of that great country so that he came to hold deep respect for all things American, while in Europe he pleased many of the rich young men of his own age by his similarity of taste in their pleasures, and though, unlike Saud, he left the corks in the bottles, like Saud his prowess in bed, was in keeping with what is admired, respected and expected of a Prince of Arabia.

He enjoyed the company and the challenge of younger men of other nations and this probably led to his wish common to young men to show his ability to compete, in his case, in the finanical fisticuffs of the gambling houses in the South of France, which became world news for a time, and not just for his winnings but for the spectacular size of his bets and for the severe assaults he could survive on his wallet. This was a lapse from the high standards expected of him and he wisely followed a word of warning in the 1970s from King Faisil that he was harming both the nation and its religion, and his own cause as well, when his time came. Far from being antagonised by Faisil's admonition he continued to give Faisil his strong loyalty and backed him to the hilt in the efforts to control Saud, and then, in his final unseating, an instance of his wisdom and good judgement. Faisil in turn sought the advice of his intelligent and much travelled brother, known for his liberalism and the adaptability so needed in the new era in Saudi with the riches coming from oil.

King Abdul Aziz had recognised Fahad's ability by appointing him in 1953, at the age of thirty-two, to the new Ministry of Education. This would be an invaluable experience to a man one day to be king, as a watchman over the welfare of the youth of the nation. In 1962, while Faisil was acting as Regent for Saud, he made some radical changes in the ministerial personnel, Fahad being appointed Minister of the Interior (our Home Secretary) at the age of forty-one. Much of what he had learnt in his travels in the modern world he began to apply to Saudi within the structure of the Islamic culture.

A typical example of Fahad's liberal approach to the old custom of "rough justice" without full evidence was his reputed displeasure and even anger at the execution by a firing squad of the Saudi Princess, the granddaughter of his elder brother, Prince Mohammed, who had refused or been passed over for the throne.

The political relations with Yemen, Egypt and other Arab countries, and with Ethiopia, Israel, and the USSR, were all involved, calling for Fahad's share in negotiations and decisions, and high-level talks with the USA included President Carter personally. During 1979, Fahad was reputed to be worn out and needing a rest, and a reduction of his excessive weight which was having an adverse effect on his diabetes, so he left the country for treatment.

Changes in ministerial policy were largely influenced by Fahad, and at the same time many business deals went his way and his family's, which resulted in returns expected of a Prince of Saudi where payments of commissions with no defined limit are part of the way of life. He became an enormously rich man and well able to create business, such as an agreement with France in 1975 of economic collaboration, as had already been established with the USA. The lion's share in the supply of aircraft and training establishments for the armed forces had gone to the US and, though Britain has little of the huge awards for aircraft, her surplus pilots are extensively used in training in Saudi Arabia.

He helped to initiate and then organise the system of state education and had been President of the committee who drew up the first Five Year Development Plan, and was closely associated with the Second of these. He is reputed to supervise this work and chair his committees in a very relaxed style, even appearing to be almost bored with it all, but such is not the case for he takes a keen and very active part in any plans and their execution. It was typical of Fahad that he did it with controlled intelligence and not by manic activity.

The decision after the assassination of Faisil to appoint the jovial and popular Khalid as King, and the astute Fahad as Crown Prince and the First Deputy, and Abdulla as Second Deputy, was made with the intention of delegating a large share of the regal duties to Fahad. This scheme quickly came into practice thus relieving King Khalid of much of the heavy burden of kingship of a state supplying half the world with oil, with the vast business associated with it, and in a country which is the centre of the Islamic world. The combination worked fruitfully and peaceably by astuteness and tolerance until time brought its changes and Fahad became the ruler in turn.

Part Three

JOURNEYS AND DIVERSIONS IN SAUDI

CHAPTER XIV

A Holiday at Haj

I

Haj is the zenith of the Muslim year, a time when pilgrims from all parts of the world make their way to Mecca, not just in thousands but in thousands of thousands. During the Haj of 1977, 1,600,000 Muslims made the journey to fulfil their religious destinies. The atmosphere is much like Christmas as, for all others not going to Mecca, it is a time of family reunion but with no cards or presents, only offerings to Allah in the form of sacrificed sheep; some 60,000 reputedly at this last gathering at Mecca were sacrificed but not eaten. Wherever Muslims may be it is the custom to look to this secular side, when the family roast a sheep, which is then placed on a mound of rice on a vast tray, the traditional dish, and all sit round and tear off pieces of the hot meat, dipping it in the rice and eating always with the right hand. The feast is on a Friday, when the ceremonies at Mecca reach a climax. Even so, since the Saudis are such notable trencherman, I would not put it past them to tuck away similarly on each day of a holiday. There is also, as at Christmas, an air of excitement leading up to Haj, for some from most communities will make the pilgrimage: it is behoven on all Muslims, as one of the five pillars of their belief, to go to Mecca at least once, if possible, but some do it every second, third or fourth year, many fewer every year, and to most it is a time of genuine and deep religious feeling.

Those who reach Mecca and pass through all the stages of religious expression reckon it to be a very deep emotional experience. Each stage has its ritual. After arriving in Jeddah, Mecca, Medina, Taif, or wherever a start is to be made from a nearby town, the first ritual is bathing before putting on the traditional white robe—a little like the old Roman toga with one shoulder showing. Some reach Mecca by car, by air or on foot but for all there is the long walk with prayers at various stages; then the perambulation around the Ka'aba, the holy stone in the centre of the courtyard of the Great Mosque in Mecca, finishing on the exact spot of starting, a very difficult feat when there are perhaps some 20,000 others going round. Of course, some of the older ones just

1. *At the Feast of Haj the masses perambulating seven times around the Holy Ka'aba in the Grand Mosque at Mecca.*

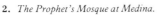

2. *The Prophet's Mosque at Medina.*

cannot make it dropping in their tracks on the way to Mecca or sometimes in the Mosque; but if it cannot be done Mohammed made express provision for those whose strength fails, the important thing being, as has been said of the Olympics, the taking part. There is the stage of throwing stones, symbolic of hurling them at the devil, and also the sermon at Mount Arafat. Other people's beliefs and religious practices, though looked on one hopes with solemnity, may sometimes seem a little ridiculous and even amusing to those of other faiths, including our own, but there is no doubt that those who grow up in the Muslim faith and go through this ritual are the better for it.

The religious observances in Mecca take three days, and this is followed by a week's holiday; there are many who regard it, as their many counterparts in the Western world nowadays regard Christmas, as a national holiday with a religious bias and an occasion for family reunion with much socialising and festivity. There are those who like to combine their religion with a spot of business, as one doctor who had been helping in Mecca said to me as he pocketed some proceeds, "There is nothing like mixing a little business with religion." Some come from farther parts of the Muslim world, Iraq, Iran, Pakistan and beyond, all of whom must enter Saudi Arabia at some point, many crossing it the long way, from the north or east over to the west. Many, therefore, have to pass through Riyadh. Some take along a load of carpets which are sold on the way for profit and expenses, arriving in Riyadh a little early and setting up a carpet market on the outskirts, and do a good trade. Most of us believed that we bought well there.

Mecca, the birthplace of Mohammed, was a holy place long before his advent, and a religion of many gods had grown up there, so that when Mohammed smashed the idols of those gods in the Ka'aba and declared that there was only one god, Allah, the local merchants thought it would be very bad for business because they were used to selling great quantities of copies of the idols to the many visitors and they objected to the change. But he had more than divine inspiration; he also had the power of a conqueror and they gave way. These days it would be a Herculean task to do away with our Christmas or their Haj.

★ ★ ★

As Haj approaches, great numbers of the pilgrims are on the roads around the city in their loaded cars and waggons often gaily lit and decorated as they move along in festive mood, yet with determination evident to see the journey through. The only businesses to remain open are the essential services and those for the supply of food. Even the hospitals have a "go-slow", with just a skeleton staff on duty. To the expatriate population it is a holiday as well, and most of us took the opportunity of exploring Saudi or nearby countries, while a few had leave for home. Some of us decided on a five-day visit to the Arabian Gulf to see the oil wells on the way and the towns of Dhahran, Al Khobar, and Dammam, and to camp on the coast just south of these at Half Moon Bay. David Wallace, Professor of Urology in Riyadh, formerly of London, who worked at the King Abdul Aziz University Hospital and the Shameisi or Central Hospital, as I did, and David's wife, Noël, formerly in London as a radiotherapeutist and now a primary care doctor at the King Faisil Hospital; also Mike Hume, formerly chest physician at Midhurst and in a similar capacity at the Shameisi Hospital; and Nick Greville, an orthopeadic surgeon of Basildon in Essex, on a two year stint at the Shameisi; three surgeons to two physicians, but we spoke of medicine only in anecdote and all went peacefully. When making trips into the desert, or even long journeys on the main roads, it is advisable to use at least two cars in case of breakdown, and a tow-rope is an essential part of the equipment, since there may be long distances between services. The Wallaces and Mike Hume were in one car and Nick Greville and I drove mine. We took a full kit for three nights' sleeping out, and left Riyadh by the Dhahran road for the east coast, crossing limestone desert for about a hundred kilometres and then across a strip of sand stretching for perhaps seventy kilometres, the Dahna, in former times the difficult part of the run to Dhahran. The sands give a feeling of the desert of the story books with splendid crested hills hewed by the winds into curves and humps and hollows, always more attractive in the evening when the fading light of the low sun casts long shadows and makes highlights of slowly changing colour in contrast to the flat light of midday.

At Khurais in the middle of the sandy desert we were stopped by the police, but only to request us to take a lad of fifteen, along with two car-wheels complete with new tyres, to his father's car some fifty kilometres on, where a blowout had wrecked one tyre, causing the car to lurch about enough to damage the other irreparably. These desert roads differ from all others I have travelled on in being lined on each side by discarded tyres at frequent intervals, and on this stretch to the east coast, sometimes every twenty yards, then none for 200 or 300 yards, and then another sprinkling all the way on each side, along with the discarded hulks of cars contorted into every shape by crashes, many head-on, with both cars written off. They lie there slowly rusting away through the years, but old or recent, all are stripped in time of anything that is usable.

Here and there, perhaps every fifty kilometres or so, lies by the roadside the decaying corpse of a camel or goat, usually the result of being struck by a car while wandering on the road at night. A camel is a big lump and can write off a car and its occupants in the act of receiving its own demise. The surface and edging are mostly good, but at times large potholes or encroaching edge erosion will strain axles and occupants as car bodies meet axles and heads meet roofs; dodging potholes in the face of oncoming traffic must have settled the fate of many a vehicle and driver. The shoulder of the road is raised at times at least four inches above the edge and much concentration is needed to keep away from approaching vehicles on the one side while not running over the edge on the other, for a run-off at speed can mean a loss of control and a run right off the road, as we saw at one stage, when a pick-up ahead suddenly shot off the road and ran over the edge into the ditch in a cloud of dust, the car turning over. We got out to help, found the car on its side and the driver standing up inside a little dazed, got him out, righted the car, and after he had his breath back, and slightly below his usual level of consciousness, he went on his way not unduly perturbed after a very luck escape.

Khurais is a refuelling and repair stop with a police station: nothing more. The lad and his tyres were delivered to his Palestinian family in their large American family car, full of a progression of anxious youngsters, all made happy as we were, our good deed for the day completed.

At some parts in the wilderness a gaz, gas, benzine, or petrol station, in its various names, is the only stop, it being sold as much by service rendered as by quantity, and for a tankful is anything from 4 to 10 riyals —it seems to matter only a little whether it is 10 or 40 litres. It is usual to wait until one's tank is nearly empty before refilling. The same volume of water at these places is very likely to cost rather more.

Hofuf, a little over half way on the journey and the principal town in the region of Al Hasa, gives one a feeling of a Hollywood stage set with its old decaying Arabic mud buildings, many still inhabited,

interspersed with numerous building projects in all stages of
completion and the usual large collection of shattered and deceased cars
with, next door to them, scores of the active, giant machines of the
building industry. Two old castles complete the picture.

* * *

After Khurais we came to the oil wells and my ignorance led to
disappointment, for I had expected to see a skyline of derricks zooming
upwards as I had found in the Texas oil scene some years before. But
here there are no vertical features—all is horizontal; here one sees only a
silver-coloured, knobbly pipe sticking in the ground, with wheels of
various sizes about it for turning by hand; commonly, a long shaft
extending from two wheels, rather like a car steering-wheel, some
twenty yards away from the pipe in the ground, apparently an apparatus
known as a "Christmas tree", and from the knobbly pipe in the ground
another, usually silvery, pipe led away, on small concrete blocks
supporting it at frequent intervals, to join a larger branch further on,
which in turn joined an even larger pipe. Around the pipe in the
ground, the wellhead, is a little low fence made of iron railing or small
piping, perhaps twenty yards long on each side, and that is it.
Somebody comes along and turns a wheel or two and liquid assets come
spurting up from the depths. The oil rushes through the system of
pipes to a local collecting area of tanks where the gas in the oil which
was under great pressure in the depths of the earth and forced the oil to
the surface, starts to bubble out of the fluid, just like the gas from a
soda-water bottle, under pressure in the bottle, bubbles in the glass. In
the same way, a man who has been at great depths in the ocean will have
the gases in his blood bubble if he comes to the surface too soon. So,
this gas must be separated out by a system of chambers in which the
vapour rises to the top of the oil and is released to the air, being piped
some two hundred yards or so away and set alight, creating one of those
great flames with a huge pillar of smoke rising from it which dot the
region, anything from one to perhaps a dozen being in view at one time.
This is a great waste of one type of fuel but until recently burning off in
this way was essential. Now, however, plants for compressing and
bottling it are completed and others under way.
    There seems, on the surface, to be no rhyme or reason about where
these wellheads are sited: they appear to be just anywhere but no doubt

PLATE 16 163

1. *Plumes of smoke rise from the oil-bearing part of the desert. Now that the gas is being bottled smoke is reduced.*

2. *At the base of a plume is a flame of burning gas issuing from a pipe led a long, safe distance from an oil-collecting station.*

3. *The large oil-containing pipes merge at an oil station where the gas at high pressure in the oil is released.*

1. *Aerial view of Dhahran with the green housing area of Aramco, the distant bare area containing dry oil wells including the earliest drill hole. To the right by the distant tower is the College of Petroleum and Minerals, see closer insert.*

2. *Our camp on the beach at Half Moon Bay, David Wallace in the foreground and back views of Noël Wallace and Mike Hume by the Wallace's car.*

the siting is determined by careful exploration and drilling, with many wells turning out to be dry. There they are, just silvery knobs and wheels, and any sheikh running a little short of money has but to roll along, turn a wheel or two, and up it comes; and to show him exactly where his well lies, amid an awful lot of desert, there is a long pole on the end of which is what appears to be an oil drum and probably is; no more than that. All are certain to be plotted carefully on maps, but in the end someone has to look for them and turn the wheels.

In some areas natural gaseous pressure is not enough to force the oil to rise up to the surface, so that air with water must be pumped down one pipe at great pressure to force the oil up another pipe beside it. When the oil has been cleared of the gas, under pressure, it runs, by further pipes, often many miles, up little hills and down small dales, mounted on its little concrete pyramids to hold it secure and unkinked, sometimes exposed, sometimes sand-covered, to reach as crude oil a terminal for refining or shipment.

Travelling by day, one sees the periodic wellhead with its fixtures and the pipelines snaking away from it over the desert, or running beside the road, on one or both sides, until they come to a junction when larger pipes lead away; and scattered about, the huge flames with great smoke clouds far and near. And by night, the bright glow in the sky of the flames over the hills, all around the skyline, looking like a thousand fires started in a line of cities blazing after aerial bombardment.

⋆　⋆　⋆

We reached Dhahran in the late afternoon, with but a brief distant glimpse at it, for we wished to press on to our camping site at Half Moon Bay, a very handsome inlet with a large surround of beach and a tidal rise and fall of about six feet, the usual in the Arabian Gulf. Here, already, were encamped in scattered tents Saudis and other members of the Muslim world, together with a smattering of Europeans. We drove about, to take the view and choose our site, as far as possible away from the debris that so often accompanies the habitations of the Arab world. There is hardly any provision in such places for rubbish; when the bedouin moved camp they left their debris lying about, because it was only a speck in a vast empty area, and when they moved into the towns where no receptacles were provided, they threw the rubbish into the streets—where else? Once receptacles for rubbish were provided and refuse collections organized they are usually made use of.

We chose our site well down on the beach, near a rather splendid Saudi encampment of some four tents and a separate green one which we guessed to be, because of this religious time, a sort of mini-mosque for prayers. They were well encamped with their own motor-electric generator and sturdy tents and quite a family was there.

With the sun about to set and darkness soon upon us, we set to and made our camp, a very feeble affair compared to the elaborate preparations of our Saudi neighbours. The two cars were angled fairly closely and in between we tied a canvas windbreak. The Wallaces used the back of their station wagon as their bedchamber, while we three men set up a row of safari beds and arranged beneath the stars our thin foam mattresses and rugs, for it was clearly going to be our coolest night in Saudi. It is part of the ceremony of camping to make a fire and so we set to and collected an assortment of dried grass, roots, sticks, and odd bits of wood and made a rather feeble blaze after all our efforts but, nonetheless, we felt encamped, and by the time Noël had prepared and we had disposed of supper we were ready for an early night, dossing down in our clothes with added jerseys, and with just one blanket above, and below a doubled rug as the main protection. Another I shared with Nick Greville, which covered at least a half of each of us.

The sky from Riyadh is a disappointment, seeming to be less starlit than London or New York due to the atmospheric dust high above the city obscuring the firmament and, as well, diffusing the lights from the large city. In Riyadh, I looked in vain for the jewels in the sky of the Arabian night famed in song and verse, but here on the beach at Half Moon Bay on the Gulf, there they were, the real thing, brighter and more twinkling than the planetarium of Madame Tussaud would have dared to reproduce. Orion standing astride the firmament, challenging, with his dagger at his belt, and nearby the Dog Star, Sirius, a flickering beacon, while Jupiter glared unblinking like some zodiacal one-eyed monster. Lying on one's camp bed with the open sky for coverlet, one watches the progress, in a fitful night, of the twinkling constellations, as the firmament like some ancient scroll unwinds slowly and then rolls up again, re-telling the drama of the universe.

The prima ballerina of the night, on making an exit, allowed the corps of stars full play in brilliant intensity and set me musing on the way this nightly drama has been adopted by the Arabs as a measure of the weeks and months and years. In the Western world we fix our time by the sun round which we go, as we all know, in 365¼ solar days, but the Arab way with its relation to the moon has much significance to all expatriates, for pay is geared to the moon, and as the crescent thins each night they hear the riyals tinkling louder, and when the moon has waned that is the official pay-day. Tales are told about this; one hears, when just arrived, that there is a little man with his telescope who sits and waits until he sees the moon no more and with a shout calls, "Pay". But it is not quite like that. The observations for the sighting of the new moon and the ending of the old must be by unaided sight; any two good citizens who say that they can see the moon no more, or likewise they have seen the new, is all that is needed. Thus the length of the months is settled and financial and other consequences follow. Since many are in Saudi for financial reasons mainly, these keep more than a casual eye on its phases, not fanciful nor romantic. The Arab year is not just twelve moonly months but twelve days more, a most popular orbital arrangement which adds a bonus to the pay.

One muses on the desire of the ancients to find imagined likenesses to some god or creature—they found a symbolic system which, though fanciful at times, we still employ—and one realises how much the Arabs gave to the world by their observations which identified and named the stars. So many have Arabic names: Aldebaran, Deneb, Vega, Alphard, Hamal, Betelgeux, Rigel, to single out just a few. This astronomy led on to flights of fancy, and astrology emerged to which the Arabs contributed much, little knowing that they would help to fill a space in future daily papers, to prescribe fortunes for the day or week for those readers, both believers and infidels alike, who are ready to be guided by omens and accept advice on the conduct of their lives.

Besides their study of the stars the Arabs of the North did much to advance the development of numbers and angles, and it was a combination of these that produced the true Arabic digits which, oddly, are the ones used by the Western world today, while the Arabs today use symbols derived from the Indian Subcontinent. The true Arabic digits (ours) denote their value by the total number of angles found in any one of them, thus:—

$$1\ 2\ 3\ 4\ 5\ 6\ 7\ 8\ 9\ 0$$

which rounded off by the polish of usage have become

$$1\ 2\ 3\ 4\ 5\ 6\ 7\ 8\ 9\ 0$$

The digits used by the Arabs are

$$١\ ٢\ ٣\ ٤\ ٥\ ٦\ ٧\ ٨\ ٩\ ٠$$

The sign for nothing • sifre, (hence 'a mere cypher' means nothing at all) can be confused with a lot of other things and, to one's good fortune, perhaps the head of a bolt on one's number plate. There is a rumour that there is a movement amongst the Arabs to revert to their original system as so much of the world uses it.

Gradually the sounds of non-alcoholic revelry faded and the lights went out, save for our neighbours with four tents and a string of lamps between them which persisted in staying alight to the throb of generators. Salaciously, I had suggested that, since there were four tents there might be one for each wife, and much to our delight, when all their tents had darkened, we noticed that one soon relit only to fade a little later; and then another in the same way, and then a third one brightened for space and then darkened. We were just a little disappointed that the fourth tent did not light up again, but later were to find the occupants were indeed quite a family.

Lying with the sand beneath us and the open sky above, it grew appreciably colder and there was much turning and shuffling as we strove for sleep, until in the small hours, I heard a noisy crackling right beside me, like a hundred Christmas parcels being unwrapped. I was too bemused with semi-sleep to trouble to enquire, but in the morning found my neighbour, Nick, cocooned in plastic. He said that when half-frozen in the middle of the night he had crawled into the container used to hold his rug, then the warmth surged through him and he slept.

★ ★ ★

Noël, a lady of much charm and determination, and a strong swimmer, is no lie-a-bed, and before we layabouts had stirred, had already braved a solo swim to the enjoyment of some early rising Arab chatterers, the juniors of the family, who had stared with much excitement at this daring novelty in the cool November waters. We were all inspired to follow later, though in and out was quite enough for me, both from the cold and a minor injury. And I must confess a slight reluctance to encounter the stinging jellyfish which inhabit these waters and whose touch causes a very painful swelling; and the sea snakes as well, whose bite injects a neurotoxin with a severe or even fatal result. We saw none in the bay, either in this water or lying washed up on the beach, though friends on an excursion a little further down the coast encountered many on the beach and others in the water. Nothing could induce me to swim some fifty yards out like Noël who would, in any case shoo away any reptiles that dared approach, and I felt a little better when following her.

The beach shelves very deeply at some six yards from the water's edge and needs watching, especially for children, but most Arabs have not learned the delights of swimming and just frolic in the sea. A speedboat trailing a wobbly water skier swished by. The next morning a lorry rumbled down the beach, complete with tents and sailing boats and a volley-ball net, their camp being soon erected after much raking and levelling of sand. We thought at least a sheikh, perhaps a prince, was on his way, but it turned out to be a man of business with his family. Two sailing boats were launched, both flat and fast, with a species of lug sail, and soon were spurting in the breezy bay.

That night we had watched the lights of Dhahran twinkling on a hill along the coast just north of us, and to the south, far off along the beach another lot of lights of what appeared to be a very significant hotel. In the morning I enquired, in feeble Arabic, from an old Saudi who said, "Yes, utel, utel." So we decided to visit it before going to Dhahran, approaching by a wide landward circuit. At first we took it to be a splendid retreat for princes or rich Saudis, but as it neared we realised it was no Dorchester-on-Sea; we had never seen the like before. It was a series of Portacabins, half a dozen high, one atop the other, on two very large pontoons which we later learned had been brought in tow in two stages from Japan. The purpose of this "hotel-boat" was to move it to any point along the coast where there was need for manpower, but so far it had stayed put at this particular spot, surrounded by a myriad of fish. Some five hundred persons could be housed on each. We walked on to the landing stage for a better view and were eyed suspiciously by the uniformed guard, but at that moment an official arrived by bicycle and invited us on board, and after explanation to the guard he took us up the gangway saying we must see the Captain. We climbed five floors inspecting this curious construction on the way and waited, watching the innumerable fish while the Captain finished lunch. He turned out to be a Phillipino and a genuine sea-going Captain who had been responsible for the long tow from Japan by way of Singapore, both pontoons at once, using a longer and a shorter cable and just one tug the whole way. The Captain's sea-going duties were completed meantime, but he was obliged to stay on as he might be ordered to put to sea again and moor somewhere along the coast. He looked the sort of man who would prefer to lift his anchor and be off to sea, so the money must have made the shore feel good.

He said that all the workers were building a concrete works some twenty miles away, travelling there each day by bus. We left cogitating over this phenomenon to combat the housing shortage, and moved on to Dhahran.

II

Dhahran is built upon a hill, and consists mainly of the expensive housing and business complex called Aramco, a name formed from the letters of its full name—The *A*rabian and *A*merican Oil *Co*mpany where live and work 2,000 or so Americans who organise and run a large part of the oil industry of the area, all of which has developed near the site adjacent to the hill where, in the early thirties, the Americans explored successfully for oil, the first successful drilling for oil in the Arabian Peninsula, the original well being now a show-piece. The other striking large component of Dhahran is the College of Petroleum and Minerals, established in 1963, a handsome neo-Arabesque building in style most suited to both place and climate, poised on the seaward crest of the hill, where are trained young Saudis in the expertise of engineering, covering all aspects, but related especially to what the name implies.

As this region of Saudia Arabia supplies much of the world with oil and so impinges on all our lives, it has a fascinating interest that can be understood only by an outline of the background. Aramco is a private company not in any way an undertaking of the US Government, as is sometimes thought, the Saudis welcoming the Americans' enterprise, energy and expertise. Few know that at one time British interests held the lease of this great oil-bearing territory, and let it go. As described earlier, Britain had been in the Middle East in Iran and Iraq for many years discovering, developing, and thriving on an oil industry, and had her hands full with those territories. After World War One the oil seepages on the island of Bahrain a few miles off this coast from where its top is visible, had been geologically looked at by Britain, but no drilling was done. The pioneer of exploitation of oil in Bahrain and Saudi was that man whom Wallace Stegner has called, "a ruddy, genial, hearty, energetic, undiscourageable New Zealand adventurer named Major Frank Holmes". He had studied petroleum maps of the Gulf and the surrounding countries as part of his wartime activities in the

Admiralty and had formed, we now know, a correct conception of the possibilities of oil existing along the Arabian coast opposite Bahrain. His convictions were so strong that, after great persistence with the King, he obtained, as far back as 1922, a concession to drill for oil in this very territory, 60,000 square miles of the Hasa, since found to contain the world's biggest oilfield. As an entrepreneur and businessman and not an oil developer he offered it in turn to the British, European, and American companies none of whom at that time were interested having no assurance that oil was there and being busy with other sites. Holmes did manage to sell his option on his Bahrain concession in 1927 to an American company to their mutual benefit, but after trying for three years to dispose of his Saudi one no one would take it up and it fell through—and oh, what a fall was there!

Yet looked at in retrospect it is easy to appreciate why. Britain had established oil interests which were sufficient at the time, and further exploration meant hazardous expense. No one knew what was under Saudi; it could have been nothing. But Holmes was right; for Britain the times were wrong, and the same thing can be said for Holmes' enterprise. The main concern of British interests at that time was more in the way of keeping out competitors than in further drilling, a consideration all companies must take into account, but it was thought to be not worth taking up, for King Abdul Aziz expected drilling to follow a concession fairly soon and that meant much expense.

The fruitful operations in Bahrain, a British protectorate then and for many years, where an American company (Socal) had their concession, gave American oil men, wishing to expand their restricted activities in the Gulf, the notion that there was, as Holmes had concluded, a strong probability of oil being in the nearby coastal territory, and they made some tentative investigations of the whole coastline being particularly impressed by the dome-shaped structure near the coast which is the hill of Dhahran. It has certain features which to their geologists implied the likelihood of oil about it. The businessmen of this consortium approached first Holmes who used delaying tactics in the hope that his own British interests would change their minds, and making little progress in that direction, they contacted St John Philby, the great Arabian explorer and friend of Abdul Aziz. Philby, at one time a British civil servant, had fallen out with British policies and, disgruntled, had started up in business selling cars in Jeddah and had manifested his attachment to the Arab way of life by becoming a Mohammedan. His

infamous son, the traitorous Kim, once paid his father a short visit in
Jeddah and said, "I do not like arrogance or ignorance," and added
uncharitably and, I believe, mistakenly that as the Arabs had both he
did not care for them and departed, never to return again, but to go on
to become a communist and sell his country out. Though the pattern
has resemblance, the son far outstripped the father in his dereliction of
their native land. The tetchy father never minded a dig at Britain and
was always keen to help his patron, the King, who with falling revenues
due to fewer pilgrims at Haj, the main source of his income, and
Holmes producing no activity, was keenly interested.

Arabians are practised bargainers, the King and his advisers being
exeptionally sharp, and there were long delays before he gave the
Americans the rights for an initial 35,000 golden sovereigns down,
counted by the King's financial minister himself across a table in a bank
in Jeddah, and with more to follow, which was later a further source of
British remorse, for just at that time the USA had put an embargo on
the export of gold from her shores, and the sovereigns were supplied by
Britain. But no one knew if oil was there, and the King was happy at the
time with his rewards which could have been shortlived. The
Americans were obliged by the conditions to get to work and start their
drilling, and after further geological exploration, including aerial
mapping of the whole area of concession, they chose to try beside the
hill at Dhahran and established a community there. Six bores went
down without success and even number seven at 1,500 feet showed no
more than traces; there was some despondency as hopes were running
thin. Just then two oil men went to Riyadh at the request of the King to
bore for water there, with good eventual results, and took an excursion
to a waterhole, Ain Heet, about thirty kilometres from Riyadh, famous
in Arabian history as the site where Abdul Aziz had watered his camels
before the raid which ended with his capture of Riyadh. (See photo
p.228.) Here the base of some cliffs had fallen in long ago and at some
150 feet below the surface the water pooled and in this cavern the
geologists found a layer of impervious rock in porous limestone which
they assessed might well reach across to the coast and trap such oil as
might be there. So encouraged they returned to Dhahran and pressed
on with their drilling and beyond 4,500 feet the oil came welling up to
start the flow which has never ceased. Further bores were made with
like success and so the settlement expanded. Aramco was formed now
housing most Americans, while the nearby coastal villages of Al Khobar

and Dammam have expanded into modern towns where upwards of 12,000 Arab employees of the company have their homes.

* * *

This day we passed on through Dhahran and skirted the airport lying on the plain hollow below the hill and towards the sea, driving into the coastal town of Al Khobar with its well laid out streets and a local touch to its buildings, a quite extensive *souk*, and a very fine hotel, with an excellent swimming pool, built on what was originally the water's edge, but now the sea has moved away due to reclamation of the swampy ground over which it had washed.

In the foyer we followed the direction on a notice pointing to "snack bar with coffee", but on sitting down realised that something more substantial was on offer—a five-course meal was tempting us; so "in for a penny in for a pound", and in we plunged into the enormous buffet, emerging from the hotel some two hours later, feeling that explorations were finished for the day; so we pottered for a while in Al Khobar and then returned to base.

On our beach that afternoon we watched the locals at their amusements. Several were perched upon an ageing pier along which ran a pipe evidently at one time used for the discharge of oil into a small vessel lying off when the exportation had started from these parts. Now it made a convenient frolicking and fishing spot for holidaymakers. On a hill of soft sand right beside the beach some fifty feet or so in height, we watched a local game with cars I had not seen before. The young Saudis would rush at this sandhill at top speed on the harder sand beside the sea in hopes that their velocity would carry them through the dragging sand and over the hill to the other side. With four-wheel drive this is no problem but it was quite an excitement for them to see whether with their rear-wheel driven sports cars they could clear the top and at the same time avoid another in the game coming from the other side, for steering in the soft sand is not easy. They kept at it until the dark descended. David and I gave a hand when one of them was well and truly stuck, and David even fetched his tow-rope to help out another who immediately set about his sport again on being freed, so we made off.

Mike and Nick made a valuable contribution at that time, by collecting all the scanty wood they could lay hands on and made a worthy blaze that evening, around which we sat about and chatted for an hour or two while moon and stars came out. Then, after one of Noël's splendid meals and much kicking at the dying embers we turned in, a lot wiser as to how to combat cold that night with adjustments to the windbreak and other details, and spent a very cosy night uninterrupted by sounds of Christmas wrappings.

★ ★ ★

The next day, Friday, was the climax of the Haj festival when families come together and sheep are sacrificed, and I watched the Saudi encampment close to us get ready for the feast. They had three sheep tied up, and from a distance I saw the dispatch of one of then by throat-cutting, the men of the party gathering round. According to their belief the blood must be drained off before the flesh is fit to cook and eat. We had wondered about paying our respects to our neighbours in the four tents, and, some time later, Nick and I walked over to them; just at that moment, along came some of the Phillipinos from the pontoon hotel who started taking photos of one another with the background of the tents. The young Arabs were upset by this and ordered them away, and rightly so for they were rather tactless, especially in the presence of women, who retreated to their tents. Perhaps no one had told them about the precautions with photos in Saudi.

After this episode we approached one of the young men gingerly, who having no English called his father, the old man of the tribe, who greeted us in a very kindly manner and called his daughter from her tent. She was not veiled, spoke English, and was pleasant with us, and, as so often turns out, had spent some time in England. I was about to say, in halting Arabic, "This is the day of your feast," but before I could they, started telling us of it, the old man saying, "Yes, we have killed a sheep," making appropriate throat-cutting gestures with his finger and a big smile, and his daughter also told us of it complete with gestures and wider smiles, quite unselfconsciously. They very kindly invited us to join them in the feast but we had other plans and excused ourselves, though appreciative of their generosity on this holy day of theirs. We arranged the camp and went that morning to Dhahran to visit Aramco.

A high wire fence surrounds the Aramco territory which is covered mainly by bungalows with numerous low trees and shrubs in the garden looking like a Florida estate as Nick, who had lived there, said, while near the main entrance lie the offices and public buildings with their hospital of some 200 beds just on the left of the gate itself. We had a preliminary drive around the attractive housing estate, and as all of us were doctors turned our attention to the hospital. The duty doctor showed us round and it is, as one would expect in such an American project, a very efficient organisation. We then went on to see Aramco's museum where are splendidly set out in picture, model, and description, the processes of the oil industry. And we were treated to an excellent film depicting drilling techniques and also the activities in the Rub' al Khali, the Empty Quarter, the southern, sandy, enormous desert of Saudi, where oil has been discovered and the search continues. The fixed exhibit is of the highest standard and one comes away much informed.

★ ★ ★

We had decided on a lighter lunch that day, following the soporific unintended feasting of the day before, and being in the driver's seat I resolutely steered towards the airport to see the building and to give my friends a chance both to eat and stay awake, but the restaurant had no attractions for me, being still afflicted by some local "bugs", and while they settled into some Middle-Eastern-looking uncertainty, I strolled outside to take the sun and look at the attractive building, wandering along its front, only some twenty yards or so wide on either side of the central entrance. I had reached the corner when around it shot a jeep and from it jumped a khaki-clad figure to stand beside his sentry box and wave in my direction. I did not at first appreciate that his interest was in me, and looked around to see to whom he might be signalling, but seeing no one else moved up with a cigarette at the ready. But it was me, not nicotine he sought, and looking pretty fierce he said, "What you stand there for?" I answered, "Just out in the sun while my friends are having lunch." He said. "Where your passport?" and I replied, "I have not got my passport here," and he said again, "Your passport!" and was obviously not trying to make a new friend. Thinking hard and fast and not wanting to lose my identity card which would most likely disappear into the maw of some branch of his administration, I remembered my library card with my photo in it, and not minding such a sacrifice produced it smartly. He glared hard at me then shouted loudly, "Passport!" I told him once again, and quietly, I had not got it with me, it was in Riyadh; he glared even harder at me and the card then stuffed it in his pocket with a lot of others, no doubt similarly acquired to hasten his promotion, and deciding discretion a better prospect than arrest, he boomed, "Bukra!" ("tomorrow"). Just what that could imply I did not know nor wanted to enquire, but tried my best at an ingratiating smile and retreated to my friends, presuming that he suspected me of being about to blow the place up with a small packet of biscuits. It was a smart reminder that anything is liable to happen at any moment for no apparent reason, and especially so in a state that is always in half a warlike mood and with recruits, not long out of the desert, ordered to suspect all strangers and so seeing a bear in every bush. As we intended to return to Riyadh the next day, I decided he could have the souvenir of our visit to Dhahran, but told my Saudi superior who said, "You are right to tell me of it should they ask but I think we will hear no more," and right he was, and what is more I never saw my card again—that could have been my passport.

We drove again to Al Khobar then on to Dammam, and though these towns owe their existence to oil there is little evidence of it for it is all in pipes and tanks. An underwater pipeline from Bahrain comes ashore at Al Khobar and joins the main pipeline running to Dammam and Al Qatif from which a branch passes to the port of Ras Tannurah where is a large refinery. A main pipeline then continues north-west all the way across Saudi Arabia and parts of Jordan, Syria and the Lebanon to the Mediterranean coast of Sidon, just south of Beirut. It is known as "Tapline" from the initial letters of its full name, *T*rans-*A*rabian-*P*ipeline. The Saudis have now constructed a further pipeline from Dammam running across the breadth of the country to the Red Sea port of Yenbo, north of Jeddah, where a big port expansion is in progress, partly to relieve port and land congestion in Jeddah and partly because of political considerations over the territories which Tapline crosses. An assortment of tankers and container ships lay in the berths of both ports, imports having a big place here as well. We wandered to the waterfront at Dammam on to a pier where some were fishing but most just strolling, a street photographer being kept busy with his Instamatic camera, the lads of all the Arab races being keen on having photos taken with their friends. No one seems to worry about the background; as long as you are taking people all is well, but if you start snapping buildings the police or someone else might well come rushing up to stop you or even confiscate the camera. The way to photograph a building is to put a friend in front of it.

The ubiquitous headcloth, head-ring and thobe, the dark eyes and brown skin, the moustache and, frequently, a beard do have a great levelling effect, the attitude of good Muslims to each other; no man is better than another. When one approaches a Saudi, say for directions, one is ready for surprises, as when we were uncertain about the way for our return, and in passing asked a Saudi in national dress. He turned out to be a good English speaker and a member of what one tends to forget about when living in the central desert regions—the Saudi Navy. He had been to Texas for English and technical instruction and knew Britain as well. We were, of course, in a coastal area with naval personnel about, for Saudi, like other states about the Gulf, must patrol its waters. Dammam was much the same as other Arab towns in its houses, offices, *souks* and style of architecture and its trees where possible, and being so young, like Al Khobar, has none of the old decaying, adobe buildings. Though ranking third in cities after Riyadh and Jeddah, it seemed a little quieter with the slamming of the shutters not so insistently on time and the traffic generally less ferocious with less likelihood of being crushed at any moment by the taxis surging up on either side. However, the cars had a similar spattering of bumps, which is a general measure of driving standards. We left Dhahran as darkness fell by the main road, a little inland, to return to Half Moon Bay to search for the camp with headlights across the beach.

That night, being now all accustomed to our beachy beds, we slept soundly, and next morning packed up in good time for the six hour drive to Riyadh by the same route, arriving back without notable incident or mishap—*el hamdulilah*, and half our own variety of Haj was over.

CHAPTER XV

Arabia Viridis

I

For the second week of Haj I had planned to fly to Abha in the Asir to explore the mountainous territory of that region, and had spoken to Charles Dearnley, a chemist in our block of flats, who agreed to join forces, proving to be the happiest of travellers, interested in everything, with a camera that never stopped clicking. Just before Haj we went down town to book our tickets in the Saudi tourist office, which turned out to be a splendid scrum with the excitement of Haj on top of the usual exuberance of Arabs of all races who were trying to book to all parts of Saudi and beyond. We succeeded without much trauma and no time to spare.

A week later, as we drove along the road to the airport for our flight, a driver coming up behind gave me a hearty toot, at which I gave way and left him ample passing room; as he drew alongside he suddenly pulled over and banged the nearside front wing, making quite a dent, and shot away. He meant it, having a rather battered car to show it was not his first time. One could do nothing about it. At the airport I parked the car on the asphalt as there were a number of cars already there, wondering if I had done the right thing.

From the air the landscape had the usual barren appearance, the terrain around Riyadh being broken up by *wadis* and escarpments, and so it went to Bisha, the only stop *en route*, which lies amidst sand and stony desert and some broken terrain with mountains over to the west, the town small and lying in the midst of an oasis. Then on to Abha whose airport at that time was a "long way" from the town. We emerged to have a taxi man at us and asked how much to Abha. He said, "Fifty riyals," so we climbed in and after about thirty kilometres arrived at our recommended hotel, the Asir, when on getting out he said the fare was a hundred riyals. We reminded him that he had told us fifty, and he said, "No. Fifty each," which was a rather different interpretation, but that is the way it is done. We thought discretion the better part of valour at this point and let him have his hundred; after all he might have said anything in Arabic.

We had made an attempt to book rooms when at the Saudi offices in Riyadh and were assured that all would be well and we would get rooms, but no message had got through; it never does, a reason being that it is usually not sent. On the way from the airport we had looked at the hotel in the centre of the town, "the Abha", and decided that it was not for us, and so had to be content with one room only which was all the Asir could offer, but we were reassured, it had a bathroom—as an extra. Some bathroom! It was a little over two square yards; it had a shower, and the water trickled through the spray even if the taps pulled away from the wall; there were lots of holes to stand on where constant dripping had worn away the stone floor; the lavatory bowl had a seat which could be found beneath the hand basin. However, the water was warm and everything functioned. The beds were hard but adequate, though scanty in bedclothes; we were not too badly placed. I slept that night in my clothes and sweater and the one blanket on top and had a good night. It can be cold in mountain country, 7,000 feet up.

We had asked the management for supper but because of Haj no meals were being served, which we thought a rum idea, so went off to some nearby shops to buy tinned food and some *khubz*, the traditional Arabian bread.

We returned to the hotel with our spoils, borrowed a tin opener and had a snack, then went into the sitting-room where the TV was re-gurgitating the religious events of the day, and our good fortune walked in.

★ ★ ★

Maurice and Louise Joubert, French Canadians working in Riyadh, had arrived the day before and had contacted a local schoolmaster who with his brother and cousin had been driving them around. We agreed to join forces, which helped both sides with expenses, made our own explorations possible early next day, and gave us the very best of company. This mountainous region which we were about to explore is known as the Asir, its administrative capital Abha, having a population of about 20,000, and about twenty kilometres away the principal market town, Khamis Mushait, which means "Thursday market", and appropriately still applies. In both towns most of the old adobe buildings have been replaced by modern concrete ones, Abha having a large, modern dam behind it for the purposes of town water and irrigation of the surrounding countryside. There are the usual commercial and administrative buildings, and in the centre of Abha a square fort with round towers built during the Turkish occupation. Through the mountains runs a magnificent highway, some 600 kilometres, all the way from Taif near Mecca, to Abha, which is being extended southwards, and a further one is being built to Jizan on the Red Sea coast.

This region of the Asir, one of the last parts to be taken over by Abdul Aziz to form his kingdom of Saudi Arabia, is very different from the rest owing to the mountains producing so much rain resulting in a natural greenness, making this the most cultivated area of the country, and apart from the cities, the most densely populated. Rain falls on many days in summer and it also gets the monsoon, so there is a lot of water about and one sees, at last, small mountain streams. Their great pride is a small waterfall, a popular site for a picnic.

The southern half of this mountainous territory below Taif and also south of Abha is the Asir. Between the mountains and the coast is a cultivated plain, the Tihama, and on the eastern side, beyond the mountains, lies the biggest sandy desert in the world, the Empty Quarter, the Rub' al Khali. Now with good roads as well as air access from the main cities of Riyadh, Mecca, Jeddah, Taif, and others far away, this region has become a popular holiday resort, many of the rich Saudis building summer houses in the mountains. Abha at some 7,000 feet is distinctly cooler than the plains. The tar-sealed and beautifully constructed road to the top of the mountains ascends to nearly 10,000 feet.

Our driver took us on the main road to Taif as far as Malha, where we first saw some of the delightful villages with their pretty houses in a style characteristic of this region, some made from mud and straw, and others of stone which lies to hand, and with a little trimming is ready for use. They are mainly square with slightly inward sloping sides and may have three or four storeys. If made of mud they have the unusual feature of stone slates in lines all round the sides, each layer separated by about one and a half feet and each juts out about a foot while all slope downwards slightly, with the purpose of spilling the rain away from the mud walls which would be rapidly eroded by the frequent rains. They serve their purpose well and many of these houses have stood much longer than those in the cities where the mud receives no protection. In addition, a lot of trouble has been taken to decorate the edges of windows and parapets with white paint or white quartz which stands out attractively against the brown walls, the clustered houses making a very pretty pattern. The most outstanding features of the landscape are the watchtowers. It is hard to believe, though one is reminded of it by the many watchtowers still standing in villages—sometimes every hilltop in sight will have one, that this pleasant, friendly region was once the scene of perpetual warfare between villages and tribes. Some of the watchtowers are square, with vertical sides, others with sides sloping to a narrow flat top; others again are round and rather conical and are reminiscent of the round towers of Ireland, used in the same way and having no door at ground level, the entrance being some ten to twenty feet up and reached by a ladder which would be pulled up from the inside, making their capture no easy feat with the defenders shooting from arrowslits, and able to hurl stones from the parapet above. One ascended inside four or five floors, by a ladder to a hole in the floor above, and at each stage of defence, the ladder would be pulled up and those below could be subjected to attack through the hole in the floor. No doubt if invaders could get in, fire below would soon bring an end to the defence, but from their large numbers these towers evidently made a very successful form of refuge.

Our driver took us from the main road on a metalled one being widened and constructed for tar-sealing, which went up the mountains, through many villages, and gradually rising to the heights of Jebel Suda where, near the top there is the village of Suda.

At the new concrete bridges we would leave the new road to cross the *wadi* and regain the old road on the other side, for the bridge itself would finish in a wall of limestone as the digging of the next stage of the new road could not be done until the bridge itself had been completed to take across the heavy implements. For centuries the people of this territory have lived isolated lives, but now have contact with Abha and other populated areas; over the generations they have laboured to produce terraces on the mountain sides to create farm land, as one has seen similarly in Mexico and Switzerland. These terraces were cultivated by hand, cattle and donkey power through the generations but latterly the tractor has crept in, although they still make use of animal power.

★ ★ ★

1. *Terraced land for agriculture in the Asir Mountains. Streaks and specks were a common feature of Saudi prints.*

2. *One type of architecture in the Asir—sloping walls, whitened windows and tops, and many storeys.*

3. *Our transport in the mountains with the 'hospital' of the driver's uncle where silver was on offer, but poor stuff and remained unsold.*

About half way on the drive to our last stop our driver pointed to where his parents' home lay. We diverted shortly after to visit his uncle whom, he said, looked after a "hospital" where we would have morning tea and where we could buy some of uncle's silver. The "hospital" looked like any other farmhouse in the region and it turned out that uncle was the village medicine man, an old *hakim*, who through the week gave advice to any of the local villagers and helped the qualified doctor on his weekly visit. We were well received by uncle and the family and shown around inside. There was a room with chair and table where the doctor would sit, and another room with an examination couch covered with a heavy layer of dust, and a bed covered in scraps of cardboard. I doubt if either had been used in recent times but they could be used if the doctor needed a siesta.

We sat outside and enjoyed cups of green tea, while uncle endeavoured to sell us his wares. The silver was all pretty primitive stuff, very high-priced and not particularly attractive and, in spite of the usual spiel that it was becoming rare and so had antique value, and that the price would rise if we waited, none of us was prepared to buy any of it. So he tried to sell us his dagger, a *khanjar*, which he wore at his belt which was also rather primitive and tatty. He was willing to part with it for 1,000 riyals (about £160), but we did not feel we were in for a bargain. I did make an offer of 100 riyals but his nephew, the driver, said, "Oh no, it cost him 200 riyals so he would not do that." Uncle clearly had a good notion of profit but I thought his business sense a little stretched at 400% profit for the quality of the goods, and he was not likely to be leaving his job as the local *hakim* for the local *souk*.

Around us were fruit trees, cultivated land ready for planting, and just beside the house a well, constructed many years back and lined with stones showing plenty of cool water twelve feet below with a bucket on a rope for household use and a paraffin engine to lift the required amounts for agriculture. We made our thanks with much sincerity but we proved a disappointing trading party and went on past more pretty villages to the mountain top. Usually by midday the clouds have settled over the mountain top, and as we were running just a little late the reported magnificent view was obscured by mist, but we did have a fine view from a little lower down.

About the top of this mountain of rather barren limestone grow plants justifying the claim about all the perfumes of Arabia; junipers and lavender were plentiful. The Arabs have long been keen on improving their food and environment by means of pleasant flavours and smells, with good reason very often, and a walk through any of the spice *souks* is a unique olfactory experience. We picnicked on high at an area much used for the purpose, and then as it was getting rather cold, descended gradually on the new tar-sealed road, where we stopped at frequent intervals as we had done all the way for the driver to point out beautiful views, which kept Charles very busy with his camera. Around us, with the terracing increasing, the men and even more the women were out and lots of children, too, the women in their bright dresses and their hats with very wide brims, often known as cartwheels, a characteristic of the region. The women traditionally do much of the farming, though now the men have a better excuse than before, for they now often go to work in the towns.

We could see Abha lying prettily in a saucer in the hills, and away beyond it, Khamis Mushait. As we gradually descended our driver at one stage dashed away to pull some twigs from a bush from which he cut off lengths of about four inches, these being the sticks known as *mishwak* which one sees the Saudis so commonly chewing in the street as a sort of toothbrush and smokeless pipe combined. The Saudis have beautiful teeth, in general, and they give much credit for this to the chewing of these sticks, but medically we might feel more strongly that heredity and the nature of the soil have rather more to do with it. The sticks are said to have in them a scanty amount of astringent which may, of course, do a little good, but the main benefit is probably due to the stringy brush-like end which forms on chewing. I tried it but found it not particularly attractive and lit a cigarette. With many of them in the past having no cigarettes, chewing gum, or sweets or the like, the chewing of the stick has been and remains a popular pastime and it probably now persists more from a habit in no way frowned on as Mohammed is known to have been keen on it. I would settle for a toothbrush, cigarette, or pipe, or some chewing gum, but there is no accounting for taste.

We made our way back to Abha, past the large dam near the town, to our hotel. Later that afternoon we visited the *souk* once more under the auspice of Yahya and his brother and cousin. We were to be given the opportunity of purchasing "even better" silver but, fortunately, his father had packed up shop and gone off and we were not put to the embarrassment of refusing him as well.

* * *

That evening we were told that the religious side of Haj had ended and dinner would be served in the hotel dining-room, which we looked forward to. Joining our party of four that evening were two telephone engineers who were surveying the whole of Saudi in connection with an extensive automatic telephone contract which they told us meant that whoever got it would have to dig up nearly every street in Saudi in order to lay the cables. I would have thought that there was not a street in Saudi which had not been dug up several times already. Now it would all have to start again.

We entered the dining-room, which was a little surprising; it had been devised in some way from a former courtyard and a wooden floor put in, but in the process of time, or perhaps they had not even noticed, the floor sloped distinctly upwards from the door and on moving to our table we felt to be trudging uphill, so much so that at dinner there was some difficulty in keeping the soup from running over one side of the plate. It felt a little eerie, rather like a ship at sea listing from the cargo shifting. The meal was well prepared and more enjoyable than sitting in one's room and opening tins, but somehow, on such an occasion after such a day in the mountains, a glass of beer or wine would not have gone amiss. But to be fair to the Saudis they have since completed a splendid new hotel in Abha of 200 bedrooms to cater for such as us and holidaying Saudis and, let us hope, just ordinary tourists to Saudi sometime in the future. Many have wondered why the Saudis do not permit ordinary tourists at the present time. This can be well answered in the reply given by a Saudi Minister when he was asked the same thing, "Why not tourists now in Saudi?" His answer was simply, "Have you seen our hotels?" Again, to be fair to the Saudis, they are doing their very best to hurry on the construction of better and larger hotels, but at the present time almost all the hotel accommodation available is taken up by those who visit Saudi in connection with business.

The next day the four of us decided to move to Khamis Mushait and our drivers took us on our way to a very pretty spot, Mahala, where a little stream arising in the mountains ran along a *wadi* to form pools with the sides covered in rushes and other green stuffs, the whole looking more of a European scene than an Arabian one. Another expatriate was there with his dog which retrieved sticks and cans we threw in. Dogs, though seen running stray about the streets in Riyadh and other towns are not looked on with much affection in Saudi, having always been considered somewhat unclean. Their suspicions have been justified, for both dog and sheep are now known to be vectors in the spread of hydatid disease which is endemic in this country as it is in so many other sheep rearing countries. Hydatid cysts are a common surgical complaint to be dealt with in Saudi. The association of dogs and rabies is well known.

During much of the driving in the mountains I had been allocated a seat in the cabin beside the driver, while outside the young Saudis, Charles, and the Jouberts, sported it in the open air on rather rough seating, but that is where they wanted to be, and with bursts of singing, shouting and laughter at times I knew all to be well with them. Inside the cabin, Yahya and I did our best to communicate, using English and a little Arabic, and I learned quite a lot from him; in the latter part of the drive his interest in Arabian affairs waned somewhat and, being a man of twenty-nine and unmarried, he told me that his father had offered him 40,000 riyals to get married but he had turned it down. His father had had seven wives and twenty-two children, and at this stage it was clear Yahya was not rushing to follow his example. The reproductive effort of the family was well in hand and his turn could wait awhile, but evidently not too long for he suddenly turned to me and said, "What is 'I love you' in French?" I told him, "Je t'aime", and also for good measure I said, "If you would care for it, you can have the German too." He smiled broadly, his best smile so far, and I explained to him the subtleties of, "Ich liebe dich". For the next quarter of an hour he practised hard over and over again, "Je t'aime", and "Ich liebe dich", not doing very well for a start, but he got it in the end and when I told him he was word-perfect he gave me heartfelt thanks and I could see that the evening was full of prospects for him, as he exercised the normal reaction of a young male. I had clearly made his day and perhaps somebody else's evening.

II

We went from Mahala on to Khamis to our recommended hotel al Zahrat which looked much the same sort of Arab hotel, and again we were lucky with rooms. They took our passports here, though why here and not at the last hotel I cannot think. All Charles could rake up, with some difficulty, was his library pass but that seemed to be sufficient. Libraries, I had similarly found in a time of difficulty, have their uses.

At this point with our driving family standing about waiting for further largesse we decided to content ourselves with what the metropolis of Khamis held, and so paid and waved them off, preceded by great handshaking, exchange of addresses and the like and went to our upstairs rooms.

We had been in the hotel only some ten minutes when the pleasant receptionist with no English came to our rooms and, at his third try, penetrated into my feeble Arabic enough to indicate that there was a man downstairs concerned about our taking his photograph. Louise said she had only taken a photograph of the mountains from her window, but the man was complaining so we went down to see him. He was a highly indignant Saudi whom we finally gathered that he was alleging that a photograph had been taken of his wife, children, and himself, on the building opposite. Louise said she had done no such thing, taking one photo of the beautiful mountain view, but then concluded she supposed it was possible they may have been in the photo as the building was to one side of the view. Rather a row blew up but Louise charmingly managed to persuade him that there had been no intention to photograph any people and she had not meant to break the rules. He kept on about it, "No pictures in Saudi," in Arabic, and I kept thinking, "What is the reason for all those innumerable camera shops in the *souks* throughout Saudi Arabia if you are not supposed to take public buildings or Saudis, it leaves not much besides friends, trees, camels and donkeys." Even on the sea coast one of my friends was pulled up for taking photos—out to sea, but since this was near an oil area perhaps a spouting of oil out of the sea may have got into the picture. This present hassle ended in smiles, handshakes, and cameras still with us.

We strolled about the town which was much like other Saudi towns, with an excellent *souk*, everything there in plenty including jewellery shops selling gold by the kilo bar, or if you cannot run to that, the talas (100gm). At the back, was the sheep and goats *souk*. The animals were fed green stuffs contained inside old tyres. The local farmers brought them to good condition for sale to the citizens, many of whom in Saudi like to compromise between desert herding and town existence with hens, goats, sheep or even cows in their backyards. I had to endure two hens and the most vociferous and persistent rooster I have ever met, and three goats beside my flat. The ladies teaching in the Medical School had two cows immediately at the back of their villa. David Wallace told

me that one evening he was invited to a rather fine house in our street
and his host asked if he would like to see his cows. David expected a
visit to a large backyard or nearby section, but a door was pulled open in
the handsome living room and there they were, two of them in a room
which he said, had apparently no way out. He thought they went in as
calves across the living room and came out as full grown animals in the
reverse direction Another lot of stalls in the market sold the large
cartwheel hats and baskets made of rafia, which Louise fell for as
excellent presents for her daughters.

Our hotel did not provide meals so we lunched that day in our rooms
having had, like the Jouberts, Haj problems with meals, and used up
the remains of some of our purchases in Abha, and for the purpose out
came our pocket knives, one spoon and a very blunt knife which I had
brought along and which I was relieved of by the airport friskers as a
dangerous weapon. It would hardly cut fresh bread. A very jolly meal it
was, which would have been even jollier with a glass of beer to wash it
down instead of the incessant juice or "cola". We lunched similarly on
tinned left-overs the next day, but that evening went into the town and
sought out the dive which appeared to contain the most benign looking
lot of cut-throats. Everything was there but it was all rather different
from the Ritz. Chairs and tables were rather rickety, stained, worn but
clean. The soup came straight up from a very large cauldron with a fire
below, such as our mothers long ago used for boiling up the washing,
and though tepid had an excellent flavour; then chicken, again all
excellent and the wild-looking men considerate and appreciative of our
thanks. Pudding was off—never on, in fact—so we bought a tin of
peaches from a shop and made do with that later. We were far from the
starvation line.

Whilst in Abha we had gone to give to the airways office the usual
forty-eight hours' notice of our return flight, and on reaching the clerk
through the scrum Charles and I showed our return tickets to Riyadh
and told him that some telephoning had been done and we had been
assured that a place would be kept for us. The clerk had no record of
any of this. Maurice Joubert was able to produce his document showing
that their booking had been made, for when, and which flight. The
clerk produced a list, said the planes were full, then produced a waiting
list for the flight of twelve to show what the situation was. The Jouberts
particularly had right on their side, we were lucky to be with them. We
all looked long at one another and then at the clerk and after a half

minute's silence he subsided, saying that as we could produce evidence
that we were booked he would let us on the plane, all four of us. Thanks
to the Jouberts, in due course next afternoon, we all boarded the plane,
only to find that there were six empty places when we took off. Anyway,
we had taken off ten minutes before the time scheduled; it looks as if
wives can get their way even with air pilots.

★ ★ ★

The mountains receded, the great plain lay beneath us and the lights
of Riyadh sparkled in a little over an hour. The Jouberts accepted a run
to their hotel in my car. On the asphalt area where I had left my car not
only was there no sign of it but there were no other cars in view either.
The asphalt was not the right place to leave a car after all. It was pretty
evident thay had all been cleared away. We had a long, fruitless search
but qualms were few, theft being unlikely, with removal by the police
more than probable, and we settled for taxis.

Because of language difficulties I did not know how to start the
enquiry for my car, but an Arabic-speaking friend telephoned around
and told me to go to the traffic office in the northern part of the city. In
the yard there I could see no sign of my car amongst the many, and in
the little office the language barrier was only overcome eventually when
an English-speaking Ethiopian, in the same plight as myself, explained
that the cars had been removed and we would have to go with one of the
assistants in the police office to the car pound. As it turned out,
authority was taking no chances about a surreptitious removal of our
cars should we find them. I thought we were just going round the
corner, but after a time, when we had left the city behind I thought we
might be leaving Arabia, as we kept on and on and finally passed into
the desert into the region of Dir'iyah, some ten kilometres out, where
we drove into an extensive dump of twisted hulks once sources of pride
in many countries (though none from Britain). I thought the worst until
my friend in distress said quietly, "That's mine. It looks OK." I felt
better but not yet good. We got out and searched for the silvery estate-
wagon, two weeks old and already thrice scarred in the battle of the
Riyadh roads, when a "Yaho" resounded and from round behind a
deceased auto came Authority. He looked pretty threatening until the
assistant with me explained the problem and we all then searched, but
in vain. I suggested it might be worth a try amidst the debris on the

other side of the road, *"La, la,"* he said, ("No, no") so we stayed put, but Authority quietly moved over and after a time came back and tried me out with various makes from the Far East. It was my turn for a round of *"La, la,"* till I gave the right answer, upon which he cried *"Fi"* ("It's there"), and so it was, living, but with its side well jammed against the hefty bumper of a large American wreck. I expressed great pleasure at the reunion—too much—for pleasure is costly. My Ethiopian helper had told me the standard fee to reclaim the car is fifty riyals. Authority looked at me and said, *"Miya"* ("a hundred"); I ventured "fifty" in a joking way in my best Arabic, but he produced an even louder *"miya"*, and we walked to a tent where I expected to find a Saudi behind a desk with a receipt book. Not a bit of it. There was a man, but in bed, under a blanket with a wad of notes in one hand, who lifted up a fifty-riyal note indicating the charge. Authority gave another shout of *"miya"*. I was not prepared to dispute, with the odds all in his favour, so I paid up, but never even saw a receipt.

The deal settled, we shook hands, all smiles, and he took my key, electing to add a further scar himself on the side against the bumper to add to the big new one on the rear door, and a stoved-in bumper as well inflicted by whoever towed the car from the airport. When freed, we again shook hands and off I drove, a free-wheeling man again, the camera in the unlocked glove-box still there to enhance the notion of essential honesty.

Saudis seldom steal, a reflection of their training and the severity of the penalty, but some have been found to do so if the chance of discovery is slight, and some have ways of adding to their basic salaries, in which they are not alone. The appearance of the Saudi police is very deceptive; they are dressed in khaki and wear soft hats, and sometimes carry a gun, occasionally a baton, but they are nearly all slight, slouchy and rather silent until the *moment critique* when there is no mistaking their powers and their intention of using them. They are in complete contrast to the large, shoulders-back British bobby who, has the air of authority and, who, when trouble starts, tries to quieten it. The sparks fly upwards in Saudi with much effect, and even-temper is not the rule; they mean to have their way and they show it.

CHAPTER XVI

Holy and Less Holy Cities

I

A University holiday in the cooler month of February gave a chance for travel, those with no clinical duties being able to go out of the country to where they wished, while those of us with a few remaining patients to look after could only manage a few days at a time from duty. David and Noël Wallace, Nick Greville with, this time, Shirley, his wife who had come out for a few months, and I, decided on a five-day car trip to Taif and Jeddah, intending to camp without a tent and using the same two estate cars, David's and mine. David and Noël slept in the back of their station wagon as before but we three others used safari beds in the open.

Mecca is a full day's drive from Riyadh and a 6.45 a.m. start, having aimed for 6.00 a.m., was good by Arabian standards. The Mecca road, made anew some ten years ago has a very good surface but the heavy traffic demands concentration from the driver. All the way we endeavoured to refill the petrol tanks when they were only half empty to insure against uncertainties ahead, failing to do this only once, with consequences. The necessities for the car need constant watching for in Saudi: the specialisation of tradesmen in towns is sharply defined and rather a nuisance, only petrol being dispensed at petrol stations, though in country districts oil may be sold as well, while petrol pumps are often part of a repair garage. Air for tyres is to be found at tyre shops, where inner tubes, tyres and sometimes engine oil may be had. Batteries are mostly to be purchased at electrical shops as is water for batteries.

The road runs for a start northwest parallel to the Jebel Tuwayq escarpment for about 250 kilometres to Shaqra where it turns at a right angle to the southwest, and then goes more or less in a straight line to Mecca about a further 750 kilometres ahead, so about 1,000 kilometres in all. There are many straight stretches, mile upon mile to the horizon with occasional curves, well-engineered, and some winding parts especially near habitation. It is a single carriageway mostly, except at some large towns, but with heavy traffic, much of it large lorries carrying goods from the port of Jeddah rumbling along at sixty to eighty kilometres or more, also a lot of large private cars mixed with the smaller variety, and the inevitable Jap pick-up. With no cats' eyes to help in night-driving the consequences are in evidence, the sides of the roads being strewn with the remains of collisions of all sorts, many of them head-on, with the two cars involved now left near to each other, on one or both sides of the road, to tell a usually unheeded tale. The wrecks and cast-off tyres are not as frequent as on the road to the east to Dhahran, but we noticed places especially on the outskirts of towns where there were collections of wrecks which could account for the fewer strewn along the road. Leaving wrecks beside the road may be a deliberate policy, to warn other drivers, but a likelier reason is that the cost to insurance or individuals is more than it is worth to shift the remains, and so they lie written off and left for the scavengers .

The road from Shaqra runs close to two long lengths of sand dune and soon crosses a long tongue of dune. Four fingers of sand run south towards Riyadh from the great northern sandy desert, the Nafud, to end almost on a level with the city. Journeys to the West and North may mean crossing one or more of these fingers of sand. After Shaqra comes Ad Dawadini, and halfway is Afif. New buildings are very much in evidence in all these towns, as in every village, with modern style villas, one, two or several larger modern public buildings and often with street lighting, double carriage ways, all indicative of a large expenditure to upgrade them, but there is always the mark of Arabia in the ill-kept pavements and road edges, and general lack of maintenance and the collections of rubbish and scattered tins in all directions.

Any town or village invariably means the presence of an ancient well, for in these desert lands with no surface water, life depended on the wells. The sites of water became known in ancient times when in the rainy season water seeped to the surface at certain points and wells would be dug there. Water is also found in the *wadis* where rain-water forms short-lived rivers after heavy rains, which on the stony surface gradually formed channels and so a *wadi*, a small or larger valley, comes into being. In former times little, if any, building was in the main channel of the *wadi*, but in modern times, throughout the country, dams across main *wadis* and their branches have been built to prevent flash-floods causing disasters, and to conserve the water as a small lake, from which it is released gradually to soak away as prolonged irrigation,

PLATE 19   193

1. *A typical wadhi or dry river bed, dammed across in parts to prevent flash-floods. They are much used as roads about the country.*

2. *The wadhi has been heaped up and this 'garden' and farm is immediately on the left in the above picture. Sheep and goats graze between the date and other trees, a bore hole has been sunk to the left.*

3. *This British made 'Blackstone' engine running on diesel has for years been the chief source of power to lift water from a bore hole and its chug-chug-chug is heard all over Saudi.*

PLATE 20

1. *For most of the year the Wadi Hanifa which this dam crosses 20km above Riyadh is dry. After heavy winter rains it was full to a height of 18ft and ran upstream for 3kms.*

2. *The dam one month later is dry, the water not having run away but soaked away in the bed of the wadhi above the dam.*

or in many places directed into irrigation channels serving new farmland made by forming banks around fields with the use of modern heavy machinery. Much new farmland, formerly the sides of *wadi* beds subject to flooding after heavy rain, has now been brought into use and on the long circuit to and from Jeddah many such areas, especially in relation to *wadis*, were seen.

The run over the extensive limestone flats to the high mountains nearer the coast can be dull but is relieved from time to time by hill and mountain landscape and by the changing appearance with the angle of the sun, and by much human interest when passing through villages and towns. Late in the journey, the land rises gradually to a high plateau and a slightly steeper ascent begins as Taif is approached, with increasing habitation of all sorts. An unpleasant wind on the plateau as well as the absence of shelter with only stunted growth there, pushed us on towards the mountains, and nearing Taif, with threatening clouds over the mountains and dusk upon us, we had a quick council of campers, which resulted in a decision, always an option, to spend the night in a hotel, heroics not being a purpose of the trip. Dusk turned to dark as we wound our uncertain way into Taif, and with a little search David and Nick found the Okaz Hotel, just the right Arabian style, a little run down but clean and comfortable with the usual considerate staff, and willing to lodge us all.

The Okaz was in a line of shops and restaurants on one side of the central square with the other side formed by the hospital. Appetites sharpened by a long drive and a walk around the centre of the town had the edge taken off by roast chicken and banana flan in the rather cool open air. An early bed was all we were fit for.

* * *

Taif is about 7,000 feet up in the chain of mountains running near the west coast, and is the seat of the royal summer residence, being decidedly cooler than the coastal and central cities. It is a well-developed town with the usual spate of incomplete or finished modern buildings and an occasional large house of the Jeddah type with several storeys, wooden shutters and much exterior decoration. There are various roads to scenic points of mountain scenery like that in the Asir region, but we could not give time to these on this short trip.

Signposting is almost all in Arabic and so was no aid to our early morning task of finding a way out of this pleasant town to Jeddah. A majority verdict was arrived at from the varying opinions of locals about our route, computed with our own ideas, and we worked our way towards the west. Tourist maps in any detail, if they existed at all, were then hard to come by. At the Ministry of Information in Riyadh, though one is kindly received, once the newspaper-reading officials come to lower the morning news and considerately proffer tea, the well of directions is not deep and even slightly muddy. A splendid book of illustrations, a bundle of fine postcards, some slides and posters, provided free with typical Saudi generosity are very welcome, but more detail as to what is where, and whether there is a hotel in this town and "Have you any maps?" did not result in an equally useful harvest, nor did shops, then at least, produce anything much better. Like everything else in Saudi no doubt it is there, if you can find it, and each quest can be a voyage of discovery, if you have the time. Today maps are more easily found.

We were plotting our way mostly with Bartholomew's large map of the whole of the Middle East, excellent in its own way but not intended as the last word on city roads. We made our way to the west of the town with further help from passers-by; then from a taxi driver who told us that the usual road was closed and pointed out the alternate route, and at a petrol station a helpful motorist with no English said he would lead us on our way to Jeddah taking us out by the road on which we had entered Taif and eventually pointing to a turning signposted to Jeddah. We followed this good road down the mountains with fine views all around, on and on until some fifty kilometres or so when we came to a warning sign repeated at intervals that infidels were not welcome, "No entry to non-Moslems", and a police stop. Not just the Christian faith but the English language also had not taken a strong hold in these parts, yet it was clear from gestures and our combined smattering of Arabic that we had reached an impasse more than religious. That we could not go forward was only too clear, none having the ambition, dark complexion, or skill in Arabic of a Sir Richard Burton.

It appeared that the by-pass road to the west to Jeddah was not for us either as it was closed for repairs. At that moment some English speaking non-Saudi Arabs came up who told us of a desert road to the east through the mountains which swung around Mecca by which it was possible to reach Jeddah, but after a conference held entirely in Arabic we were told it was impossibly rugged for our two-wheel driven cars; we must return up the mountains to Taif where the usual road to Jeddah, the one that the taxi driver in Taif had correctly told us was closed, was the road for us; it was indeed closed but would be open at 6.00 p.m. but then only for two hours as during the day it was being enlarged near Taif to a dual carriageway. We must, they said, go back to Taif by the way we had come! But how?

⋆ ⋆ ⋆

We had expected to find petrol on the Mecca by-pass and we had not refuelled in Taif and now neither of us had enough petrol to make the mountain ascent even with the help of the two gallons in David's emergency can. Was there a village, we asked? The only one we had seen of any size was about five kilometres back with some construction going on. Yes, we might find some there at a camp for the "Chinese" who were building a new road. So, after a general quick meeting of our grand committee at which no one was for sudden conversion, we pinned our hopes on the "Chinese" and turned back some five kilometres, reaching the village Sharaye, an oasis with some old adobe buildings and a mosque, and there, before it all, was a construction camp. Luck was early with us, for, on the drive in, we met a jeep driven by an English-speaking Pakistani material engineer, Said Anwarkan, a road builder who gave us hope and led us past abandoned petrol pumps which, on our own, would have fooled us completely, on to the machine shop where he produced a very kind Taiwanese who, after hearing of our plight, offered advice and petrol, had a quick word with one or two of his colleagues, said he would help us but would not sell us any because of regulations, though he would give us enough to continue. They would accept nothing but our profuse thanks, while a sturdy Taiwanese with much delight and many "Aows" gave us sixteen litres each. The engineer told us that there was a desert road some twenty-five kilometres long in the direction mentioned by the officials at the Mecca-stop, that, contrary to the officials' opinion, we could easily manage it in our cars and it began at the end of a shortish stretch of excellent new tar-sealed dual carriageway which they had just made. The foreman then indicated to his assistant to fill our tanks to the top which was done with more delighted "Aows" and gentle cheers from us. After a briefing on the route we set off with waves and thanks to all our friends.

We made a good fifty metres. All of us were feeling a little jaded, and

David led us on across a tar-sealed road at about one mile an hour to find that he had gone over a foot drop at its far edge, not noticeable in the dust and glare, and had finished with his rear wheels held suspended in mid air resting on the rear overhang and solidly stuck. It was not our day. He might have stayed there all day but for the kindly Pakistani engineer watching us drive off, who smiled sympathetically and with David's hook and nylon ropes, included for such moments, and a piling of rocks under the rear wheels, hauled him clear with a great tug from his four-wheel drive jeep. My little bus did not have enough power.

As an engineer who must have faced many such moments of imperfection with deep understanding he asked us all to tea in his prefab bungalow. He and an equally calm colleague, Mohammed Sulaiman, brought some peace to out-vexed spirits and only time prevented us from accepting his invitation to lunch; so he offered to route us on our way leading us on to the tarmac to the east some five kilometres, telling us then that the desert road would be at its end. We whipped along and at its end found a construction site and took the desert road which initially was wide and well surfaced—at last on our destination to Jumum some thirty kilometres on—we thought.

Shortly afterwards we met a car coming towards us with two more Pakistanis who stopped, and to our enquiries said, "Yes. It is the way to Jumum; it is very rough ahead, but you might make it." Some twelve kilometres on, the road roughened up a lot when bumping along came a Jap pick-up with two Saudis and a youngster aboard, none speaking English. The driver, an older man, waved to us to stop, insisted that we would not get through to Jumum saying his passenger was from there, knew all the routes well and he insisted we wouldn't make it.

We had heard it all before, and now had visions of the long haul to Taif up the mountains, but the very kindly old Saudi said that if we would follow him he would put us on the right road, and that also we had heard before; but there seemed nothing else for it, so we agreed to follow him. He went off on a pretty rough old desert road at a cracking lick for a man of many years, slowing or stopping to let us catch up, waiting for us on the main road and after only about one kilometre stopped and showed us a better, wider road marked by a stone painted yellow and on it a red arrow for direction, which sign he indicated we would meet ahead to guide us on the way. This was the right road, a good road, a little rough but we would do it easily, and with handshakes and a wave he set the infidels on their way around the Holy City on the other side of the mountains, another example of the consideration of the Saudis.

After a short drive we lunched, to gather strength. The old man was right, it was an easy and interesting route through the mountains with only one stop for directions from two men driving camels. The moment was notably instructive for one of the camels seized the chance to flop down and lie over on its back and roll about like a horse giving itself a good rub. We had seen lots of camels before and saw many more on the trip, but this back-rolling was a new phenomenon. Camels have great bare patches on their elbows and knees where the skin seems to be padded suitably for when they lie down on their bellies; with their long legs, I had imagined that like a giraffe they would have difficulty getting off their backs but not a bit of it—she was up like a shot and on the way again. We found the asphalt once more after some directions from a passing car and were on our way to Jeddah, with the radio and television masts on top of the hills as pointers.

★ ★ ★

The approach to Jeddah by this route is not a scenic drive, with factories, rubbish tips and building conglomeration strewn about. On nearing the centre of the city we turned northwards towards the direction of our intended camp on the beach. Our route passed the King Abdul Aziz University Hospital and Medical School where we stopped to greet our friends to whom David had written and to fix a time to join them the following day. The route north out of the city was spattered with detours, due to road expansion, but we came after some thirty kilometres to a sea inlet, the Creek, with roads on its sides described appropriately as Southern Creek and Northern Creek and, after exploring this fine amenity bestrewn with houses and boats including a sailing club, we went further north on a fine tar-sealed road eventually locating a rough once-sealed road going in the general direction of the seashore. Dusk was with us and we drove on and on towards some low buildings and in about a quarter of an hour arrived at the seashore to find a strange, large, incomplete building looking as though a hotel had started and run out of money; nearby was a string of very rough shanties for beaches shelters. Also nearby was a very large modern factory building in construction.

Subsequent enquiries revealed that the large derelict building, evidently a good source of elegant green roof tiles for the casual raider, is another example of a "Saud folly". As described earlier, the great King Abdul Aziz had nominated his eldest son, Saud, as his successor, but King Saud did not turn out the way his people wished and his name then, generally speaking, was not mentioned in Saudi society. The story of his profligacy has also been described earlier. Most of the vast luxurious palaces he built are now unused. When he died work on the uncompleted seaside palace stopped immediately and it has been left to rot. Had it been completed it might now have given seaside joy to many an honest citizen. The building seemed to have a long string of rooms on both floors and we hazarded a guess that many concubines would have had a grand sea view while the owner would have had neither the time nor the right direction to enjoy it. We chose a site about a kilometre away, pitched camp, and a good meal from Noël and Shirley put the cap on a long and eventful day, and so to bed.

At 3.00 a.m. with Jupiter at the zenith, I awoke to harsh voices and commands in Arabic with David and Nick replying in sturdy English, and they seemed to be reaching some finality. My bed being a little separate from the others at the rear of my car, I had been overlooked, and no good purpose would be served by delaying the raiding party for fresh investigations or offering coffee; so I rose only at their departure. It appeared that I had surfaced from a long deep sleep only at the last moment when the police, coastguard, or whatever, had been silenced, partly satisfied and perhaps defeated by the production by David of a letter in Arabic from higher authority mentioning princely permission for us to visit Jeddah and its Medical School and to enjoy the surrounding district. Though it is unlikely the authority had visualised us camping on the beach near Saud's Folly, the power invisible had served its purpose, and with a short *"bukhra"* the power just visible before us faded into the night. Another power invisible had worked on me in the night for I awoke with the worst sandfly bitten face ever.

II

Next morning we made our way back to the Hospital and Medical School to be received by Professor Horton of Surgery, recently of Bristol, and Professor Haddock of Medicine who had spent much of his later life in the tropics.

Jeddah started their University with Islamic Studies, the Basic Sciences, Engineering, then a Medical School. Instruction in all subjects is given in a one-storeyed prefabricated building for the most part. The one-storeyed hospital of 200 beds, with only some forty in active service then, is very spruce inside and serves well. One year before that there was bare earth on the site. There are adequate rooms in the Medical School and a good two-storeyed library and even the beginning of a small pathology museum, all specimens being from operations as there are no post-mortems in Saudi to provide others. The patients are comfortably housed, the labs and X-rays are established though small, the three operating rooms are serviceable.

All this is temporary. Jeddah has plans, shown to us, to build soon a very large modern complex of Hospital and Medical School on a part of the old airport which is within the city. We compared our problems and found them very much the same, agreeing that the Saudis have done splendidly in a short time though they had some way yet to go in changing from a desert people to be part of the world of modern technology. We all have great hopes for the present graduates and medical students. Jeddah's medicals were just starting their clinical instruction while in Riyadh three groups had then passed their finals.

A former student and house surgeon of David Wallace's in Riyadh, Rashid Nabibulla, attached to the surgical side at Jeddah guided us around the centre of the city. It was the evening rush hour, the streets were jammed with cars and at one roundabout, just as I cleared it, a driver crossing behind me faintly touched the rear end of my car. It was only just audible. I thought nothing of it for he was careless enough to touch me behind and it was his doing and I was not going to stop to investigate trivialities. We had just cleared the roundabout when he came at me and forced me over to the side in his little goods vehicle, jumped out and said something in Arabic, then shouted *felus* (money), with appropriate rubbing of his fingers and thumbs. Nick Greville, my passenger, and I could find no mark on my car so he must have shaved my rear bumper. His car had a faint mark on the front off side about 2in. long and about $\frac{1}{8}$in. wide. He was responsible, because of trying to cut in too sharply behind us. Nick and I gave him a piece of our minds in English of which he got the drift, and a Saudi and an older Arab standing by looked at the cars and jeered at him and waved him on as the one completely responsible for such a knock but he persisted. We told him to call the *Bolis* and he told us to do so; it went on thus to an

impasse. Our other car had gone on ahead in the maze of traffic but now
Rashid came back to see what was wrong and saw the situation. Rashid
is a gentle quiet young man, but I soon realised that there was a good
deal more in his depths and was glad to have him on our side. He laid in
magnificently, all stops out, but our adversary still would not budge and
started to sulk. He wanted *felus*. I doubted if he was a Saudi and Rashid
said later that he thought he was from over the mountains in the south
from the Hadramaut.

Just then a police car came along nearby. Rashid went over to speak
to the officers, and on return gave a long, high-powered burst of
advanced Arabic to the young man on the make who suddenly folded,
got in his vehicle and drove off. Rashid said the police had agreed to
come as soon as they had settled with another accident. He had told our
man on the make that we would wait. Any accident is a trial on the spot
with the settling done by the participants who, if unable to reach an
agreement, call the police to do it. Traffic even in a rush hour has to
wind its way around the contestants, a crowd grows, horns hoot, and
snarls begin and time goes floating by. This was our introduction to a
try-on of the kind which led many Europeans, with a little less right on
their side than we had, to pay up and get away. This time we felt he had
neither a case nor a licence and wanted nothing to do with the police,
who stand no nonsense.

★ ★ ★

Jeddah is a more cosmopolitan city than Riyadh. For hundreds of
years pilgrims from many countries have been coming through Jeddah
on their way to Mecca, leaving their imprint. Here are all the features of
a Saudi city but in this, the largest, the central buildings are more
numerous, compact and higher in the principal shopping and business
area, with rather a Western look but a mingling of Arabic styling.
However, the potholes, the broken roads and pavements and the
winding alleys and the erratic traffic are all there. Further on we came
near the waterfront, where once masses of shipping lay for days waiting
to unload, but now with containers and good unloading facilities, the
turn-round time is much reduced.

Rashid led us on to his sister's flat for tea. We removed our shoes in
the hallway before entering the living room which was very comfortable
in a mixture of western and Arabic styles and the slightly broader life of

Jeddah was made apparent by two wooden, carved semi-nudes standing in the corner. None of us had seen anything like them in Riyadh. The tea was of the usual dilute Arabic type with or without milk or sugar. The family came in to meet us all; Rashid's brother a former student of engineering but now in the family business of ladies' and babies' wear, with shops in other centres. In a few days he was on his way to London on a buying expedition and that may not have been all. The family gradually came in, Rashid and his brother in Saudi dress, and then his pretty, attractive younger sister, Fakhara, training as a schoolteacher, shyly speaking good English, and then the married sister's little children and their cousins of the same age, also shyly peeping at the strangers round the door, wide-eyed, unsmiling, and dashing away to return for another peep until growing confidence saw them settled on the edges of the settee in pretty dresses staring away at us; finally our hostess, Fiza, joined us with smiles, but no English.

They insisted on us staying to supper *(asha)*. Conversation was no trouble with the bi-linguists in the family, but smiles from the children were scanty until they were taken away to show themselves off in their *abayas*, the black shawl used as a head cover like a mantilla. Like their older counterparts with a new dress, Fatima and Sana came in all smiles and with great confidence, sitting with the superb carriage of Arabian women, folding their *abayas* over their heads and about them in that built-in feminine way, with wide smiles and taking all the applause as their due. We spoke of men's dress and shortly after Rashid brought in a *mishla*, the long gown rather like a university graduate's gown but reaching to the ground, in black, brown or cream and usually with gold edging, this particular one being black and of fine material for summer use. Shortly after, the son and heir, a sturdy, chubby one-year-old, was produced.

A little later we pushed back our chairs and in the centre of the floor was laid a plastic strip of floral design and in came large dishes of boiled chicken, excellent creamed rice and side-servings of gherkins and the like, and a very hot tomato sauce. Cutlery and plates went round and we set to, with extra helpings. Then came fresh fruit, bananas, oranges and apples, and coffee to complete the meal. Nothing was much different from our own meals except for the way of serving and that we sat on the floor, for it was the way in which, they said, it was invariably their custom to dine in the home.

Fakhara, noting my lack of success in finding any comfort in the cross-legged position, put me on a low cushion with a side-table. Rashid asked us if we would care to wash our hands. The cultured Arab host is little different from his western counterpart in his expressions, being perhaps a shade more delicate and considerate, and such an offer gives the usual alternatives of washing hands, which one does after a meal in Arabia and making good use of such moments in other ways. A distinguished medical Briton was asked three times after a dinner and reached a point of being asked if he was sure he would not wash his hands, before the penny dropped and he spent it. There is one word of great importance which has spread over much of the world, being widely understood and which gets one out of difficulties, as I have found, and that is "toilet", heard and recognised everywhere and spread, I fancy, by so many American travellers. "Powder Room" is utterly American. The equivalent in Arabic is *el hammam*—the bathroom.

Shortly after, the man of the house came in from spending time with his friends on the street front of the apartments on padded angled benches, exchanging puffs on the hookah, or hubble-bubble pipe, the *shesha*. When I had to return for a moment to my car for a document I was invited to take a puff or two. The mouthpiece is passed around with a wipe, amongst the gathered friends. Our host, as he entered, was holding Tariq fondly in his arms and in greeting us all asked me whether I had enjoyed my puff outside and would I like to try it again properly, a chance I was not going to refuse. The monstrous silver-coloured weapon about 5ft tall with about a 10ft long flexible, cloth-covered tube ending in a long wooden-ended mouthpiece rather like that of the bagpipes. We had watched workmen in Taif making these long python-like tubes, winding them around a pole.

Having a smoke Arabic style is a performance. The tobacco is a special variety known, with variations, as *tumbak*, the tobacco for the usual man's pipe being known as *dukhan*. *Tumbak* is a dark, damp lump consisting of tobacco and a mixture of fruity ingredients whose nature we were not able to discover. The lump of tobacco is placed on the top of the large standing piece, in former times on some red charcoal embers, but the modern style is to place the tobacco on an electrically-heated coil in a tin, with a variable resistance on a control wire to get the tobacco going, and when smoke signals are to your satisfaction, you turn it down a trifle. Starting up involves some tremendous inhalations to draw the smoke along the extensive dead space of the apparatus while the air is pulled through the water-chamber which cools the smoke and extracts a lot of rubbish, a much more effective filter than the feeble ones on our cigarettes.

After some maximum inhalations, enough to make my shirt feel tight, I was suddenly knocked back a little by the arrival of some dense smoke, but I persisted. My hosts asked me how I felt and I truthfully could answer, "Everything has become much clearer, much sharper," and one wondered if some of the plants in the tobacco could possibly have been a mild variety of "grass", while one of my fellow travellers suggested it was only because I had not taken any deep breaths in a long time. He was probably right. Persistent adjustments to the electricity produced a much better puff of smoke with a pleasant, cool, faintly scented aroma, though the needful, powerful draw made it feel as if my chest was full of smoke, but irritation was minimal as was any general effect on the senses after the need for the initial heavy puffing had ceased. Nick took over and looked a picture but felt much the same. A happy evening drew to an end with Rashid and his brother in another car leading us out of the city to set us on the way to our camp site.

★ ★ ★

The previous night we had been welcomed shortly after pitching camp by five dogs, two fawn coloured, whippet-like types and three white-chested black puppies. How the combination came about was anybody's guess. They were thin and scavenging and spent a time rattling the empty soup and meat tins, neatly piled, departing a little way with their loot to lick them clean. In the night one of them tried the end of my safari bed and then a lick at my protruding feet, but quickly returned to the tins. This night we had changed our site and the sandflies did not trouble me at the other end.

On both mornings the party took to the sea. My first venture was only a short paddle because I had a shoulder problem which hindered swimming, but the others waded out to the swimmable sea, which was a long way off. We could see the light coloured sea-bed before us running to the dark water where the reef ended. All this coast has a coral reef extending for a variable distance and I watched David and Noël on the first morning with shoes on to guard against the rough sea bed and any spiney fish, still wading out on and on, not much more than knee deep, further and further, until at some 200 metres from the shore they climbed up at the reef's edge and were in only a few inches of water, though beyond them was the sudden steep drop, swimmable, sinkable, and explorable with goggles and pipe or oxygen which some of our Riyadh friends had done, noting the usual ledges and caverns, and one also noting a large shark suddenly swimming along beside him. These sharks are reputed not to worry humans, there being plenty of other little titbits for them in the warm seas, but one felt disinclined to see if they had yet breakfasted. I felt sure that given the chance they would want a souvenir of Noël and Shirley, so the deep water was out of bounds for us.

Sharks, though one enemy in these waters, are by no means the most unpleasant. Sea snakes are common in both the Red Sea and the Gulf and some of our friends report swimming along with sea snakes suddenly confronting them, reputedly gazing at the reflection of themselves in the swimmers' goggles. Again they are reputed to be friendly unless accidentally hit or disturbed, but since their bite injects a very powerful neuro-toxin causing bodily paralysis, they are not the sort of pets to cultivate, though keen types do tell of swimming about amongst them to no harm.

More deceitful in their way are the graceful Portuguese men-of-war—the jellyfish with long beautiful tendrils, looking the most harmless creature in the world, but let a tendril touch you and you have a painful swollen limb and may be very ill. Rockfish are the other chief menace of tropical waters and they lie on the bottom with sharp poisonous spines sticking up, giving a very painful swollen foot if stepped on, so that shoes in these waters are a must and you may be warned off areas known to be feeding grounds, as I found in Tahiti.

The next morning I began to wade to the reef's edge but after passing the hundred metre mark felt a little tired with the effort of walking through water and, with the return walk and a drive to come later, I settled for a swim on my back and a piece of coral. Coming on to the beach one is careful not to tread on any of the large crabs which live in burrows along the sand just above water level. Whilst drying I reflected on the glories and pleasantries of the shark, snake, and rockfish-free cooler waters of Cornwall and other much abused British resorts. Home has its compensations.

III

We had gone into committee about our return, adopting Noël's suggestion of going round Medina rather than face the desert road we had come by round Mecca, as well as the vagaries of opening and closing time on the other Taif road. This meant a much longer beat but a good surface all the way, and a good time-saver, as we came to confirm, with much less traffic then the Jeddah-Riyadh road. We liked the idea of completing the circuit with new places to see and a possible glimpse in the distance of the second Forbidden City, Medina, though this meant a two-day return trip instead of our originally planned one day, but uncertainties the other way could possibly mean even three days, so we settled for the Medina road.

With limited driving on the first day we rose late and spent the morning with a swim, shell and other souvenir gathering, and reflecting that the Arab people were, in general, a very messy lot with their tins and refuse even at the seaside and in high righteousness and huff we gathered up all our debris, deposited it in a large oil drum, hopefully put there for the purpose. I chipped a toe in the process being sockless and in sandals—maybe the Arabs have got something after all.

We set off along the coastal road north on a mostly flat landscape with hills and mountains far over to our right and an occasional glimpse of the Red Sea on our left reaching the junction, Badr Hunayt, where the road divides, one branch going to the left to the port of Yenbo, and the other to the right which passes through the mountains to Medina. After a refill we moved on towards Medina and were in for a surprise. This route is one of the most beautiful of mountain passes with an excellent road surface, well engineered with fine bridges as it passes from the side of one *wadi* to another, the mountains rising to a great climax with what looked like near vertical sides to some magnificent peaks passing into the clouds.

Various busloads of the faithful clearly making a pilgrimage to Medina were part of a fairly heavy traffic. We passed some very pretty villages in oases, delightful pieces of old Arabia, all little disturbed by modernity save the road itself and a few points of trade and refuge for travellers. The sinking sun added its glory to it all. We suddenly left the mountains and there before us framed by a hill on either side, lay the city of Medina with the lights beginning to twinkle in the high central buildings and the city spread about them at the start of a long plain. The light was fading as we drew nearer to the repeated signs in a string

1. *Our camp by the Red Sea where the police came by night.*

2. *The road to Medina where it leaves the plain and starts to go into the mountains.*

3. *Breaking camp in the early morning east of Medina. Nick and Shirley Greville to the front and the Wallaces to the right.*

of languages, at first 3,000 metres out, "No entry for non-Moslems" and with a final police stop and a raised bar quite unattended!

We took the short way to the by-pass around the city, mostly behind a hill which lay on our right with the airport on our left outside the restricted area, the by-pass being some eight kilometres long and lit by standard lamps the whole way.

We cleared the area and decided that as we were camping we would choose a site well away from the Forbidden City, with no cause for any casual authority to make a 3.00 a.m. inspection and catechism. As we left the hill, the city at its western end appeared again and then slowly faded into the night. After what was judged to be a safe distance we started to look by use of our headlights for some turning to find a camp, but had to drift on a long way until a track was spotted leading to a flattish lava-type rocky area, and after a search on foot we made a very suitable encampment. The ladies prepared supper, the men gathered dry bushes for a camp fire to follow the meal and we sat reviewing the day as the traffic, well beyond disturbance level, rumbled on its way, while we watched the distant flashes of a storm to the north-east, though too far for any noise of thunder. We sorted our safaris and settled in.

* * *

Three o'clock in the morning was not our hour. This time it was not the power military but the powers heavenly that had caught up with us. Again Nick's voice came through my sleep as he bawled out, "It's raining." It did not need his vast experience as a highly seasoned ocean racer to have arrived at this assessment of the weather situation; no one could dispute him. The glorious canopy of stars had vanished and the dark clouds spat threateningly at us. We outsiders bustled to, packed our bedding, and donned our raincoats and I produced my umbrella which, when it was put into my car on a hot day in Riyadh, had made me feel a little silly. We waited in our cars and hoped. Our nocturnal luck held once more. The light sprinkle blew away; Nick summed up the skies and thought that just a fringe of rain cloud had passed over us. So we went to bed again, to be disturbed no further, but later learned that a very heavy cloudburst had struck the Jeddah area that night and rain continued through the following day. We had departed from the sea coast just in time.

Next morning, after breakfast, I strode to the top of the little hill which had sheltered us from the brisk wind of the previous night and looked about to see vast mountains far to the west, crops of hills all around us breaking out of a stony plain bestrewn with desert tracks to anywhere, a main road to the mountains unwinding like a ribbon on a spool, a village in a small oasis in a *wadi* near our road, and a risen sun flooding all with reddish light; a superbly handsome stony desert landscape when all are full of breakfast with two cars to escape in, but a merciless threat in the heat of the summer with uncertain water and no supplies.

We settled for the tents of Shem and went on our way, only to feel a touch of desolation when we had gone on a few miles. Nick and I were leading in my car and our customary glances in the mirror showed no signs of David following, so we turned and found him one or two kilometres back, pulled into the side with a flat tyre. His problem was to free his spare as, with trouble breeding trouble, the impact of his rear-end on the road-edge during our efforts to by-pass Mecca had jammed his spare tyre in its holder. He softened the tyre by releasing some air and eventually levered it out, while Nick and I returned to a petrol station we had seen a few kilometres back. We had primed ourselves in the Arabic words for pump, air, and tyres but it was clear he had none, in spite of his not being able to follow my Arabic. So we returned to help David put on the spare tyre to watch it flatten nearly to the wheel rim when the weight came on it. We seemed to be stranded in the desert.

However, shortly after, a Saudi pulled in behind us and then another also in a pick-up truck. They saw our problem, produced a pump to fit in the spark-plug hole and blew up the tyre. They would take no gifts but one eventually joined us in a cup of *ghawah* (coffee) and went on his way only when he saw us out of trouble. Once again we had met with nothing but kindness in our difficulty. We believed from the way the two cars pulled in behind us that the petrol station owner whom we had approached had told them of our distress and they had looked out for us to help.

We stopped some long way on at Equalat at a tyre shop where the owner was able to supply David with a spare tube and fitted it in a very workmanlike manner in a few minutes and, thus restored, we settled for lunch in the adjacent large *wadi*, near the long bridge spanning it, and by a small oasis of palms and tamarisks, and an old stone-lined well with a new pump. The *wadi* had a large area of static water and an area of soft sand by which some Saudis were paddling and, as David pointed out, no doubt infecting themselves with bilharzia. Shortly after they drove off, but the tyres dug into the soft sand where they stuck, one man and a boy not being enough to push them free. We all had a long look at each other and thinking of our puncture and petrol incidents David said, "I suppose kindness should repay kindness." We crossed the *wadi* and heaved them out and they went on their way waving to us. We felt honours were getting even, but still in favour of the Saudis.

Nearing Buraydah we came to some fertile *wadis*, with many trees, and old and new farmland. Then came a glorious stretch of sand dunes with the road winding up and down and curving about through the windblown sands, a handsome scene for upwards of some ten kilometres, with some pretty oases with adobe houses here and there in troughs between the hills, where water would accumulate. Suddenly we saw the city of Buraydah bathed in the sunlight of the late day, lying on an elevation and framed between two long sandhills, losing sight of it as we descended to the habitations scattered on the outskirts of the town.

Buraydah is the centre, together with its twin town Unaizyah of the region known as Qasim, once a power centre of the Rashids whom Abdul Aziz defeated in his bid to make a new Arabian state and stop the tribal warfare. The name Qasim has been adopted for the aerodrome which serves both towns. All about is farmland and in passing through Buraydah I saw for the first time in Saudi, a combine harvester. It is a medium-sized town of the usual appearance though some of its houses had rather a different feature with balconies all round. The whole area is very sandy but seems to be well-endowed with water and is renowned for productivity. We did not tarry on our way to Zilfi, crossing more sand and noting the well-built walls of cemented stone enclosed in chicken wire for further strength to hold back the dunes encroaching on the road. Those who have travelled in the snow countries know the anti-avalanche walls with a similar purpose, but with sand no roof is needed as the infiltration is stealthier and any slipping of the sand does not reach the dimensions of a snow-slide.

After crossing the sands there came a very fertile valley with on its left side the Jebel Tuwayq escarpment met once again, but here less high, and on the other side the long neck of sand which we had crossed earlier.

Zilfa was another small town with new buildings, dual carriage-way, anticipatory ranks of standard street lamp lighting well beyond the present limit of buildings. The road continued on beside the

212 **PLATE 22**

1. *Michael Ford, an oral surgeon colleague (left), with the Northern Irish manager and his wife on the late King Khalid's farm near Riyadh.*

2. *The huge arm ¼-½km long spraying crops.*

3. *On the late King Khalid's farm, water pumped from a vast underground cavern comes up steaming at 75°C and runs into a pool to cool then to be piped off to the sprays.*

PLATE 23 213

1. *Dr A. A. Mishari, gynaecologist and a farm owner on a farm completely developed and run by Northern Irishmen.*

2. *Holstein cattle from Australia, accustomed to heat feeding in the cool of a barn.*

3. *Another farm developed and run by Masstock of Northern Ireland. A line of irrigation points can be seen.*

escarpment when, at a break in its face, it climbed up to the top and thus went on to be the road to Dir'iyah and Riyadh, the southern end of which was all familiar territory.

Darkness had come and we were watching the road and the passing traffic like falcons, for though the road signs were good the absence of cats' eyes and erratic traffic called for the greatest care. We passed Dir'iyah, the ancient and long-abandoned seat of power of the House of Saud, with the village on our right and on our left the great new buildings of the seat of restorative power, the new Medical School and University Hospital, just recently named to honour the services of the then ruler, the King Khalid Hospital. Here is this great complex, rather remote, at the start of the desert but with the rate of expansion of this city it will not be long before it is engulfed by buildings. A few kilometres further on are the palaces of the late King Khalid and the new King Fahad, while other palaces abound in this area. Somehow the house of Saud has found a neutral territory at one side of the massive heap of modernity built upon the former palm-strewn area with adobe buildings which the Sauds took over two centuries ago. We entered Riyadh at 9.00 p.m. that night after a round trip of about 1,800 miles.

In 1982, a new, handsome dual-carriageway was completed, which runs out of Riyadh more or less in the direction of the Camel Trail, reaching the Jebel Tuwayq escarpment a little north of it, the views from it above the old Trail being just as handsome and without the climb. The new road sweeps down a great cutting in the side of the escarpment passing on to sweep across the old Mecca road and then on to cross the Red Sands. It finally joins up with the old Mecca road at Zalim, nearly two-thirds of the way to the Holy City, making for better driving and cutting a big slice off the long run.

CHAPTER XVII

The "Empty" Quarter

There is not much chance on a week's holiday, and even less on a day off, to jump on a camel, and in the tradition of the best explorers, strike out across the Rub' al Khali, the Empty Quarter, the largest sandy desert in the world. Few Europeans ever did it by camel in months, though in recent times motor vehicles with wide tread balloon-tyres and four-wheel drive and trucks full of oil men's kit venture into this sea of sand and make the journey somewhat commonplace for the technical elite. With neither apparatus nor privilege I still had a wish to see the Rub' al Khali, having soaked up tales of the trials and superhuman endeavours in these wastes of sand of Doughty, Thomas, Philby, Thesiger and a few others who, with fortune on their side and toughened on preliminary testing grounds, by enormous endeavour achieved their objectives, to survive one of the great feats of human endurance. That needed the stuff of youth and a lot more.

I remember making the crossing by air from Cairo to Karachi, in about 1950, on one of the hops to the Antipodes, which took us over the Arabian Peninsula, in those days at about 16,000ft, giving a much closer view than from the fringe of space today, and thought, "Those poor souls down in all that brown and yellow sand. I never want to go there." Well, here I now was in spite of the earlier antipathy, and any crossing for me must be by air again. Researches into the timetables showed that one could get a plane in Riyadh, taking off at 7.40 a.m., and a little over an hour later reach Sharorah, the only air-stop in the Rub' al Khali, some 500 miles due south and about fifteen to twenty miles from the ill-defined border with Yemen; it seemed very likely one would see all there was to see of the thriving metropolis of Sharorah from the air and savour at the airport the general view at and near ground level of the Rub' al Khali. I decided to put it to the test, all for 280 riyals, on a morning off. David Wallace and George Russell had expressed interest and came along adding pleasure by their company.

The rule to remember at airports is that if you go from the airport building to the plane by bus, never rush. We were last in the queue in the departure lounge, partly because our Arabic is less than undistinguished and our English is a little different from the announcer's. The stampede for seats was a strange phenomenon for me; my travels have taken me around the world by air several times, but the Saudi scamper was a new experience. Once out of the bus there is a hell-for-leather scuttle to the foot of the steps—even those are taken in a few athletic bounds—and the window seats have gone with a bang. It was the Saudi equivalent to the post-Christmas-sale-opening-time onslaught of the big London stores. Whether the rush is for the unaccustomed view or they just don't get blasé and like looking out, it is hard to say, but, whatever it is, they have no coy repressions about it—they like window seats—anyway, who doesn't? The bus was there, so we took our time and were last on, so first off at the steps to the plane, and did not raise our pace above a brisk walk; but, even so, there were eight to ten who passed us, up and in, though we still managed to get a window seat each. The flight-path took us over the centre of Riyadh and after so much sweating to get to know the city, it was an interesting pay-off after four months to see what was now almost like the back of one's hand. We had made one oversight, taking the sunny side of the plane, with the sun still low so that only the near ground could be seen clearly, further out being quite hazy; but even so we followed the Mecca road from Riyadh as it crosses the Wadi Hanifa, a run we had made several times in our jaunts, and then came the start of the long escarpment, the Jebel Tuwayq.

The *wadis* in the limestone looked like enormous bare trees with trunks, branches and twigs formed by surface erosion from the infrequent though heavy rains which when repeated over millions of years form wider and deeper channels, the water gradually soaking into the ground to form underground streams and pools.

The sands came into view as we left the limestone-like waves on a golden sea, wave after wave in an east-west line, nothing but sand in sight all round to the skyline as the plane flies on. This is the largest area of continuous sand in the whole world and all of Britain would fill less than half, and France could be just tucked in. It looks at first as if nothing has ever grown in it for millions of years, but when we came a little lower faint specks of bushes could be made out on the ridges, more on the southern slopes, and enough here and there to fuel that superb machine of nature for the desert, the camel, who if given enough greens, can do without water for long periods, taking the water out of the green stuffs. How these plants can exist in such a place is extraordinary; they must be able to lie dormant between showers just like seeds which can retain the life process for years without nourishment. There must be, of course, a little water under the sand, just reachable by the plants' roots, the process of capillarity bringing it up from even greater depths, and any dew will help. Another surprise, as we were to learn after landing, was that plants are by no means the only forms of life.

The rolling waves continued and on the return journey I counted them, seven to one minute, and thirty-three minutes to cross at 480 mph. From this rough calculation, and a check with a map, we estimated the distance to where we met the escarpment as 250 miles; this made a total of about 230 waves, with a distance between the crests of the sandy rollers about one mile, but how long could not be estimated since they stretched away one after another to the horizon on each side. Those are the great waves, but there are many minor waves between the crests. Just imagine being an explorer crossing that lot! Thesiger did it and along this very line from near Sharorah to Sulaiyil.

We began the descent, and Sharorah loomed up, with various military encampments about it, in consequence of there being a Communist regime in the Yemen whose undefined border is only some twenty or thirty kilometres away. There were only two large separate buildings; one, we learnt, the Emir's palace, and the other flats with shops below—no hotel, and who would want to stay? But should you arrive there and get stranded, Saudi Air will find someone to put you up and they will welcome your company till bedtime. There are a number of houses and sheds scattered about and some military works with some guns of the ack-ack type near the airfield, and doubtless lots of other things we could not see, besides a very serviceable airstrip for our 737. Most of the passengers on our full plane were going on to the next stop Najran, an attractive oasis with agriculture, from where a road to Sharorah is slowly being made. All the materials for the buildings, houses, sheds, heavy implements, the tarmac and concrete for the airstrip, and the rest has to come in by air or across the desert by lorry.

We left the plane to walk to the shelter, which is divided into three railed sections with an alley way for ticket holders, and roofed over with corrugated iron like an open barn, and all Sharorah was there for us to see. A low rocky ridge nearby with two ancient wells accounted for the site being habitable. We met a typical Briton who gave us his brief history. He was a technician from Lancashire with four years in the Middle East, one being in Sharorah, working fourteen weeks then three weeks back in the UK. A Marconi man, no doubt doing something in an expert way with communications, radar or whatever. His work was on the ridge about three kilometres away, but he lived in the town and had rather liked the place, although he had had enough of it. He was at the airport to get his rations, which were flown in frozen every day. "There they are," he said, "in that green box," to his great relief, only to have him return in about ten minutes to say that his rations were not in it and he was getting concerned, which did not surprise me for missing lunch in Sharorah would produce more paranoia than in an old people's home.

Doctors, when travelling, are pretty cautious about revealing themselves as such, for the sake of a rest from it all, but when he asked me what we were doing I foolishly thought it was safe to explain that we were three doctors having a morning off to look at the Rub' al Khali and Sharorah, while the students were on holiday. That was enough. He gave me the full story of the pain in his side which, in the circumstances of his isolation, I was glad to hear and could reassure him that it did not sound at all like a kidney stone, the possibility of which had been worrying him. David Wallace then called me over to two others, one a Scot and the other an American from Florida, the latter on finding David was a doctor produced the story of his rupture and so David passed him on to me; I arranged to fix him up in our hospital a little later. I was sorry for George—no sign of a mother and babe—but we had done pretty well; two patients within ten minutes of landing in the midst of the desert.

You will always find a Scotsman established anywhere you go the world over. Our new friend had spent many years in London, coming originally from Dundee, but even George from Aberdeen could not place his origins in Scotland. He had been two or three years in Sharorah and ran the airport as an all-round engineer and manager, keeping it going for them, liking it, saying it had a nice climate except for being a bit hot when the temperature got over 50°C (122°F) in the shade! It had been to 150° once, he said—a bit warm. There seemed plenty to do with his work, radio, tapes, and friends. As we were talking, our plane from Riyadh flew off to Najran, and then a four-propellor transport, a slow old bus of the Royal Saudi Air Force took off, and we saw it again on the tarmac in Riyadh on our return, no doubt collecting supplies. Our Scot said that there was a lot of life in the desert. "I would not put my hands into the sands about Sharorah." "Why not?" "Vipers, the sands are full of them, thick as thieves and most deadly. You can see their holes in the sand," he said, "They come out at night, after lying hidden all day from the sun." One man had recently been bitten by a camel spider, which caused a great swelling of his hand and later of his legs. They had a desert fox around who scavenged, but how he got there he did not know. Lots of birds, big ones, flew through at times—no doubt the bustard, which is the one the falcons hunt—and they have their own peregrine falcon about the area. All these creatures lived on smaller creatures in the desert which seemed to be teeming with life. As far as human activity was concerned, the man from Lancashire told us that there were thousands of Yemeni refugees camping just over the ridge, all fugitives from the Communist regime and that they were now used as soldiers for Saudi guarding the adjacent border. None were in uniform but were going round like cowboys with pistols on their hips, he said.

We sat in the sands and chewed over all this with our sandwiches. It was pretty clear we were having a very dull time of it in Riyadh.

Shortly afterwards our plane came in from Najran and in due course we went to the gate and had the routine search for weapons and metal objects. I was asked by the gateman for my passport, which I did not have, not having left Saudi soil, in fact not even having left the small enclosure about his gate. He seemed to remember and let me through, and my two companions produced enough papers to satisfy him for us all, so we climbed aboard a full plane and into not the best of seats. Our air hostess, to whom we had chatted for a time, was a member of a country formerly part of the old imperial order and she had a lively appreciation of her duty to three crowded-in Britons. She put her head to work with her male counterpart and before long we were offered three seats in the sparsely-occupied first-class section, (with not even a song called for). We greatly appreciated this kindness and enjoyed the wonderful view, again in considerable comfort, this time with the sun in our favour, of the waves of rich golden sand below.

We crossed the sands to the lowest point of the limestone escarpment of Jebel Tuwayq where beneath us we could see Sulaiyil, with the tar-sealed road coming from the north turning west out of the town to run up the Wadi Dawasir. We followed the edge of the escarpment to

Riyadh, an equal distance further on, and so to the east round the top of Riyadh with familiar features and a glorious view of Dir'iyah in the Wadi Hanifa with our new University Hospital close by, and on to our landing at about 12.40 p.m. We had left Riyadh five hours previously, crossed the Rub' al Khali twice, picked up two patients, glimpsed the life of Sharorah, and though not quite in the same class as Doughty or Thesiger, had put in a very satisfying morning's work nonetheless. My car was correctly parked this time, as was David's, and we dispersed to more mundane medical adventures in the afternoon.

Being still on semi-holiday, I made an attempt on my own to reach Ha'il by air. The travel agent, the evening before, said the only chance was to go to the airport and try to get a ticket there. I got up when roused by the call to prayer at 5.00 a.m. (no need to set the alarm), and by 6.00 a.m. one hour before take-off, confronted the man in the airport building at the stand with the number of the flight to Ha'il. "Nothing doing," he said, "fully booked." A well-groomed non-Saudi Arab with a ticket was already waiting for the crumbs of a cancellation. The young man behind the desk was not overflowing with words, not from any inability to speak, but he did offer, "Wait twenty minutes." So I asked "Sales" and he said if they could give me a place he would sell me a ticket, which seemed reasonable. So I waited and watched and noted the time by the large clock in the booking area which was stopped at 11.25 and three other lessers clocks which had all stopped, one at 2.30 another at 8.00 and another at 4.15. The time was about 6.10 a.m., so I stayed there without much hope, but with a lot of interest, as various types came through, then a richer type with six porters carrying large bundles of curious luggage, while near-pandemonium went on as those with tickets but no booking for Ha'il tried to force the issue. Saudis are not trained queuers and the technique is to arrive at the back of the scrum, thrust your ticket as far as you can through any weak point in the wall of heads, backs and backsides ahead of you; they need a lot of persuading that there is no place for them. The young man became very fierce twice, giving the sign with his hands that all was finished, and still it went on, so he gathered his completed papers and walked away to send his own company off while another stepped in to check the next plane's passengers.

Still a few hung about; it was now full daylight and I, too, had seen enough, and went on my way regretting a lost chance. I had left without luggage or a coat of any sort as I could have had the whole day in and about Ha'il and would have returned next morning to Riyadh to tidy up there.

That evening in Riyadh the long-awaited clouds gathered with ensuing spectacular thunder, lightning and deluge continuing through the night and morning. In Ha'il it had started earlier that day, and exploration of the day and night life of Ha'il without a raincoat might well have left a poor impression. The Arabs would say that Allah was watching over me. We would say that the Devil looks after his own.

CHAPTER XVIII

Ha'il, Home of the Rashid

On a week-end later, I took the plane to Ha'il, some 700km to the north-west of Riyadh, and enjoyed the views of the northern part of Nejd plateau, passing over the fertile region of Qasim by Buraida and Unaizah with their aerodrome between, the roads familiar from the air but the numerous tracks known only to the locals who bump around the countryside in their pick-ups.

Ha'il lies on a flat with hills and mountains around it, being said to be the bed of an extinct volcano. The Great Nafud, the huge sandy desert, starts some 30km to the north of Ha'il, and has a line of wells extending across it, which makes the crossing possible. Some time later, I had dinner in Riyadh with a prosperous former inhabitant of Ha'il who told me that thirty years ago he helped to drive 200 camels across the Nafud to a man in Jordan, taking two months. Crossing in a plane today the passengers do not bother looking out at it. Ha'il grew up here long ago because of good wells at this point south of the sandy desert, and now two new dams allow good farming and horticulture all around.

As I looked about the airport for an office to book a return flight I was hailed in English by a fine young Saudi, who said that the office was in the town and would I like a lift there, which I gladly took. He was an offshoot of Al Rashid, the former Emir of Ha'il, the formidable opponent and arch enemy of King Abdul Aziz who had fought him over many years and finally defeated him. One can well imagine King Abdul Aziz and his sons, still living, who faced this enemy or heard their father's tales and bitter words about his formidable rival. The young man told me how Ha'il had suffered somewhat from this old rivalry for the victors had long been watchful for any resurgence and slow to give Ha'il the usual handsome grants for development. But that was now all over and in the last few years Ha'il had gone ahead with extensive building which was in evidence everywhere. The old adobe strongholds had largely gone; all that remains of their former glory is one fort perched upon a hill with a high wall running from it. The large, square,

PLATE 24   223

*Abdul Aziz ibn Rashid, until he was killed
in 1906, was the powerful adversary of
Abdul Aziz ibn Saud.*

eight-towered castle in the centre of the town was the work of Abdul
Aziz, and from here he kept his hold on this former hostile territory.

The Ha'il Hotel to which my new-found Saudi friend drove me is
two years old and is no Hilton, though much better, with touches of
Arabic style in the buildings, rooms, menage and meals; but it is already
showing that hallmark of so much that is Arabic—a lack of
maintenance, particularly in the *hammam*, or bathroom, which had
evidence of insipient seepage on the plaster work, with taps that were
becoming detached and mirrors that were spotting badly. My room was
comfortable and the attention the essence of consideration.

The shops and *souk* were the usual Arab style but with a touch of
their own about the doorways and roofline, much of the old lying
amidst a modern growing town. Late that afternoon I made my way to
the hospital, a rather run-down, verandahed, one-storey building about
twenty years old, staffed entirely by Muslim doctors, Egyptian and
Pakistani, most of whom I met, and then visited their departments and
patients. They were very considerate, and all ready to tackle
emergencies of any sort, doing a good job in not the easiest of
circumstances; a group of doctors working in isolation but aware of
what was going on elsewhere in the world of medicine, who brought a
great deal of relief to the afflicted in this locality. Patients needing

advanced specialist treatment were mainly sent to Riyadh.

That evening in the lounge of the hotel, which appeared to be about the only social centre for Saudi or expatriate, I chatted for a time with a fine young Saudi, recently married, who confirmed that his wedding followed the conventional pattern. He said that in the service held in the bride's home, the Imam asked only the girl if she would wed him. "Why not you also?" I enquired, and he said, "There is no need to ask me, that is what I came for." He confirmed that at a wedding there may be just a few relatives—or a thousand friends as well, if that is what you wish. He had not seen the bride's face except in the bedroom after the service, and he was delighted with her, but at that point his description ended in loud laughter and he said he would now say no more. He did say that in his own district and as far as he knew elsewhere, it was still rare to see the bride before the marriage, except in cousins.

A variety of expatriates strolled in and took some coffee and to one of them I spoke at length. Ha'il had recently hit the headlines in the British press on account of its distillers. He told me that the making of *sadiqi* had gone on in his establishment, his acquaintainces sending their friends around to buy up all the sugar available. They had four-gallon drums full of it. One of them was due to go home but was doing so well that he stayed on and on and to his downfall, for he was caught. The local expatriates, he said, had no sympathy with them for selling *sadiqi* to the Saudis. They had been sentenced to two years imprisonment, but following protests this had been remitted to six months. Their cells had been without windows, with poor electric light or none, and there was little excercise. He confirmed that they were beaten in prison, perhaps a hundred strokes; later he had seen their backs. The shares in the distilling industry in Ha'il had hit rock-bottom and were likely to remain so.

The next morning I made a run to the remnants of a former town, Qufar, some 10km in the direction of Medina, once the counterpart of Ha'il, but decimated allegedly by plague perhaps a hundred years ago, and subsequently abandoned; and now there is little left but some crumbling walls and tattered towers amongst which the tamerisks flourish, leaving scarce "a rack behind". Arabs, on the whole, are rather primitive historians, showing little interest in the past, and it took some questioning to find the situation of the deserted village. None of my new-found doctor friends knew of its existence.

While I was standing by the new telephone exchange to decipher the

Arabic lettering, a young Saudi came to my rescue; his consideration was not equalled by his English, and wishing to help he drove me to the northern part of the town to the home of his cousin with good English who had studied engineering in the States and visited England. He suggested that we visit the old deserted village of the family of Ha'il. Wells were plentiful as indicated by the many palm trees. Most of the adobe buildings were intact save for some minor crumbling and he said that it nearly broke his heart each time he came as it was his birthplace and his attractive happy home until he was twenty. This was the first time he had gone into the house since taking up new unattractive quarters ten years ago.

We went into the small room where the family life had revolved, the floor straw-strewn, the ceiling of writhing tamarisk bows with palm fronds laid above, the walls begrimed with the smoke of a hundred years or more, two small high windows, and in one corner on the ground lay, as on the day they moved away, the square granite stone with a flat topped surface within which was the little cup-shaped cavity wherein they had ground their coffee beans. He opened a tiny cupboard let into the wall in one corner and sadly said, "Here I kept my beads." In this room they had sat around fed, drank their coffee and knew the binding fun of family. Progress seemed to have gone backwards here.

Other houses lay amongst the palms, one or two inhabited, and my young friend said he and his cousin intended to patch up the little defects wrought by time and use their family possession for the summer. The date palms still made a profitable farm; one ancient well had been filled in but a later stone-lined one had a diesel pump to bring water from 20 feet down.

We drove on to a newer district fringing this old-time Ha'il and found ugly cement and scattered rubbish not helped by the community of the Saleb, the Arab gypsies who came into the peninsula centuries ago, possibly from Palestine. The younger brother took me to his home, to the outer guest room, which was carpeted and pillowed in the usual way. I was in the thick of it, for he and his brother had little English and their old father, a dear old *shaib* of eighty-three, blind but most of his mind still active, spoke no English at all and I could just barely follow his slow Arabic as he told me how he had known Philby, and then asked me how was Churchill. He had fought with the French at Damascus against the Arab tribes for money, needing it badly for his family, and had regretted it ever afterwards. He had known King Abdul Aziz and had fought against him in the army of Al Rashid. Fate had made him twice the ultimate loser. I tried him in my indifferent French and this began to seep back in simple phrases clear enough to confirm the story of his warring travels. He sat against a wall and let his sons make the verbal running but roused to mutter some point he thought might be of interest; one was: "A woman came here long ago and I saw her." I took this to be Gertrude Bell, later the Secretary in Baghdad and a distinguished traveller who had crossed the Nafud to Ha'il. The Blunts, husband and wife, had been much earlier, in the last century, and seemed most unlikely. The tea passed round several times, and in this truly Saudi household I kept the soles of my shoes turned well in. We chatted on in oddments of three languages and they told me a lot about Ha'il and the old battles.

The time had come for me to go to the airport, my friends offering to run me there, some 2-3km out. We could see on the low hills on either side a number of black bedouin tents the like of which I had seen elsewhere near the town, and I said how good it was to see the bedouin so close in. They corrected my impression, "No, these are not bedouin, those are the locals gone out." Evidently they enjoy returning to the desert, for many in Ha'il started there, and at the weekends they use the tents frequently to have a taste of the old life.

At the airport I had some difficulty with the return ticket but my friends and the kind engineer in the Saudi Air Force did their best and eventually I was fortunate in getting the last seat. I sat about and watched the play, for here, on this particular day, there was none in sight but Saudis and myself. I saw a portly Saudi stepping on to the baggage scales anxiously watching the spinning numbers—his counterpart could be found anywhere in the western world. I observed graceful manners of farewell and greeting of the youths and grown-ups, the men with family and friends and the incessant farewell kisses, two or three to each cheek, and occasionally the mouth; and all the family, young and old, displaying so much affection to all ages, the ancient customs of the Arab peoples, conveying no more that the heartfelt handshake of the Anglo-Saxon world. I mused over the light-boned form of most of the Saudi youth, but as elsewhere, the abnormal podgy child or lad. Then passing through the throng replete with handbags and children tugging at their skirts, shrouded over with their long black veils, passed their women into the ladies' room, all a disorderly and friendly progression to the exit and the take-off.

CHAPTER XIX

Saudi Lakeland

New arrivals to a parched Saudi in the hot months tend to have a virtuous concern to avoid wasting water. Disillusion comes on seeing great pools from burst main pipes in roads yet no one rushing desperately to repair them, water-hydrants and water-carriers splashing untold gallons about, innumerable bore-holes throughout the city and in *wadis*, with water gushing out freely to irrigate road side palms and shrubs and gardens, and private swimming pools galore. One becomes relaxed and fills up the bath or prolongs the shower, especially when one learns of the scores of oil-fired plants about the coasts converting sea to fresh water. No one talks of a shortage of oil.

Two British water engineers put things into perspective. The saying goes, I was told, "Oil for a hundred years, water for a thousand." Water is there in vast quantities much greater than the oil, deep down in the pores of the limestone or in huge caverns needing to be pumped out if one or two hundred feet down, but under pressure, like the oil, if tapped from the depths. However, if millions of acres of desert were converted into agricultural land by tillage, chemicals and pumped water, the supply would not last a thousand years, far from it. The surface is as parched as the depths are saturated, and though Saudi has no natural surface rivers, it has underground ones, as well as waterholes and lakes. Over millions of years, rainwater as it seeps through the limestone dissolves some of it, and gradually little channels of water from which become streams and these in time may create bigger spaces to become caverns like the Cheddar Caves in England. The roofs of the caves may finally fall in, thus forming a waterhole which is constantly refilled from the sides and depths.

One such waterhole is the famous Ain Heet, halfway between Riyadh and Al Kharj where geologists found important data to encourage them to continue to drill for oil at the distant gulf coast, and where Abdul Aziz watered his camels before taking Riyadh. Here the sides of an

1. *The water-hole at Ain (spring) Heet near Riyadh, where Abdul Aziz watered his camels before his attack on Riyadh, and is now used as a swimming pool by young Saudis. Here the American geologists noted the grey slate layer, seen well in the photo, indicating a top impervious layer thus encouraging them to drill from 1,500ft to 4,500ft at Well No. 7 where they struck the great oil field 250 miles away at Dhahran.*

2. *A desert outing with David Wallace (half in view) and John Hadfield (surgeons). Some of the younger men climbed up the face close to the point marked by a streak.*

escarpment fell in at one point from the collapse of an underground cavity formed by water which seeps from the highest land of the central plateau towards the east coast. This underground stream flows on and comes near the surface in the lower flat land of the ancient oasis of Al Kharj, 35km further to the south-east where there is a sizeable town of that name, and 6km south of it the water comes to the surface in two large waterholes about a hundred metres across. The good tar-sealed road south from the town centre passes close beside them to the advantage of many visitors.

We had decided on a visit to Al Kharj and the waterholes on a Friday, four cars leaving Riyadh by Janub (south) Street, and after a drive of about thirty-five kilometres we turned to the left by a radio tower, a prominent landmark, and by rough tracks across the desert we arrived at the entrance to the waterhole of Ain Heet. We left our cars at the point where the King had halted his camels, descended steeply under the cliff with a wide large arch of rock overhead and fallen rubble of small and large stones lying over a broken surface. Most unexpected were shouts of delight echoing up accompanied by the sounds of splashing, and it was clear that young Arabia knew what to do with a large waterhole. As we descended young Saudis came running up over the rocks in their wet bathing shorts as others went lightly skipping downwards from rock to rock. It was quite steep and we Europeans, unaccustomed to these jagged paths, fumbled and stumbled with much caution and even so I took a little tumble. They were diving off the rocks and joyfully shouting away at the top of their voices and swimming capably. The water, they said, was quite warm, at about 150ft below the surface. When we had puffed to the top again a party of Germans had arrived and joined some young Saudis with lots of photos and good fun. Refreshed by fizzy liquids we went on our way to Al Kharj.

The railway from Riyadh to Dhahran partly follows the direction of our road and for some distance after Ain Heet we ran along beside it. This is the only piece of active railway track in Saudi, although over in the west, in the Hejaz, are the remains of the track running through from the border of Jordan down to Medina which Lawrence and others spent a lot of time blowing up in World War I, where, as well as track, there are dynamited engines and heavy gear still lying about. The railway from Riyadh to Dhahran is a 357 mile track built between 1947 and 1951 at the request of King Abdul Aziz, being put through by Aramco

1. *From Riyadh to the coast at Dammam run two trains, each day, one fast and one slower. It is a single track 3′ 6″ and has a double track at Haradh for passing.*

2. *Speeding near Riyadh.*

at a cost of $52 million. In 1963 the government took over the railway, compensating Aramco for it, and it still provides a twice daily run, one fast, one slow of about five or seven hours, each way between the two terminals.

The approaches to Al Kharj are heralded by an increasing number of oases of date palms and then come fields with greenery of various sorts, both horticultural and agricultural. David and Noël Wallace led a small cavalcade through the town, none of us knowing the turn to our destination, the "lakes", and we passed through the town to its further end where were some very attractive buildings with a fine football stadium. We turned and paused to sort out our direction and to have a drink. Just at that moment a large four-wheel-drive car pulled up, the American occupants being in a similar dilemma about the way to the waterholes. A minute later up came a little plump, jaunty Saudi policeman on a motorcycle, who called us to him and made signs that photography had been going on saying, *sura* (photo). Most of us were unaware of this and protested vehemently about it, but he was having no nonsense and signalled to us that we must all follow him. So, with a fifth car added we made quite a procession behind him to the gates of the highly pleasing piece of architecture to find that this was a sort of military establishment.

We were ordered to park our cars and get out, whereupon a pleasant but dutiful sergeant came and started in on the details. It was pretty clear they meant business and waterholes were off for the day. We spent the next hour and a half giving our names, surrendering our cameras, under threat that if we did not we would be searched for them; two cameras had no film in them, but still they took them, including that of our new American friends: they protested vehemently that they had not taken any photos, that they had only just arrived and talked to us, and far from being intent on spying were employed by one of the princes to train the National Guard. The sergeant took this information with measured look, but with firm insistence on the surrender of their cameras. The Americans were standing no nonsense and showed a lot of old-fashioned truc, throwing in their prince's rank. They had a point and it had an effect. In the long run, after all our names had been taken and attached to cameras the Americans made a final vehement protest saying that they insisted on their cameras before they left or their prince would have something to say. The sergeant looked long and saw the light, and allowed them to take their cameras and go their way. With so many guns about we thought they had handled it pretty well, had shown the right amount of threat and made their point successfully.

On our side Noël put up the best show of fight and contempt for the triviality of the proceedings, and our Egyptian guest's quiet Arabic helped to calm it down a lot. We were told we could have our cameras back in three days but the films would be taken out and developed; it was unlikely that we would see any of the films again, which included photos of other trips a number of the party had made. They would let us have the cameras back in three days, though we had to turn up at Al Kharj to receive them; we were then permitted to go on our way. There is a rule in Saudi that no military objects may be photographed and also it is unwise to photograph public buildings. It turned out that one member had tried to take a picture of the handsome football stadium and that it was this that had set in motion the whole event, perfectly innocently, but once reported it had to go through.

Three days later David Wallace and I drove out to the gates again, telephones rang and after some delays and language difficulties we were told that the films were not ready, the cameras were not available until the films had been seen and we must come back in a week's time. The films had to be taken to Riyadh for development. We felt that right would be on our side in the long run if the results of the developing and printing of the photographs in Riyadh were anything like the ones we had submitted ourselves not much would be seen anyway.

In due course, a week later, David, this time with his son, went out and was duly handed the cameras but no films—all except one camera, that is, and he was told that that would have to be sent to the United States for the development of the film there, and the camera would be held. It is clear that the members of the military must act according to their bounded duty. It is sometimes forgotten that there is a state of suspended or open conflict between the Arab states and Israel, and attempts are made to buy photos of the views of Saudi from pretty well every aspect—maps also if they can be located may be freely bought.

We discovered that the way to defeat the Saudi logic about photos, if one wants to photograph any prominent building, is to stand one's friends some ten feet away from the camera with all the appearances of photographing a friend, which is permitted, and the policemen will not worry you. Remove the friend and they are upon you with speed. Stegner in his book *Discovery* said about the Americans when they started their oil explorations in the 1930s on the Gulf, "They did their level best when some Arab customs jarred their sense of logic." Charity is needed on both sides. They often cannot follow what we are up to.

* * *

At a later time still not having visited these waterholes, I made a further trip together with two friends who had not seen them either. Mike Ford, the University Oral Surgeon, and Bob Hunter, a Scottish constructional engineer, and I, made a bad job of water-divining, concentrating, on our drive south out of Al Kharj, on the right instead of left side, and shot past the spot. After another 8km of eyes-right our committee of three decided we had gone a bit wrong and enquired from two non-Saudi Arabs at a petroleum station, who, though so close, had never heard of them. However, a Saudi put us on to the right direction, and we had the spot roughly sited.

Being now very close to Dillam, the ancient capital of this district, we diverted to see it first for it was the scene of Abdul Aziz's first battle with Al Rashid. After taking Riyadh and expecting Al Rashid to come after him sometime, Abdul Aziz had moved south to rouse the southern tribes to support him, and was 100km away at Huta, south of Dillam, when his scouts told him that Al Rashid was upon him. It has been earlier described how he hurried his small forces to Dillam which had already declared for him and placed his men in the palm grove about the town, along its wall and in its little forts. That day he made a small revolution in desert warfare when the young man's courage, skill and bluff won again and his reputation shot up with the tribes, many of whom now joined him.

The scene of this skirmish attracted us, and with a brief and limited look at the town we set about photographing the little crumbling mud tower and wall, nothing else, when the second skirmish of Dillam began. Up drove a young Saudi in his pick-up and stopped us with muttered protests of *sura* (photo), and said he wanted our films. Old Arab ruins are photographed in thousands by the workers of all nations in Saudi without protest by the locals and in many places with encouragement, one of us having stood before the ruin, but not as he drove up. This one kept on a bit and from the seat of his car demanded our films. Clearly, photography in the Al Kharj district was not meant for us. Before he might try to come and get them with the many other photos on our films I suggested that we drove on. He did not like it and shortly after followed us in his pick-up and tried to divert us to the roadside but we went ahead. Like Al Rashid we had been repulsed from the town, but this time we had some booty as a record of past and present battles. With feathers ruffled we drove on to look once more for the waterhole and took a track with an apparently good surface between the two main tar-sealed roads, but when about 300 yards from the further road we hit deceptive sand and stuck. It was not our day. Efforts with stones and bits of wood beneath the tyres and jacking the wheels onto the wood were to no avail. Mike and I walked to some distant farmers who were amused but had no tractor, so we advanced to the road and had the luck to hail down a four-wheel-drive lorry with two kind Egyptians aboard who gave us a tow to the hard surface and went on their way, as did we, having asked for trouble by going on an unknown desert road on our own; but the weather was cool.

Lunch with fluids smoothed our feathers and soon afterwards we found the waterholes just 6km from Al Kharj as they should be, and close by a low range of hills with a building housing two pumping engines from which four large pipes poured water into a small channel running to Al Kharj. At the edges of the holes there is a sudden steep drop so they have been enclosed in a wire fence for the benefit of the absent-minded. Locals ascribe the holes to the fall of a meteorite, but scientific counsels say that they are due like all the others to falling in of the roof of an underground cavern. Once the water level was almost at the surface but now the sides descend sharply some fifty feet or more to the black water far out of reach of swimmers with no means of scaling the sheer walls. But bathing is not far off for fans, for the little rivulet of pumped water some two metres wide and half a metre deep, provides further down its course several stretches for cooling off as some glittering dark figures were doing. Still further on its course the little stream had rushes, bushes, and grass upon its banks and to the locals of Al Kharj it is a favourite picnic spot with the remnants of many happy afternoons, the carcasses and skins of sheep lying around, marking their habit of leaving the clearing-up to nature. A second waterhole, nearly dried out of about the same size lies nearby.

We drove on to the hill above the waterholes to take the view of the wide flat before us and here was a scene which might have been on Salisbury Plain. Al Kharj to our right, like a distant Salisbury with not one but two towers, and not a mosque but a factory; then before us was a fertile plain with belts of trees and farmland dotted in between, and

PLATE 27   235

1. *The largest lake at Layla.*

2. *A typical concrete-sided water course at an oasis such as al Kharj.*

3. *The water-hole at al Kharj with the pumping station above.*

though not visible just then, we knew that a herd of milking cows were grazing along with sheep. Though an ancient region of fertility due to its water, its extensive cultivation dates from little more than thirty years ago when King Abdul Aziz set out a policy, with aid from the States, of developing the "wet" area as a Saudi agricultural project. In the background the hills rolled away to the distance, the semblance to an English scene enhanced by many dark clouds with shadowy lines beneath suggesting rain on the furthest hills. We gazed for a while in this reminiscent atmosphere in nostalgic silence, then moved away towards Riyadh before darkness.

★ ★ ★

Over 300km south of Al Kharj across areas of limestone and sand, in the al Aflaj region is Layla, a town where, readers of Thegiser will recall, he had a hostile reception by the Emir and the Ikhwan alike at the intrusion of an infidel, and where the shopkeepers would accept his money only after it had been publicly washed. When Thesiger arrived at Sulaiyil, 300km further south still, in the Wadi Dawasir, after crossing the Empty Quarter from the Yemen, the news had been sent to King Abdul Aziz by radio to Riyadh, and he was at first furious and about to make an example of Thesiger to other infidels, when Philby successfully interceded with the King, then drove do⸱n by car to Layla to meet Thesiger and to intercede with the local Emir. Thesiger had seen the lights of an unknown car as he was reaching Layla and heard the revving of a far-off engine indicating it was stuck in the sand; being a camel man he admitted to being a little pleased, though most desert-outing drivers today will feel a touch of sympathy. Philby's car was rescued, and the two men met next day in Layla. These two acts of Philby may well have saved Thesiger. We found the locals a friendly lot of infidels, and they could not pocket our unwashed coinage fast enough.

Mike Ford and I had driven down on a Thursday afternoon in the one car as we were on asphalt all the way but for the last six kilometres or so, reaching Layla at sunset, thereupon deciding to leave the waters until the next morning. After some friendly chatter in and around the central market square we sought a camping ground just north of the town and off a tar-sealed road to the left in behind a small camel thorn bush. It is better not to be far from a main road but away from its noise and lights. We found an area of firm surface some thirty to forty yards off the tar-seal and made a camp. I like to rough it with a safari bed, foam mattress, sheets, blankets as necessary, and my usual pillow and pyjamas, with a well-stocked larder and plenty of light from the car. We dined well and with the moon up Mike decided on an exploration of our surroundings, coming back with a full report and no snake bites, while I had lazed back listening for any yells. It is rare in these limestone areas to see snakes by day, but being night feeders there is just a chance of a bite at night. In other areas there are distinct dangers at night when thick footwear should be worn. Lawrence made reference to his worrying about snakes when he lay upon the bare desert. I had contented myself with the slaughtering of many dung-beetles which emerged from the sand in our presence. Some old familiar waltz tunes from the BBC World Service floating out of the car radio put us in a sleepy nostalgic mood and after I had laid some time gazing at the brilliant heavens, sleep came easily.

Just as a year before at Haj beside the Red Sea, I awoke to voices; some quiet Arab chatter, car lights, and Mike's, "Who is it? What do you want?" Once again the watchful police had spotted us but this time gave us no midnight aggression in any way, nor even worry. They seemed to realise we were no Hajis trying to make a life in Saudi, and, after more chatter amongst themselves, made off and we returned to sleep. In the old days many Hajis settled in Saudi, but now the visa control is strict with such vast numbers coming in every year, and Saudi accepts new citizens only after five years' residence and strict scrutiny.

We broke camp early next day and sat ready for the off to find that the ageing battery had not stood up to the drainage of its stores the night before. We blessed the fact of having remembered to camp on a hard surface, found just beside us a desert road, and easily pushed my light little car on to it, where, after an extra shove, she started on the run. It would have been a long walk. We drove through Layla and on a further four kilometres, and then turned off to the left on to a wide, well scored desert track which led us to the lakes.

We had been a little surprised the night before by finding a string of locals who did not seem to know of the *buhaira*, lakes, or *uyun*, springs, but one or two had been helpful, and we surmised that it was our Arabic not up to the local accent, or just our Arabic. Here in the midst of the usual run of limestone desert the trail suddenly ran down into a rough oval of low cliffs whose lower margins shelved into a line of reeds and there within green banks lay the sparkling water of a nursling lake, Ain Samhah, about one kilometre long and 400 metres at its widest, and on it spurted a speed-boat trailing a water-skier. Our Riyadh medical cousins at the King Faisal Hospital make regular week-end trips to these waters, keeping a boat at Layla which they tow to the lake. We drove halfway round to a cleared flat area by the lakeside where some Saudis, including a good swimmer in the University team, and some Britons, were wasting no time. The British were from the Military Hospital in Riyadh and had brought a bus-load of Philippino nurses for an outing. On the other side was a small tent for the water-skiers. Saudis came and went, amongst them one of my students from Riyadh.

Mike and I drove around the whole territory of the lakes and enjoyed the moments of discovery, coming upon six lakes in all, some tiddlers we would ordinarily call ponds, the second biggest being about 150 metres across. For a time we watched some Saudi lads diving off a rock about twenty feet above the water and making the familiar calls and yells of all languages. Campers, all expatriates, were dotted about infrequently. This beauty spot draws Saudis and foreigners alike to look long at the sight of sheets of water in an arid, riverless land. Let us hope it stays that way, as unspoilt as it is now.

This water all comes from below and the lakes were formed in the same way as those at Al Kharj. The locals say that there is no bottom; perhaps by their system of measuring with a stone tied on a long piece of string none is reached. More accurate sources say that the depth is much the same as at Al Kharj, about 350 ft.

We drove to the other side of the main lake and joined the Feisal group with the speed-boat, meeting two Saudis in traditional dress, fine young men who turned out to be local police "high-ups", both having visited Britain to advance their sleuthing skills, with a dearth of crime in Saudi. We regretted that time did not allow us to accept their invitation to lunch, the *ghudda*, which would have taken at least two hours; on our way home we ungraciously concurred that it was one thing in the Al Kharj district where our visit was almost ended, but in Riyadh we would have put aside much to be invited to lunch with the local police, where considerations of possible future collaboration and benefits would have overcome any present problems.

We set out on the return journey deciding on a quick half-hour lunch beneath some shady trees not far from the road and drove on to find one, going on and on and on, on this splendidly engineered piece of tar-seal across desert land where trees were few, and when there were some we could not get off the banked-up sides. So we settled for a roadside snack in the car's shade and did ourselves well to a chorus of toots from passing vehicles but no trouble from the local watch calling for high influence. The further drive to Riyadh of four hours by way of Al Kharj was without incident.

CHAPTER XX

Saudi Derby Day

The long-awaited day of the annual camel race had arrived in April with an event at 11.00 a.m. which we decided to forgo, and another in the afternoon at 4.00 p.m. this being the largest race for camels in the country and our objective.

Large assemblies are not in general encouraged in Saudi, even a private assembly for a conference needing official approval. There are some occasions when all are free to pack in as in football stadiums, athletic meetings, for some royal occasions at race-tracks, at executions and at this annual camel race; but all such events either the police—even a few at conferences—or the army, and, if the King is present, the National Guard, turn out in force.

We went out of Riyadh as a small caravan of three cars, men and women, along the Dhahran road to the east and then turned northwards on to a road that leads a long way on to the King's extensive farm. Some twenty kilometres along the road were the tents of the meeting on an elevation above an extensive plain. As we turned off the asphalt down a dusty avenue towards the tents the National Guard were lining each side, ready to receive the King, looking splendid in their red *guttras* with the head-rings well down on their foreheads with a golden badge below, nearly at nose level in some, like a version of the forward sweep of the British Guards' peaked hats.

We parked well back and footed it over the dusty tracks to the crowds of all nations lining the tracks on either side of the royal tents on the elevation; men of all nations, many Saudis and other Arab nations, Westerners, Koreans, Indians, Germans and Japs and the large flat-topped mound with well-smoothed sides and a large low tent—the stand for the King, the Princes and the VIPs, with a large number of the National Guard around its sides and lining the way down to the low arena before us, and a few Rolls Royces indicating the presence of the

Royal party. About a kilometre away out on the desert we could see the camels and their riders, some 306 starters we were told, some standing quite still, others wandering about a little, and a few of the camels couched, all awaiting the royal signal for the four o'clock "off". Before us was a heaped-up line of sand marking the edge of a semi-sealed road with the cars of the Guard moving up and down keeping an eye on the crowd and the whole road edge lined at intervals of about ten feet by the Guards with rifles and fixed bayonets. The road ran for some distance to our sides, ending before the royal stand, and parallel to the road on its further side was the finishing stretch of the race-track, lined on each side with a low wall of heaped sand. The finishing post was immediately opposite the stand and thereabouts was a line of the Guard without fire arms, whose purpose was not clear till the end of the race—they were camel catchers. A group of about a dozen heavily-veiled Saudi women with their children stood well back on a mound at the end of a line of male spectators, in sad contrast to the Western women with their families wandering about in T-shirts and picnicking just anywhere.

A helicopter came in and landed on the track in front of the stand and then took off to hover before the line of runners, which I thought to be the ABC equivalent of the BBC roving camera as other television cameras were mounted near the finishing post. The helicopter followed round the course some distance behind the runners and I was assured that it was the Royal Air Ambulance ready for the King, but also kindly allotted the duty of attending to any casualties amongst the jockeys. However, some of my friends told me that they had seen views of the race on TV taken from this helicopter, so it appears to have had a treble duty.

The crowd was thickest around the mound and the finishing post but was also fairly thick on the side of the long 40-metres-wide finishing straight at least 300 metres away from us. It was a sizeable, jovial and patient crowd, mainly Arabs, though plenty of Westerners mostly in picnic attire. The Guard lining the road in front of the crowd had plenty to do keeping the eager Saudis from straying. Next to us was a Saudi version of the famous Prince Monolulu who featured as a character at British race meetings for so long; a self-styled expert who entertained the crowd, but here, with no betting allowed and no sale of tips, his talents could not be exercised but were restricted to diversions. He was a dark-visaged old Saudi with great, long, gapped fangs, more so from the lower jaw, thrusting up like those of a wild creature. He was full of personality and fun, talking entertainingly and setting the crowd alight about him, using a pair of binoculars like an Ascot devotee to spot the incidents before and during the long race and bringing a laugh even to members of the National Guard near us.

The camels were all lined up facing towards our right to start the great sweep of the 20 kilometre race; 306 camels spread in a line over a great wide plain—and precisely at 4.03 p.m. came the "off", a good piece of organising in Saudi terms, and in any terms for that matter, and a reflection of the presence of the King who is conscientious in his schedules, as in Shakespeare's version of the duties of a King. He had already that morning attended the 11 o'clock race. Now the long line started moving slowly forwards, the rising dust, the helicopter and the cars following tracing the whereabouts of the riders who had soon gone from sight round the first bend.

There was no indication at all of relative positions, no signals, no loudspeakers, and it was a long wait, even the Guards smoking away; one with an unlit cigarette held for a long time between his lips accepted a light from me with "Thanks very much" in good English. The dust clouds came nearer, the old dark Saudi excited and explaining the unseen, then the first rider showed up well to our left some fifty minutes after the start. He was only about 200 yards away and about the same distance ahead of the next rider. The track is a huge oval widely open at the start and the finish narrows down to much the same width as an ordinary horse race-track, which is adequate, the runners having thinned out so much over the long distance. He was riding easily with plenty still left in his camel; the animals do not gallop in such a long race. He came on moving at a brisk trot using his camel stick with great gusto, on the neck, on the rump and anywhere, having pulled the best out of a good animal and he was greeted with loud cheers.

As he passed the winning post his camel was seized by one of the members of the National Guard allotted to that duty as was each subsequent camel, some with great excitement as they dashed on taking some slowing down, like a long distance runner after 20 kilometres. They were remarkably spread out. The first ten riders came in comparatively close, not more than some 300 yards separating them, one being a small lad who was given a lot of time on television that night; he was said to be eight years old and looked it, and came in riding in magnificent style, beating away at his animal and taking eleventh place, looking as if he had been born on a camel, cheered all the way on to the finish.

Another young lad came in fairly well up later on. Many of them as they came into the straight were beating at their animals to try to improve their placings, for the first hundred riders received a prize, so position mattered. One young Saudi near to us suddenly burst through the ranks of the National Guard and passed his *agal*, the head-ring, to one of the riders who had dropped his stick to urge on his favourite. The crowd about us gave him a cheer, the Guard let him go as he came back, and his fancy came in a few places up the list. Another camel came along with the young rider dismounted and holding on to the animal's tail, being pulled along as fast as his legs could go. It doesn't matter how you finish in this sort of racing; as long as the camel and his rider pass the post together they are given a place accordingly.

Some of the riders sat right on the hump, some a little forward and a number of them were almost over the rump of the animal—there is more than one way to ride a camel. What was extraordinary was the difference in the quality of these animals and perhaps their riders, for the time between the first and the last camel must have been at least twenty minutes, which was between a third to a quarter of the time of the race, and the distance between the first and last animals was some four or five kilometres.

The newspapers reported the rewards for the desert Epsom; the winner of each of the two races of the day would receive a car and a money prize, for the large race 25,000 (£4,000), and there were available 600,000 riyals (near enough to £100,000) to be divided amongst the first hundred runners and we thought this was probably divided proportionately to their placing in the race. Why prizes for a hundred? The intention is not just to encourage the best to win but to encourage other riders to keep coming annually, that being only the fourth year of the event.

While a lot of stragglers were still coming in after the first hundred, some officials moved to a small mound beside the track in front of the main stand and on this there seemed to be some distribution of a few prizes, and before the last rider and beast had staggered in, the royal party with the King in the middle in his black robe and surrounded by Princes, friends, and closely-packed National Guard, moved to his Rolls Royce and the annual camel race was officially over as he drove off. The Saudis also very quickly dispersed as seems to be their custom

1. *This driver aged about 8 came in 11th out of 300.*

2. *It is not necessary to ride the camel home, only to cross the line together.*

3. *Even crossing the line holding the camel's tail qualifies.*

4. *Three race-goers but no bookies or tote, but the National Guard keeps a close eye on proceedings.*

at the conclusion of any event, whatever it be, including eating; the British moved around in the usual fashion to greet and to talk, and some started picnics; the Saudis, at a dinner have their chat first and then, when the meal is over rise and go.

"Do not tarry after food," is an Arabic saying.

There was an aftermath the next day. We had gone out through the same territory—but far beyond it—for our desert trip the next day, and in the evening as we came past the site of the race we could see across the desert about a dozen camels being walked away in a bunch, while on the road we passed a series of little pick-ups each carrying in the back a camel couched and tied down with ropes right over, the long neck reaching up like a chimney and its superior nose sniffing the wind, and finally near Riyadh we spotted the climax of a small pick-up holding two camels which must have represented a superb feat of container packaging, getting two camels lined up straight and squeezed side by side into the back of a little pick-up. We would have to wait another year so see the like again. In 1982 the entries for the big race had reached 1000. Prize money does it everywhere when coming by the sackful.

CHAPTER XXI

Desert Outings

The desert is like a great sea suddenly stilled, but a lot of movement can be got out of it from the momentum of one's vehicle. Flat areas are like calm water but ups and downs have to be steered like a boat; sudden sandy stretches need watching for you can get trapped as on a shoal and you may need hauling off, and high winds may toss you about and half-blind you like a helmsman by spray or mist. The flattish areas, like calm waters can be a little dull in the ordinary way, but may be welcome after a rather long tossing.

The *wadis* are ideal for land-cruising with their varying terrain, and the unexpected, whether it be a choice of tracks or one just going on and on to nowhere. The equipment and precautions are much the same for sea or land, needing a little homework on what you intend to try and how long you may be out, and some plotting of the route, on a map, if you can find one; then the filling and stacking of food boxes, maps, digging-out tools and tow-ropes, spare fuel, and large amounts of fluid in the warm weather. If you intend staying out one or two nights the list gets long, but is quite a challenge with immense satisfaction when you find you have included all you need. To some a desert outing is just a matter of getting somewhere to have a barbecue or a gigantic guzzle, to others it is an exploration combined with something of a rally or mystery drive and food may be snacks only.

On most Fridays (the Saudis' Sundays) many of us would go out into the desert for a picnic and as the mood took us to explore anything anywhere.

Soon after my arrival, David and Noël Wallace took me on the most popular of desert excursions—to the Camel Trail, just an hour's run from Riyadh with something accomplished by climbing it and studying the superb view from the top. We crossed the city by way of the flyovers, past the largest fruit and vegetable *souk* and on through the suburbs, across the bridge over the Wadi Hanifa with nearby on the right four substantial houses reputed to be the homes of the four wives of a rich Saudi who is duly giving each equal consideration. Then on through the long straggle of houses as the town spreads into the desert where water must be carried by large tankers to each villa, works, chicken-breeding houses, barracks for the guards and military, and the groups of shanties of scrap-wood, flattened tins, corrugated scrap and sacking, for the humble, low-paid, hard-working Yemeni who live with the minimal or no rental and return to their homeland comparatively rich enough to support a wife and family.

The land is marked for about eight kilometres out by little white cubes of stone to show the owners—all Saudis, for only Saudis may own land or buildings. Desert at this distance from the centre of Riyadh is priced at about 1,000-2,000 riyals per square metre. Where else can a rich Saudi place his money—other than his businesses, farms, or London, New York, Paris and the rest? At 25km out on this vast central plateau of limestone, the Nejd, comes the principal escarpment, the Jebel Tuwayq, where the earth long ago crumpled, split and left an overlap in its skin of ancient sea-bed in the form of a long curving line of cliffs some 400-800ft high and 800km long, with a gentle bulge eastwards. Debris of eroded stone skirts the great bluffs up to half their height. This face must be descended to the long flat below, and the excellent modern road now winds down, lined by innumerable empty soft-drink tins, cast out of the windows of passing cars, a practice now officially declared untidy and campaigned against in the general clean-ups of the cities. Not far on the descent a tar-sealed branch to the left sweeps down to other flats and *wadis* used on lesser outings, a short run going to Al Hair on the Wadi Hanifa, whence an asphalt road runs about 30km to Riyadh.

The main Mecca road swings to the right, the escarpment on the right and, on the left, hills sand-smudged about their bases, the final scattered sandy remnants of one of the long fingers reaching southwards 400km from the Great Nafud, the huge sandy desert of the north. Clumps of tamarisks and palms ahead mark the little farms dotted about

PLATE 29

The four adjacent houses of a rich Saudi endeavouring to treat his four wives equally well.

1. *The Camel Trail zigzaging up the side of the Jebal Tuwayq escarpment, built by the Turks during their occupation.*

2. *A frontal view of the Camel Trail showing where it starts at the cars and reaches the top at the angle on the right.*

PLATE 31 249

1. *A view of the plateau at the top of the Camel Trail towards the gap in the hills through which various long journeys can be made.*

2. *The top of the Camel Trail with the Arizona-like peak and, far beyond, the flat horizon.*

1. *The highest point on the Red Sands nearly opposite the Camel Trail. A figure can just be seen on the left.*

2. *Lunch on a typical Friday (their Sunday) desert outing under a camel thorn tree with Dr George Russell of Aberdeen at ease in the centre.*

on the flats where pumped water is plentiful. On the right side, the side
of the escarpment, rises the great cup on its trellis mast for radio-
telephone by satellite to Jeddah, and on the edge of the plateau above is
a tall mast with a receiver to pick up the signals from Riyadh. The first
farm on the left is a ministerially owned horse-rearing establishment.
Some twenty kilometres on, the valley widens and in its middle,
pointing upwards, are fingers of eroded stone with webs of debris
between like a scene from the Arizona desert. On the right the
escarpment now rises as a sheer face carved by the heavy tools of time
into pinnacles and columns. At 55km from the centre of Riyadh, on our
left, a wide gap in the hills appears which can be used at these times for
runs on ancient desert tracks for 50-60km, or as far as you like.

To our right the line of the escarpment was unbroken but we could
spot on the scarred face a faint zigzag, the Camel Trail, a track winding
up the face which was built during the Turkish occupation to make a
shorter, direct route across the desert to Riyadh from the west, instead
of the longer two sides of a triangle taken by the old darb and the
present road we had just used. We turned from the main Mecca Road
towards the face about two kilometres distant, with strings of tracks on
the flat limestone pointing to the foot of the Camel Trail, and made our
bumpy way over small channels cut by waters after rains and between
scattered scrub and trees. A small herd of camel wandered about lifting
their heads in curiosity, and ignoring the occasional crow perched on a
back, making a meal of the ticks. We pulled up alongside half a dozen
cars of earlier arrivals and had a ration of ice-cool drinks before we
started on the climb. We were perspiring profusely, but in this hot dry
air with evaporation so fast, one is barely conscious of it while standing
about, but the thirst still needs to be satisfied.

Above us loomed the trail winding its way upwards by fairly gentle
slopes, well buttressed in places by laid walls of roughly fashioned
stones. We began the climb of about 800ft, Mike World, a young
physician in our party with years in his favour, being half-way up and
no stopping, while we sweated and stepped slowly over rubble and
rough-paved surface laid long ago in the time of the Ottoman Empire,
and where camels once languidly strolled upwards with their burdens.
David and I made four stops for breath and to wipe ourselves dry, for in
this late summer heat we were pouring it out faster than evaporation
could clear it away. In winter I made the same ascent with little sweat
and no stops. Even an estate agent would be at a loss for words about

the view from the top, with the cliffs ahead, the flats with their farms with bright green crops amidst the fawn terrain, the rolling flat-topped distant hills, a long finger of sand on the skyline, and down below us coalescing runnels marked out by dotted lines of desert scrub where traces of water near the surface permitted life. Specimens of Riyadh's universal population wound their way up and down in little knots while cars would come and go. Some wandered away back on the plateau where fossils were said to be plentiful, but we tottered down and settled for further fluid therapy. On several later occasions I was to revisit and to climb the trail, each time to be stimulated by this glorious view of the Arabian desert.

We returned across the track to the Mecca road and went on for 5km, then turned west to go past the oasis villages of Muzahamiyah and Ghatghat, the site of Abdul Aziz's second Ikhwan settlement, where a revolt by his warriors was smashed by him and the village razed. A pretty little village has grown up there again, populated by a number of men and youths who told me that their forebearers were Ikhwan. On another occasion when I drew up there at a small shop for drinks and a chat with the locals, Frank Murray of Portsmouth, on his first visit to the further-out countryside, was uncertain what to make of the local lads frisking about until one of them turned to him and in splendid English asked him where he came from, and on learning it was Portsmouth, asked, "And how is Bournemouth?" The spritely lad was a local schoolmaster and had recently taken classes in Bournemouth. Frank suddenly felt quite at home. This first day with David we drove on to the stretch of sand we had seen on the skyline from the top of the Camel Trail, the Nafud Qunafadah, and walked about on the endless dunes, but it was hot and we turned back a little to an oasis in the shade of a line of tamarisks where we opened our boxes of desert specials. Later we walked about the little farm behind the trees with its old adobe buildings, its pump and cistern and water irrigation channels. A late tea saw us steady enough for the slow drive back to Riyadh in thick traffic as night came on.

Another day, after visiting the Camel Trail, in the late afternoon we moved on to these sands which when lit by a low sun have a reddish hue and we call them the Red Sands. We climbed a largish sandhill to sit and look at the escarpment. Rain had fallen unusually early towards the end of October, enough to bring a hint of green to the middle and far landscape and to enliven the scattered scrub upon the sand where a shepherd had moved his flock of thirty, or so black with white-faced sheep which from a distance seemed to be nuzzling the bare sand. Unusually, several Arab families were on the sands, the father, two or three wives, and children in assorted sizes, the girls dressed in the brilliant reds, blues, and greens, in contrast to the long, plain, white, nightshirt-like thobe of the boys. Arabs are not noted for leaving their towns at the week-end, at which time they like to visit relatives and talk and eat, but more are beginning to enjoy the desert again. On this beautiful evening, like the best in a good English summer, they had left their cars by the roadside to sit on the sand and admire this great spread of landscape as the plain, the cliff-face and the blossom of clouds above played out nature's full repertoire of colour. The yellows, reds and blues of the day's end faded to the grey of evening and the silvery moon hinted that darkness would soon be on us. We lay long on the sands, saying little because nature was saying it all. Jerry Bevan had detached himself to scale his own higher peak and lay brooding on the majestic scene, while on a neighbouring peak three Arab boys had perched to look on their world at its best. One of them could contain his friendly instincts no longer and rushed over to join our own "stout Cortes" still silent on his peak, to offer his hand, cigarettes, and a thirst-quencher, and to sit and commune with this stranger in his land. We sidled grudgingly to our cars for a final round of liquids before making our way home along the Mecca road. That evening we were passed continually by cars and trucks piled high with people and paraphernalia, often lit with coloured lights as they journeyed on their way to Haj, the greatest concourse and the spiritual climax of the Muslim world, fifth pillar of wisdom, in which we had no part. But we had made our own pilgrimage that day to witness Allah's works as he has displayed them a million years now gone and, *"in sha lah"*, for a million years to come.

On yet another outing we crossed the same Red Sands which here are about thirty kilometres wide and continued beyond them until we were some seventy kilometres from the main Mecca road, then turned right towards a prominent rock on the plain close to an escarpment about two kilometres away. We were about 140km, away from Riyadh, having been on asphalt all the way except for the last two kilometres. The large rock had shattered, crumbled sides with some flat surfaces remaining on to which many curious, jumbled figures had been scratched including those of ostriches, now extinct in Saudi, with their young trailing along

1. *Pre-Islamic rock carvings about 140km from Riyadh. On the right modern Arabic has been written on top of an ancient carving of a camel with a very long neck like a giraffe, and a high hump.*

2. *Horsemen.*

3. *The rockface with the greatest number of carvings being recorded by some Italians with a professional touch.*

like a line of ducks, wolf-like creatures, other animals, and then line drawings of humans similar to those we made in early childhood. Many more were on the flat faces of the adjacent escarpment. No picture had a sexual motif that I could detect, certainly nothing to match the Cerne Giant of Dorset, perhaps indicating that the primitive artists were strongly under some influence keeping them on the straight and narrow, so possibly Muslim; but scholars rate them pre-Islamic.

Some Germans left soon after our arrival but shortly three Italians appeared, one with a camera and large tripods which he lugged up over the rocks and set up opposite the best face by a very fine piece of equipoise making our snapshot technique look pretty primitive. I wondered if he was going to use flash, ignoring the brilliant sunshine, and hoped that he got some good results after such a professional-looking effort. Ours were not too bad. There was not a tree that could provide shelter, so for lunch we put a canvas shade between the two cars and poured fluids into ourselves, but the heat was getting up and drove us home rather early.

Another time some of my friends, about ten in number, took a route through the gap in the hills opposite the Camel Trail, where we had also made various expeditions, and they went on some fifty kilometres along a *wadi* road, coming eventually to a small village where they stopped, and some small children came over and spoke to them. Shortly afterwards a man decked out in a bandolier full of cartridges and carrying a gun came towards them, causing a moment of concern, because he might have thought they were casting a bad spell upon the children. Not a bit of it. He had come to invite them all to his house as guests. They all went over to find a party of about thirty men sitting around drinking coffee and all kitted out in their bandoliers, criss-crossing their chests, and rifles on their knees. A trap? Again, not a bit of it. It turned out that this day the old man of the tribe was forsaking his office and handing over power to his eldest son and there was a celebration to mark the event. The mutton and rice were about to be produced, and they invited all the Europeans to join in the feast. Everyone sat down in the palm covered shelter with the children around, while the women, occasionally glimpsed in the back of the kitchen, prepared the meal but did not join in, though the European women were welcomed and feasted like the rest. Photos were allowed, and a few weeks later my friends made the trip again to present the results. They said they had never been more welcome anywhere. I was very sorry to have missed that day. As long as the desert holds the Arabs it will hold its surprises and lessons.

Another good *wadi* run is to go out on either the Mecca road or the Dir'iyah road and go from one to the other by way of the Wadi Hanifa. The *wadi* beds have always been ideal routes in most regions for crossing the country, like rivers in wet lands, and the route out of Riyadh by way of the bed of the Wadi Hanifa, running north-west and later west, was an old pilgrim trail or darb to Mecca and was walked or camel-ridden by innumerable pilgrims and others, walking being the holier way. If taking the Dir'iyah road out, one keeps to the main highway to Jubailah, some thirty kilometres, and here turns left and carries on for about twenty kilometres, passing through Uyaynah, the village of the original Mohammed Wahad; one turns off the asphalt on to the limestone of the Wadi Hanifa, very wide at this point and gradually narrowing until the Wadi Khumrah joins it six kilometres from the tar-sealed road, where the junction is marked by a block of cemented stones, appropriately known as the Mecca Stone. One of the tracks at the end of the drive up the Wadi Khumrah, which we did on other occasions, finished at the edge of the Jebel Tuwayq escarpment where an ancient water-course has gouged out a valley to leave a drop like a small Niagara, which must be quite a sight after a heavy rain, for even without water the whole landscape is superb. Here fossils abound in the limestone, and birds, lizards, scorpions, and a few camels, have it all to themselves.

The Wadi Hanifa climbs to the top of the watershed where there is a pass in the escarpment, and the track runs down the other side between spectacular cliffs, and mostly on flat stretches with what looks like an easy quick run to the Mecca road, and so it is if you take the right track, which I did not on one occasion, taking unawares a turn to the right which led me on and on parallel to the Mecca road in what seemed a journey to the moon, being more than thirty kilometres instead of the two kilometres by the correct darb. If one takes the right route one joins the Mecca road about twelve kilometres north of Durma, an expanding minor metropolis on the old oasis, on the run in to Riyadh. The round trip back to the city is about 180 kilometres. This pass in the escarpment is the only break for a long distance on either side, and save for the man-made Camel Trail up the face nearer Riyadh, is the shortest way, and so was the darb used by pilgrims going west which is still used by the locals, as well as visitors looking for a good day's outing.

PLATE 34   257

1. *Not all dashes over Saudi reach the other side, here I was stuck 6km out from the road and I had to leave the car in the desert for 3 days to await Frank Murray in his 4-wheel drive car to pull me out. I was aiming for the petrified forest.*

2. *Dickie Rees, standing, and Frank Murray in his 4-wheel drive; towing was successful but about ¼ hour later on our return Dickie stuck also and had to be hauled out.*

The "petrified forest" is another area of some popularity, favoured for souvenirs of long ago in the shape of lumps of petrified wood, small or a foot long, brownish and rather pleasing. With no trees about, it is more attractive for its fossils than as a picnic area.

* * *

Eleven in the morning was the appointed hour when I was to lead a caravan of cars to the desert. I collected my Indian assistant, Madhu, at her villa a few minutes before, and after a kilometre, true to tradition she remembered she had forgotten the present for the three-year-old's birthday which we were to celebrate at a desert barbecue. We set off again for our rendezvous, still without fear of being late, for when all the boxes of food, barbecue apparatus, fourteen children and twenty-six adults had been assembled by 12.30 p.m. just an hour and a half behind schedule and not bad going, we set off towards the Mecca road.

We were a multi-racial group: three Saudi families, Indians, Pakistanis, Egyptians and three Europeans, some forty in all including the youngsters. Those with young families to think of are not so adventurous as those younger or older without such obligations, and as I had already spent some time exploring the surroundings of Riyadh, as well as Saudi in general, I had been invited to take them to some suitable place for a barbecue, near sands for the children and a good shady place for lunch which is the main meal for Arabs and no puny affair.

When travelling with my European friends we have usually kept some sort of order behind a leader but this day my friends were dashing ahead of each other from time to time, perhaps a more interesting way of travelling. As we neared the Camel Trail, some fifty kilometres out it was my turn to spring ahead to line up the cars as the way ahead was unfamiliar to most of them. We went on another ten kilometres to the beautiful finger of sand dunes, the Nafud Qunafaydah. Here we all drew up and deposited ourselves on the dunes with the beautiful vista over to the escarpment behind us. We had already frittered away much of the lunch hour by delays, so we turned back four kilometres to an oasis farm where a long line of tamarisks gave shade and screened the breeze while its soft whispering made lunchtime music.

A wide clear area in front gave plenty of room for cars and for children to kick a ball and everything else. Then out came large mats

and barbecue devices and with much huffing and puffing the charcoal
eventually took light and some twenty fried chicken were on the way.
About 3.30 p.m. we attacked the vast spread of rice, salads and
everything to go with them, children first, and using mainly hands as
tools. It was worth waiting for. A very large chocolate birthday cake was
spirited up, the candles lit and blown out and thrice repeated, then
much singing of Happy Birthday to our three-year-old star, daughter of
Mikhtar and Denise Youssef. The cake vanished in many pieces into
eager mouths as tea was served. Such good food needed deep
consideration and appreciation, so only half a dozen could face the slow
walk to view the farm at our backs with its date palms, goats, water
pumps, and cistern, amidst a few adobe sheds near a house. We waved
to the old farmer who returned our greeting. The men had mostly
gathered round a game of chess with witty comments on the moves as a
champion took on the amateurs and the ladies chattered, and the
children climbed over cars and fell over everything, leaving a trail of
chocolate everywhere. It was extraordinarily friendly and welcoming.
Kindness is a deep Arabian characteristic and it was well seen that day.
I was later to have several outings with them and their consideration
and kindness were always outstanding.

    After two hours, a return to the sands for a romp was the general wish
and most of the debris was put into a sack-size thin elastic bag in the
back of my station wagon, which had so far served well for sleeping
babies, and was considered the only remaining space in any car. As we
heaved it in, it burst a little at the seam on one side. At the sands only
four cars turned up, but we climbed again for the exercise and the view
as the sun set, another glorious feast this time of colour, when another
car brought the news that the large American model of our anaesthetist,
Mohammed Saraj, had stuck back at the oasis, so we returned to give a
hand. Mohammed had tried to cross at a right angle the deep dip where
the desert land met the main road and had stuck fore and aft with the
large rear overhang embedded. He had to face some heavy-handed
humour for this was the sixth successive time on outings that his large
model had ended up stuck in some way in the uncertain desert tracks.
Much toil and jacking-up of the car had enabled some sand to be
scraped away at the rear end and rocks had been piled up in front of the
wheels to give the back a lift as the wheels rose on them; the jack was
lowered and Mohammed tried again without luck, so, with all the ladies
and children removed to a safe group, the men gave a heave at the back

of the car while Mohammed opened up full throttle. Stones flew, dust rose in a cloud into which Mokhtar, our Egyptian anaesthetist, whose shadow is no mere thread, disappeared from view and the car moved and was up on the bank to great cheers, while Mokhtar's outline slowly reappeared. A small, high-slung car has its uses in the desert.

We were now all sorted out and on our way through the approaching night to join the heavy traffic back to Riyadh. The bag in the back of my car had split open further and the aroma of that massive meal wafted around us; no adjustment of the windows would disperse it. In true British fashion, I was not prepared to dump such a mass of plates, paper, rice, bones and flesh by the roadside; no refuse heap or receptacle had yet shown up, we were in heavy traffic, and night had come. We stuck it out. Madhu said she felt a bit sick and wondered how such a splendid meal could smell like that. We survived to Riyadh where I took her to her villa and set off for my flat to dump it in the large bin provided by the city at our front door, a by-product of the clean-up-Riyadh policy which had just been embarked on by a British firm—and very successful too. Unfortunately, the bin was gone, doubtless appropriated by someone with his heart in the new campaign, two lids remaining as little recompense. However, the bins were recent innovations and the usual habit had been to dump everything beside the door, when twice a week, if lucky, a refuse round collected. That lot was not going to remain in my car, so I heaved it out with its burst side upwards and made to move away when the underside ripped apart and that lot went down my legs and over my feet, over the back of the car and scattered on the road. A quarter of an hour later it was in a great heap beside the door and I slammed the two lids over it leaving it to the experts in the morning and went into the flat for a bath and a profound night's sleep. I need not have bothered cleaning it up; as I came out of the door in the morning to go to work it was an impressive sight, outdoing anything the street had seen before. The cats and dogs had enjoyed their own barbecue that night and the final remains lay scattered across the pavement on to the road, clearly a job for the experts only, who through the day took it in hand and with a very hefty hint left us a fine new bin for the future. It was a splendid barbecue.

CHAPTER XXII

Sport in Saudi

Passing away the long hours in desert lands has always been something of a problem and in the past was dealt with mainly by indulging in food, sleep, talk, and sex of some sort or other. Arabs have never been disdainful nor dilatory about any one of these things.

Prayer, with its regular visits to the mosque, involves something more than giving praise to Allah, and a great deal of sociability is to be found among people coming and going to prayer. Since there are no pubs or clubs, the craving of men for shared activity has to be satisfied by other means, and before and after religious observances they exchange gossip and undertake a measure of business. Reading of the Koran between times was one of the few occupations for many Arabs, though some would spend time playing chess, and even the desert dwellers had a game which was a kind of draughts or chequers with squares drawn in the sand, using bits of camel dung as counters. The Prophet frowned on dice and games of chance: how deeply he frowned on the partaking of a little wine is less certain. But all is now changed with the change of life style. Means of transport and attending to it, whether camels or cars, has always given men much to argue about, and when a raid was in the air there would be, before and after, hours of "natter". The Arabic word for "let us talk" is *nattakallam* and the British soldier's "Lets go and have a natter" has undoubtedly produced our present slang word of "natter". Nowadays, cars have taken the place of camels for dashing about and promoting divertionary "natter".

Even in remote villages, what is happening in the rest of the world can now be followed on television to an increasing extent and what is not allowed to be seen is heard on radio. Now more sophisticated pastimes are indulged in. Small boys at school get training in football, during a period devoted to the sport each week, scheduled among the more conventional lessons. The youngsters are naturally quick in their movements, playing barefoot, and the small ones courageously tackle

262   PLATE 35

1. *Football is the most popular sport, schoolboys in the Asir have a weekly session at school.*

2. *Awaiting their turn on the football concrete pitch.*

3. *Any unused piece of ground will do for a game. These young men are playing in a park in Riyadh.*

PLATE 36 263

1. *With nowhere else to play, the streets serve well enough, as in Britain. But the accidents from the traffic are frequent.*

2. *Plenty of enthusiasm with shouts of 'Liverpool'.*

the large, while constant loud cries without which no game is ever played are reminiscent of past desert raids.

The Saudis are hooked on football, and are beginning to become keen on swimming, wrestling, and tennis, which are becoming quite popular with students. Private swimming pools are present in their ten thousands, but only slowly are public pools being constructed, and many have no opportunity for this best of all sports in a hot country. In Jeddah scuba diving off the reef is popular and swimmers in Riyadh baths train for it. Horse-racing is well established, and the camel is now being brought into use on the same race circuit, since there are no opportunities now of raiding. Amongst British expatriates rugby football in the winter has taken on well in Jeddah where there is a very keen league, a sandy surface keeping the injuries down but slowing the pace a little. Around Riyadh, rugby is almost impossible as the ground is nearly all a sandstone-limestone mixture and too hard to fall on, but cricket flourishes about Riyadh, especially with the Indians and Pakistanis and Sri Lankans. The favourite pitch is a stretch of old tarmac with some flat desert around it, better if unused but if still in use that presents no problems. A piece of matting goes down, some holes are knocked out for stumps and off they go, and when a car comes along the players in the middle stand aside to let it pass and then they get on with it again. The natural surface of the Nejd, thought too hard for rugby, is too soft for cricket even with a mat on its surface as the bowled ball does not rise high enough, and so asphalt with matting is needed. With the Americans at Aramco at Dhahran baseball flourishes.

In Riyadh, Jeddah and Dhahran the hard and sandy terrain allows a good game of golf with certain local advantages. The Riyadh Desert Golf Club is just over thirty kilometres north of the city, being on land reserved for the new airport which is building but will not be ready until 1984, or thereabouts, being a vast area of some 250 square kilometres of flattish desert. An enterprising American engineering contractor concerned with the new airport construction and a keen golfer, saw the chance of a few birdies and got to work on sketching out a nine-holer, later to be a full eighteen holes of 6,637 yards, and had his men scrape and roll out the fairways, the natural sandy or stony desert forming the "rough", the only disadvantage of "rough" being that the ball stops in its tracks after landing, while in the newly-rolled fairway a fortunate twang off the tee produces a result better than that on a flat downhill terrain in a British drought with a wind behind, and the

PLATE 37 265

1. *Pakistanis on a tar sealed road with a piece of matting at cricket.*

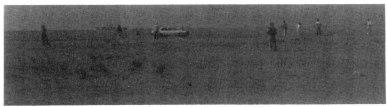

2. *When a car comes along the game stops long enough to let it pass.*

3. *One of several swimming pools and tennis courts at the Military Hospital in Riyadh.*

4. *In the foothills of the Asir mountains the space in the centre of this school (where the medical students were investigating) serves for football, volley-ball and net-ball.*

1. *The three main cities all now have golf clubs. Haddon Speakman of New Zealand is ready for it outside the air conditioned club house.*

2. *'Chuck' Ellis of the States usually beat me, but win or lose there was much enjoyment from being in the vast empty space.*

3. *Having landed on the 'brown' of small stones and oil, sometimes firmly rolled, but usually needing the T-bar as shown on the right to smooth a path from the ball to the pin.*

average smiter feels rather grand out-distancing a Nicklaus at his best on grass. Even a well-topped prod at a teed up ball, with the head well lifted up at the moment of striking, can result, in the absence of bunkers, in a nice slither towards, or even on to, the browns, There are ambitions to plant palm trees and shrubbery and to dig out deep bunkers as civilising touches but, for me, I am all for the wide open spaces with desert landscape all around, while a red ball on the immense fawn terrain even far off the fairway means a trivial hunt. I went three months before losing a ball. There is one snag, greens are but a memory and one plays to "browns"—small stones oiled to bind them a little—but the constant variations of browns are not known on grass. The browns are rolled and some pack down but some do not, so that the same pitch shot from about thirty yards can bounce across the green and finish ten yards the other side or, on another green, embedded deeply like a "sucker" on the edge of your own side. If you try to run up the ball, it may pull up sharply or run right across the brown.

To clear footmarks, a large T-shaped piece of iron piping is used to smooth the way from hole to ball, but no matter how hard you drag and smooth the surface the texture is such that the putt may finish halfway to the hole or as far again on the other side of it—not always but often. The browns would result in many suicides on the American Professional circuit, but if you allow an average of two or three putts and occasionally some four or five per hole, it will help to keep your hair on and add to the fun. After all, you can drive 360 yards and tee-up for every shot, so there are compensations.

If the soil on a desert course is predominantly sand then a little mat is carried and laid on the surface and a tee placed on it, usually the top of a mineral water bottle turned upside down. In the harder terrain around Riyadh mats as well as tees are used by many to save the club head from too much trauma when banged into the stony soil in spite of the tee, an art I rather excelled in.

To add further to the fun are a number of little mounds in sandy areas with vegetation and burrows into the sand, in which anything may lurk—desert rats, gerbils, sand vipers—though none ever sent me scampering off and surrendering the hole to my opponent. Scorpions can rest beneath stones, but not often, and camels will appear at times about the landscape and some are known to lie on the browns, turning on their backs to have a good scratch and perhaps get an oily applications to any mange. So far no golfer has succumbed to snake, scorpion or camel bite, and no handicap allowance is made for snake-bite, nor can anti-snake bite kits be purchased in the club-house.

This neat little building was put up by some enterprising engineer and contains perhaps the least attractive hole on the course—the nineteenth, where no shot is stronger than tea, coffee or "Saudi Champagne" (Pepsicola). But there is a pleasant air-conditioned sitting room, and a shop where the usual balls, red or white, and occasionally second-hand clubs are available, as well as T-shirts with remarkable claims printed on them and splendid golfing hats inscribed in large letters "Riyadh Desert Golf Club", Saudi Arabia, with a teed-up golf ball motif and a peak with as handsome a spray of leaves as any five star general ever sported.

Even if your well-struck drive has been known to finish up behind you after striking the concrete block of the ladies' tee or some stone ahead, or a momentary dust-devil creates a totally blind shot, there are shaded seats with water dispensers and paper cups at reasonable intervals.

Golf has a status connotation in much of the Far East, and there are many Korean members, pleasant and speedy players, who have a variety of original styles and come out with the customary sort of remarks after hitting the ball or failing to do so. No club would have any status at all if there were no Scots members to give it the stamp of authenticity by their patronage, and to liven the club-house with a good story, and there are various British and Irish and as well many Americans about. Some day we may hear the skirl of the pipes drifting over the stony, fawn fairways and browns. In summer months the Korean enthusiasm lives on through the heat, as they start their round at 4-4.30 a.m. to finish in good time for their day's work. At 40-50°C the snakes, scorpions and camels have it all to themselves at 9.00 a.m.

If you decide to join it will cost you 100 Saudi riyals throughout eternity, but each time you play you will assist the club by 10 Saudi riyals. When I joined at number 325 about a third of the members had gone home and at number 500 the membership will halt for a while. The club is amongst the most exclusive in the world, for you need a work permit for residence in Saudi Arabia and your name on a prospective list. However, wives and girl friends and other visitors can play as the guest of a member for 30 Saudi riyals at a time.

When I was leaving for Saudi Arabia I asked a group of golfers what club I should take and, quick as a driven ball, came an answer—a sand-iron! Strangely, this particular club I,did not use at all there because of the teeing-up rule, but with the threat of bunkers to come I would keep one handy. Saudis have not yet taken to golf, but in sport they are like the Indians and Pakistanis were about 150 years ago, and I am sure it will not be long before we see them thrashing away in some bunker calling on the assistance of Allah like all the rest.

Part Four

MEDICINE IN SAUDI ARABIA

CHAPTER XXIII

Some of the Medical and Surgical Problems of Saudi Arabia

Life in the desert was hard, precarious, and cheap, because of drought, famine, disease, and devastations by raiders. It has been estimated that four out of five infants died in the first year of life, mostly from diarrhoea and vomiting which causes a severe loss of fluids, irreplaceable in primitive conditions, and, with further loss caused by the great heat, quickly kills. It is still a very common disease in tropical countries, with a high mortality, not enough doctors yet realising, quite apart from public ignorance, that if water and salts are replaced promptly by a needle into a vein the infant has a fair chance of surviving, and that some of the medicines so commonly prescribed may do more harm than good, at least until the dehydration is corrected.

Effective treatment of the desert people in the past for any illness, other than some handiness in the management of wounds and fractures, was not obtainable, though, as elsewhere in those days, they had some herbs and other substances which by modern methods of assessment were not much better than impotent. However, in this respect they were no different from much of the rest of the world, in which a similar state prevailed, and even in the best centres of treatment there were few drugs that could provide effective help until the great upsurge of pharmaceutical endeavour in this century. Iron to help anaemias is as old as is belladonna from the deadly nightshade to help colic and cough, chalk to help some types of diarrhoea, and various vegetable products such as senna for constipation, mercury for some ulcers—and for syphilis brought to Europe by Colombus's crew as something new from America. Quinine for fever is another but much more acceptable present from the New World, digitalis for the heart from England in the seventeenth century, some leaf astringents and mild antiseptics for wounds in various countries, and the greatest of all and still the queen of drugs, opium, together with her offspring, long known for relief of pain; for severe pain there is no medicine to equal the effects of the product of the poppy. These are the main medicines remaining from a vast pharmacoepia of uselessness, and the rest have mostly dropped out of use. From the time of the introduction of anaesthesia in the forties of the nineteenth century and antiseptics in the sixties and so to this present century, doctors have become armed with hundreds of highly effective weapons.

The Arabs of the northern lands travelled widely and brought back much information from as far away as China, increasing their pharmacoepia with such preparations as ambergris, camphor, cassia, cloves, mercury, myrrh, nutmeg, senna and sandalwood. Apart from oil of cloves, which is used in dentistry (though could be more effectively replaced) and senna, still one of the best drugs for constipation, the rest play little effective part in therapy. The apothecary is an invention of the Arabs and so are the pharmacists' preparations of alcohol, elixirs and syrups, all words being derived from Arabic.

The Arab of the desert today has much more of this great range of modern medicines available to him by dashing off in his pick-up to the nearest town or taking the patient there, but he often comes rather late and often after a try with some of the traditional measures. It is likely that long ago the Arabs, especially in towns such as Jeddah and Mecca, had access to supplies of opium, but it is unlikely to have been available in the interior.

For the relief of pain they used instead an ancient, extraordinary method still widely practised today in the desert and villages, very simple and physical and in line with their environment, which must have something to recommend it in view of its long and continued use. They use the cautery to burn the skin over the site of pain with hot irons, and in a curious way it does seem to give some help. Without drugs, it has been their only trick. It was widely used by the ancient Greeks and Romans, and during the last century was in use in Europe, the surgeon to Napoleon, Baron Larrey, wrote a book on the uses of the cautery; his descriptions do not differ much from those of the Arab surgeon, Albucasis, in his extensive manual of over a thousand years ago. Today, many patients present themselves at hospital with a variety of complaints showing scars of burns, some old from former trouble, or recent from a recurrence of the same, or new ones, distributed over the sites of their pain, sometimes in patterns or just three or four points about the area.

The method is fairly simple: the village expert, perhaps the local wise man or the *hakim*, or another, puts his set of irons in the fire until red hot (and unlikely to be tested on the back of the hand of the expert), applying it to the victim, who in the old days was expected to bear it without flinching. In Larrey's description he makes a big point that if the irons are at the correct temperature the pain can be surprisingly little as the nerve ends are destroyed so quickly they stop registering. Judging from the extent of some of the patterns of present day applications there must be something in that, for it is hard to conceive how anyone could possibly stand up to it otherwise, and the victims of the cautery seem to behave much the same as the rest of the world in their reaction to a sharp needle. A party of British sailors shipwrecked on the Arabian coast last century were kindly cared for by the Arabs, fed on dates and milk, and on being taken ill were given the ultimate in hospitality by having their bellies cauterised. The ensuing traditional language of the sailors on such occasions was not recorded.

If we grant that the treatment may not be as devastatingly painful as we imagined, what is the point of it all? Does it do any good? Strangely, the answer is that it does appear to, for they still submit to it in large numbers rather than face possible surgery with a knife in a hospital, which may in contrast be painful. There is no accounting for taste, as even the Romans were known to have observed—perhaps while applying the cautery.

How does it work? Possibly one aspect is much the same as applying a hot-water bottle to the abdomen or back, or an ice-pack to a headache, and the hotter or colder the better. They are forms of counter-irritation which some say may do something to diminish or divert the nerve impulses in the spinal cord or brain from the painful area, or on the other hand they may be explained more simply by the idea that a new sensation or even a new pain will distract the mind from the long-standing one which has been tormenting mind and body. Lesser applications in the form of lamps, bottles, linaments, as well as cold by ice or a cold spray, are all thought to work in the same way. The direct effect of all these is only skin deep, while the source of the pain may be in the muscles or the bone.

A sufficiently long application of ice can act in quite a different way by cooling the whole limb, so that amputations have been done painlessly by this method, a good description of this also being given by Baron Larrey who used it when amputating the limbs of the wounded soldiers of Napoleon during the retreat from Moscow. Many a cold spray has put a footballer quickly in action again after a painful injury, and even the frightful pain during the passage of a stone from the kidney has been relieved by this treatment. The root causes continue, but the old pain is less noticeable. Distraction is an effective reducer of all lesser pains, whether in the shape of an interesting book, music, some company, the appearance of a loved one, an outing, or, if the pain is worse, an argument or a fight. Training the mind to ignore pain can also work for some, as with fakirs who sleep on nails, thrust needles through limbs or cheeks and generally enjoy themselves in ways excrutiating to others. Hypnosis will allow about a third of the population to undergo major surgery, without pain, while having no effect at all on another third. Acupuncture is a means of relieving pain in some and is thought by orthodox medical people on the whole to be a mixture of hypnosis and distraction, though its practitioners have other theories for such success as they achieve. So we must not condemn as barbaric the Saudis who use this strange method of burning by the cautery to relieve pain, when it has been for so long the only method that they have had.

One question that matters is, does it do any harm apart from creating delays in seeking better treatment? There are few effective treatments which, even if very rarely, do not produce some adverse features, but the cautery produces surprisingly few, other than undue pain and a temporary ulceration of the skin, which often becomes infected, and nothing like the debility and deaths which resulted from the bleeding used as a "treatment" for centuries in Europe. One bad complication from it arose in a patient whose condition was of general interest: I thought that with King Abdul Aziz's sons now ruling the country in their sixties that all the old King's early warriors had passed on, but one day an old patient, said by his elderly son to be 115, lay semi-conscious as we passed his bed; his right leg had been amputated through the thigh and his left showed an encircling white ring of scar around the calf. He was a very rare patient for two reasons, one medical, in that he had complained of pain in the calves on walking as older patients will when the arteries in the legs become hardened and narrowed with a consequent reduction in blood supply. He had been cauterised for the pain in both calves in the form of a ring of burning around them, the cautery going deeply on the right side and producing a thick scar down which in the way of all scars the skin gradually contracted and came to act like a tourniquet, cutting off the blood-supply so that leg went gangrenous from the line of the scar down and had to be amputated. The left leg showed a similar white band but the burn had been much shallower and had not produced as much scar. The non-medical reason for this patient's rarity was that this worn-out old hulk was all that remained of one of the *Ikhwan* (brethren) who had fought in seventeen battles with King Abdul Aziz and had lived at Ghatghat, the second of twenty settlements for his *Ikhwan* established by the King and the one which, when the inhabitants rebelled against him, he razed to the ground. The ruins of the old mud town are still there to one side of the present village and the old man must have been about the last human remnant of it all. My students were interested in the cause of gangrene of his leg, but knew little and seemed to care less about this aspect of their country's history. Their feeling for history is not strong.

The other question is—did cautery actually cure the disorders? Here the answer is almost certainly, no. Because the patient got better, they believed that the burning was the reason for it, and this is the great fallacy into which so many people fall, many doctors included. Something was done, the patient felt better immediately, or gradually became so; therefore it was due to whatever was done. We have seen that many pains are relieved by distractions or displacement from the mind, which is no cure of the underlying trouble. But many diseases are cured by nature's powers of healing within the patient, some to go forever, some to go and return at a later time, as with peptic ulcers as many sufferers know only too well, while headache, tonsillitis, the common cold, and rheumatic pains of muscles and joints, are amongst the most common to run a course, clear completely and return again. These natural cures are the basis of so many false "cures" from the stars, radio waves, and rubbing with an old sock, to Aunty's favourite herbs from the garden, and not excluding some quite firmly believed in by the medical profession for a time at least, both medical and surgical. The establishing of true cures involves a long, complicated process of testing by skilled investigators and at the end some with a very definite "Yes", some "No", and quite a lot as "uncertain", until repeated trials over a long time usually settle the issue.

Is there a definite answer to this system of the cautery still practised widely by the desert Saudis? This subject was discussed at the Saudi Medical Conference at Jeddah in 1977, and I can give no better opinion than that of an older much respected Saudi doctor who has seen it all and stated that the cautery had provided aid in times when there was no other method, but with the coming of better modern measures to relieve pain and to treat the illness, these should in time replace it.

Is there an answer to the hundreds of other "cures" which very often do help to relieve pain but which do not effect a cure of the basic trouble leading to the pain? Yes, is the very definite answer. In the end, if the disease is one which undergoes a spontaneous cure by the processes of nature, the patient is happy with his remedy and his return to health, but if it continues and worsens in spite of everything, he takes himself off to the doctor in fear or pain, which is why we see so many patients with the burns of the cautery, or, in the western world, a history of having had acupuncture or a visit to a psychiatrist. After all, we are much the same the world over, including doctors; we all want to funk it for a while in the hope that all will be well, and usually it will be. We try an aspirin.

Religious attitudes condition outlook, thus deeply religious Saudis may prefer to die, be buried and to rise in one piece on the Day of Resurrection, like some Christians, and so the removal of a large portion of the body such as a limb, even for gangrene, may not be acceptable. Numbers of elderly people may refuse any treatment, even life-saving, to die quietly at home, as anyone has the right to do in any country if that is their wish and they know the facts; but taking that attitude on behalf of their children raises great problems everywhere. As confidence in modern medicine grows these practices are changing.

Not all services are available throughout Saudi, but modern emergency treatment can be given almost everywhere, patients with advanced or special problems being transferred to city specialists. The unfortunate side of advanced treatment, as seen through western eyes, is that too many bigger hospitals want to have every service, with their own dialysis services for kidney failure, their own cardiac surgical units, and their own neuro-surgery, mainly because they can afford to have the buildings and equipment. However, to be effective the buildings must have brains within them, and to find highly trained staff—not just doctors, but also experienced nurses and technicians—for many scattered and similar units will be difficult if not impossible. A little less individualism and a greater amount of co-operation and concentration of services would appear to be more productive.

* * *

Because Muslims in general have the opportunity of making a fairly prolific score with the sexual act and its consequences, many are prepared to try for records, in numbers, with the money to pay for it, and they may well continue until nature puts a stop to it. Such are their sporting instincts that it is not uncommon to find men in their 70s and even 80s, though I never heard the 90s and 100s mentioned, coming along and complaining of sterility. King Abdul Aziz was no exception, being badly depressed in his later years, resulting in his becoming unproductive in the end. Sterility is a common enough complaint, with much of it not in the fading elderly but in the enthusiastic young who have never got started, some producing no sperm because of a variety of congenital defects, untreatable or never treated, or from past inflammations of the genital tract due to venereal diseases, bilharzia, tuberculosis, or even buggery. A great deal of neurosis is due to concern with sterility. Only some can be helped with treatment.

★ ★ ★

Stones in the urinary tract whether in the kidneys, bladder, or the tube connecting them—the ureter, are very common in all hot countries due to several factors. Some have a congenital disposition that way, but everyone, with sweating in the hot months causing great loss of fluid, has a much smaller output of urine which, in consequence, is high in salt content. During the hot weather one of my friends measured in himself this change and found that he was drinking an extra three litres of fluid in addition to his usual two or three litres, and his urinary output fell from the usual one and a half litres to about half a litre. He passed two small stones during his stay, and none before or since. As well as this fluid change, abnormalities of calcium (lime) absorption result from changes brought about by excess sunlight, possibly the high sugar intake from the frequent cups of sweet tea and sweetened minerals, as well as the high carbohydrate content of their modern diet of everything that the world has to offer, and with an excess of sugar in the diet calcium is absorbed from the gut in larger amounts. The moral is, drink plenty of water in the hot weather and increase the amount of salt in the food to make up for that lost by the excess sweating. There is no need to add the salt to the water, which makes it rather sickly-tasting, unless a very heavy bout of sweating causes a little dizziness, when an emergency addition of salt to a glass of water can work wonders.

Addition to the food is, in the ordinary way, enough. Another cause of an increase in urinary stones the world over is the present rich diets that people in a greater part of the world can now enjoy; an increase of uric acid stone is running parallel with these richer diets. The foods now available in Saudi will do nothing to lower the incidence of uric acid stones.

The surgery for stones is fairly straight forward in the hands of well-trained surgeons and most of its goes well enough, but if the kidneys are excessively damaged from the effects of the stones and even have to be removed in advanced stages of disease, resulting in little or no production of urine, the patients must have the blood cleared by the process of dialysis. There are several centres in Saudi where renal dialysis can be given to patients and their lives extended, but that is not the end to available treatment, for there remains renal transplant surgery which has been long discussed and is now being performed by the live donor method, that of a suitable close relative giving one kidney. The surgical process of putting someone else's kidney into a patient is not a particularly difficult operation and is well within the skill of most surgeons engaged in the usual run of major surgery, but the difficulty arises in trying to match trained staff with expensive medical facilities, and the operation has little chance of success without this and without the many other essential measures needed. Procuring kidneys to transplant is a major difficulty in Saudi where there is a religious antipathy to the disturbance of a dead body by a post mortem, so the main source of kidneys from patients dying from accidents is not available. Kidneys, like so many other needs, cannot be bought in Saudi, for there is a world shortage of kidneys and each country has to provide its own requirements, or eventually make good the loan if kidneys are borrowed from a kidney bank serving several countries. However, live kidneys from relatives can be used if the kith and kin are more helpfully disposed than some, and come forward in sufficient numbers, for any old kidney from any old relative will not do, and there are many difficulties, including a correct typing, as with the kidneys from unrelated persons derived from post-mortems. All these matters are, as it is often put, under consideration, and meanwhile live-donor transplants are being done. Word received in 1985 is that King Fahad, very recently, has granted permission for the use of cadaver kidneys.

Some of the bacterial diseases are more common in the tropics as everyone knows is the case with the dysenteries. Surprisingly, one disease often thought to be the result of cold and damp aggravating the invading germ, rheumatic fever, is common in Saudi, many cases of rheumatic heart disease being seen where the valves of the heart are extensively damaged and require surgery; more of that later. Protozoal diseases are seen particularly in the form of amoebic dysentery, with liver abcesses needing drainage by surgery, leishmaniasis of the skin (two cases cropping up in the European population known to me), while malaria is rife in the south-western part of Saudi, the Asir, where the mountains are high and the frequent rains create pools where in the warm climate the mosquito breed freely. We would see the occasional case in Riyadh and would be on the look-out for it in patients with large spleens. In the first expedition from Europe 200 years ago to visit the coast of the Asir and the Yemen from which most of our patients come, Niebur was the only one to survive out of the six sent out by the Danish King, and he wrote a fine record of their adventures describing how three caught the fever, ascribed then to staying out in the cold air and getting a chill, and died from what is now recognised to have been malaria.

Madura foot, due to an organism somewhat akin to the ray fungus of actinomycosis, we would see occasionally, resulting from the germ entering a small break in the bare skin of the foot. I saw about eight patients in five years in Saudi but one doctor, Dr. Sheikh Majoub, had seen scores. There is a medicine useful in early cases but amputation of the foot is the commonest answer.

Worms, whether living in the intestine or getting into the tissues of the body, are more common in the tropics, and two are noteworthy. Country districts have their familiar and reassuring sounds similar to the bird-song that can be heard throughout England, the pipes from the hills of Scotland, the rivulets of the Welsh valleys, and the lowing cattle of Ireland. In Saudi it is the chuff, chuff, chuff of the old Blackstone diesel engines bringing up the water from the depths of the *wadis*, a very pleasing sound on a hot day and most reassuring as it reminds one that this deep water is quite fit for drinking, if sometimes a little salty, being fresh, cool and free from dangerous germs and worms. Riverless Saudi has always relied on wells, and any danger from the water comes later and is the result of contamination.

How different from the hot countries relying on rivers where the banks are breeding grounds of many forms of life and surface contamination is common. Thanks to her underground waters Saudi has been almost free until recently of one of the great diseases of the tropics, bilharzia or schistosomiasis, whereas in Egypt with its Nile, and in the Yemen, that land at the end of the Arabian peninsula of mountains from which rivers run down nearly to the sea, the disease is endemic and has been since recorded time. An Arab of one of the northern states with a poor opinion of Egyptians scathingly wrote to his master about 1,200 years ago that "even the men menstruate", referring to the blood coloured urine passed by sufferers from the disease. It is caused by a minute swimming worm which passes through the skin, especially that of the hands or feet of those working in water or even bathing or paddling in pools. It sheds its tail after penetrating a little vein and is carried by the blood to all parts of the body, but only those lodging in the liver survive.

What happens then is one of the great love stories of the world of worms and is worth telling. The survivors of the first stage of one of the most extraordinary of journeys, now marooned in the liver, are not short of rations, for sustenance is all about them. They gobble up the surrounding red cells of the blood and make a home in it, slowly changing into worms, about one or two centimetres long, living two to three years—a male, short, broad and knobbly with a sucker at each end, and a female, appropriately slender and smooth but a little longer, with two weaker suckers although up in front. Now they have grown up some of them leave the nest and go swimming together down the great vein draining into the liver where they get ideas and, to make the rest of the journey more of an Anthony and Cleopatra affair, the male turns himself into a small canoe by curling his ends towards each other which causes a little cosy gutter along his length into which the female nestles for the rest of the trip. It is hard to believe. Thus the loving pair make their own Nilotic passage paddling their way upstream by stages, anchoring to the vessel walls for the night as the mood takes them by means of the male's suckers. On and on they go in their vermicular idyll out of the main stream at last to find their way through tiny venules and, depending on their affinity, some types go to make a final home in the bladder wall (*schistosoma haematobium*), others preferring the wall of the large bowel and rectum (*schistosoma Mansoni*). With the pair now wedged tightly in a little vein in the bladder or rectum the lady decides to go it alone and pushes on until she is once again snugly tight, and though she is still slender, suspicions about her are quite correct, she is with egg, and she proceeds to lay a chain of them. Some eggs with the help of their sharp little end penetrate the vein and go on right through the wall of the bladder lining, resulting in a little bleeding, hence the blood in the water. If the worm is of a different type which prefers the bowel, the same process goes on, only the blood may be hidden in any ensuing diarrhoea. In either case the eggs are then cast forth in urine or stools, wherever the previous owner (mostly in men) chooses to relieve himself, but that is not the end of it.

Within and about river banks and pools of casual water may live fresh-water snails of various sorts, one particular variety being just what the little eggs are wanting. As soon as the eggs are in fresh water their covers burst and a little creature covered in fine moveable hair-like structures emerge. These are gobbled up by the snail where they, too, like their forebears go for the liver, where myriads of further cysts are produced, and on the death of the snail they are liberated into the water. Each one of those, in nature's lavish way, produces thousands of little worms which wiggle about waiting for an unsuspecting worker or swimmer with a nice piece of skin to penetrate, and that is where we started.

This most extraordinary odyssey with its various metamorphoses goes half the way in some 200 million people at any one time in the world according to the World Health Organisation in 1965, and creates a vast toll of ill-health and loss of life for thousands. The Japanese have their own variety of worm (*schistosoma Japonium*) which is now endemic in some neighbouring countries and, like Mansoni, settles in the bowel and tends to produce rather severe symptoms. *Japonicum* is associated with an interesting social history, for, as D. R. Bell puts it, China used to be a major area, but thoughts of Chairman Mao are claimed to have eliminated the problem, while in Japan it is becoming uncommon, partly due to golf, for golf courses have often replaced previous damp transmission sites.

As doctors we see the effects of the worms and eggs upon the various organs invaded, livers blocked by scarring in quite young men and even some in their teens, the blockage causing excessive vomiting of the blood. Operations can help some for a time and though the liver cells may be otherwise healthy the scarring is so severe life is much reduced. Similarly, the urinary tract may be scarred so badly that the bladder is destroyed and may need removing, stones form in the kidneys and bladder, cancers of the bladder may come on and other organs may be destroyed.

In spite of the pure waters of Saudi, I saw many cases of bilharzia, like my colleagues, producing damaged livers and urinary tracts, and the numbers are rising. How does this come about? The dark villains of the piece are the invaders, some Saudis themselves from the south-west bottom corner, the Asir, the land of mountains and rains where the snails essential to the cycle breed, and whose inhabitants have spread over much of Saudi to get more lucrative work, and those coming from outside Saudi, the Yemeni from mountains, and the Egyptians whose Nile banks are fertile breeding grounds for the snails. Invaders bring their diseases with them and this is about the worst, though some might say that gonorrhoea and syphilis that sneak in also are as bad. In areas where there is casual water as in some oases, anyone casting excreta carelessly and carrying the disease can set the cycle going, for investigations have shown that the necessary snails are already there.

The problem is to be tackled by regions testing for carriers and treating them. Whether an attempt to eliminate the snails is possible or practical is being considered, as is the question of examining for carriers on entry at immigration. Whatever is to be done "'twere well it were done quickly" before the disease becomes endemic. It is a sad sight to see a youngster, with his anxious relatives about him, vomiting up his life-blood, while we can do little to help him.

* * *

Any country which has sheep, goats, cattle, and camels, along with mankind, as well as the dog—man's friend in some countries but not especially in Muslim ones which, with some justification, have always regarded the dog as unclean. The hydatid worm has two parts to its life-cycle, like the bilharzia worm, only this time it is the dog which harbours the worm and casts it forth in its bowel motion to become scattered by the elements on to possible food such as grass or fresh vegetables, or just on to the hairs of the dog who when handled in affection passes them on, and subsequently they can enter the mouth. Sheep, goats, cattle and camels can also act like man in the second part in the cycle. When the eggs enter the digestive tract they can finish up in any part of the body, most commonly the liver or lungs, where they may grow into cysts from tiny to big as a turnip, and from one to hundreds. The completing phase of the cycle is when a dog eats the offal of sheep or goat, cysts or portions of them can be included and the whole thing starts again. I spent a lot of time operating on hydrated cysts in Saudi, for all the elements are there. As a medical student and young doctor in New Zealand in the 1930s I saw numbers of the cases, for it was a common disease then, but my NZ colleague in Riyadh, urologist, David Mee, also an NZ graduate, who was having a break for a year from Hamilton told me it is now a very uncommon disease, and he had seen only two cases, both those being in Cambridge, England! This clean-up is due to a remarkable pursuit of the worms by public health doctors and officials, which had started when I was a student. Dogs are purged with great regularity, about every three months, to get rid of the worm, and they must not be fed casual lumps of offal. Generally, every step to combat each phase of the life-cycle has been taken. New Zealand has about three million humans, 60-70 million sheep, large numbers of dogs, but few goats, and in an ideal breeding ground the disease has been practically eliminated. Saudi has plenty of resources. It is up to them.

★　★　★

One of the main causes of death and disaster in Saudi is road accidents, a world-wide problem, and where so many drivers from 12 years old upwards, untrained and unlicenced, jump into large powerful cars and drive off, the casualty rate is bound to be high. Let us face it, in all countries no matter what their laws, religions, or motives, some alcohol is found, and alcohol is found to be a contributory cause in too many accidents in Saudi. As well as their concern for the religion and law, the authorities are gravely concerned at the consequences of drinking and driving. With present driving at its best exhilarating, at its worst a nightmare, I cannot but see that drinking makes it much worse. As in all countries, the usual other factors, including the state of the roads, of the machines, and of the drivers and the speed at which they travel, have to be considered also.

Health statistics in Saudi are difficult to come by with any accuracy and trying to trace the health of Saudis, quite apart from the very large and rapidly changing expatriate population of all nations, is very nearly impossible. As for getting an accurate follow-up on treated bedouin, chasing them all over the desert with one of those overpowering questionnaires containing a hundred questions, such as, "When did you last belch?", with a choice of six possible responses, there is not much chance of success, for generally you will not find your quarry, and if you should, he will not know what you are talking about (and he might just be right for they are no fools). I remember Sir Thomas Carey-Evans, son-in-law to the former Prime Minister, Lloyd-George, and a surgeon of note in Iraq and other places in peace and war, speaking at the end of a lecture concerning a vast analysis of the belches, rumbles, and general dyspeptic symptons of a shipload of lesser gastric sufferers, with charts and with figures to the nth degree. He said that statistics were no doubt wonderful but not always easy to obtain, and he recalled how one day, when he was in the desert with his tented field-hospital, a bedouin was brought in with a completely blocked outlet to his stomach from a chronic ulcer; after restoring him, they operated and relieved the obstruction and put him to bed in a tent—the only patient, complete with intravenous drips, hot-water bottles and the lot, and retired for the night. A chance for such an operation in the desert, even any operation, was uncommon at the time, and they rather celebrated. In the morning they got up to see how their patient was progressing. He had recovered fast, very fast, there being no sign of him. In fact, there was no trace of the whole hospital, for during the night the Arabs had quietly stolen the lot. "Talk about a follow-up," he said, "I never saw the patient again, nor the hospital either."

In spite of the difficulty of obtaining accurate statistics, it becomes fairly easy to get a general pattern of the frequency of most diseases after a time when you are living among those who have them. I have looked after patients in the teaching hospital, the King Abdul Aziz, and taught in the emergency hospital of the city and district, the Shameisi or Central Hospital, and in the Military Hospital, and have seen a good cross section of the admissions. Also we all spent many hours talking about health matters. All this put me in a good position to give a reasonably accurate impression of the disease patterns, right from the top.

The much-famed eyesight of the bedouin, if it ever really existed widely, does not seem to have been transferred to the towns. Opticians flourish and Saudi men and women of all ages wear glasses in what seems to be much the same numbers as in Britain. About a third of my classes, both men and women, wore glasses. Cataract, aggravated in its development by the bright sunshine, is common, as in other sunny countries. Sir Richard Burton noted that cataract was treated by roasting mule's teeth and administering the powder. They do better today with modern surgery. Noses are much troubled by the dust of Riyadh, with rhinitis common and nasal polyps abounding, while good business is done in hearing aids. Trachoma is rampant, nearly everyone being affected in some districts, and it causes much blindness. Goitre as simple, nodular, toxic, cancers and rarer forms kept us surgeons about as busy as in Britain.

Cancer of the gullet as well as cancer of the stomach seemed to be of about the same frequency as we were used to, but cancer of the large bowel and rectum, one of the commonest cancers of the west, is so uncommon as to be rather an event when one saw a case. In Oxford, my assistants and I might see thirty or more cases in a year and other surgeons could be seeing like numbers, but in my first year in Saudi I did not see one patient with a cancer of the colon. On the other hand lesser diseases of the rectum and anus such as piles and fistulae are very common, but, to my knowledge, none of the surgeons saw a case of diverticulosis in that year—all of this very much to the confusion of those who say it is mainly a matter of roughage; eat bran and you will have a healthy large bowel and rectum! There has been much thought given to food but there is still much food for thought. Acute appendicitis is very common and the rich diet may have something to do with it, who knows?

Duodenal ulcers are frequent enough, and rather contradict the theory about worry and overwork, for Saudis are not given to either if they can avoid it. No one knows the basic cause of duodenal ulcer though we know, or at any rate believe, that worry and overwork make the symptoms and possibly the ulcer worse, as they do with other diseases. As much is left too long we had to do rather more cases of pyloric stenosis than at home.

Hernia at the groin is common but there is not the great frequency of hernia at the navel seen in Africans.

Gallstones are common, too, seeming to be about the same in numbers as in the west, perhaps due to the western diet, available in full measure with shops stuffed with all that the food suppliers of the world can think up. Gallstones occur in women who have not borne children and in men in about the same numbers, but, once the children arrive, women come in greater numbers with their gallstones. Fair, fat, fertile, forty, and female, is an old adage of British medicine to depict gallstone sufferers, and this is a rough average syndrome in Britain, where fair complexions, predominate, or did so once, and the other four points are also likely to be found. But in Saudi nearly all gallstone sufferers are dark, often thin, and any age after thirty, with again, fertile females predominating. A one-time generalisation was "a tooth a child", because of dental caries in the mother rendering up her calcium, rightly or wrongly assumed, and now that teeth are better looked after we might generalise in the same way, "a gallstone a child"; the large families, produced even by one woman in Saudi, might be responsible, with the help of the right diets, for the rise in the gallstone population. How many gallstone sufferers there were before modern times we have no means of knowing, but gallstones were forming a long way back—they have been found in Egyptian mummies of the ancient variety—but if the bedouin had them they just had to suffer, were probably cauterised with no curing effect, and many of them would die from the complications.

Cancer of the lung is, in contrast to the West, very uncommon, but the Saudi youth seem to be doing their best to change this, for they are heavy smokers on the whole, and it will be interesting to see what the next twenty years turn up. Chronic bronchitis, as seen so frequently in the cold, foggy, industrial countries (the English disease) is uncommon, though tuberculosis of the lungs and elsewhere in the body is common enough, a programme for eradication being not yet fully underway. Tuberculosis yields a harvest of cases for the bone surgeons busy with operations they have nearly forgotten with the success of the vaccination programmes of the West.

Older men develop enlargement of the prostate gland both benign and malignant in what appears to be about the same numbers as elsewhere, and there is modern apparatus to deal with it.

Cancer of the breast is less common, in contrast to its great frequency at home. I saw two patients in one year in contrast to perhaps 30-50 a year in Oxford. Some say that this is due to the high fertility rate, for cancer of the breast is more common in nullipara, but Saudi has its share of spinsters and those with few children. Most women would appear to suckle their children and so keep the breasts at their function. Analysis of data is difficult.

Cancer of the womb is very uncommon compared to that seen in the women of the west. This is attributable to several factors which may have something to do with it, but so little is certain about cancer in general. Some say that the womb is better for being put to use early and often, like the breast. Some say that in the circumcised male the smegma bacillus, said to be a trouble maker to the womb, is absent. It is said that venereal disease, though it occurs, is very uncommon in Saudi and that the incidence of chronic inflammation of the mouth of the womb is low; it well may be so, but venereal disease does occur, though it seems to be less frequent in Saudis. Other Arabs seem to have their fair share.

Diabetes is common, and whether it was before the change to the modern diet cannot be known, though it did occur. One test for it was to put out in plates two lots of urine, one from a healthy person and one from the suspect of *sukkari* (sugary), their Arabic for diabetes. The plates were then watched to see which one the ants would go for, if either.

Arteriosclerosis is rare and to see gangrene of the leg from atherosclerosis is extremely rare, but diabetic degeneration of the small end vessels occurs as elsewhere so that gangrene of toes and feet in diabetics with the ankle pulses easily felt is common enough. Degeneration of the coronary vessels is equally uncommon and so coronary "thrombosis" is rarer, while on the other hand rheumatic disease of the heart is common. The gradual effect of the introduction of so many items of western diet will be interesting to follow.

Mental disease is quite prevalent, my colleagues told me, but there is only one mental hospital in the whole of Saudi, in Taif. Mental disease is generally treated as it is in the rest of the world today by using the many wonderfully helpful new drugs. The lesser depressions are common enough, as are neuroses, while the severe mental cases are sometimes admitted to a local hospital for a short period, but must then be managed at home or admitted to the Taif Hospital.

Snake bites and scorpion bites are very uncommon considering the many thousands of bedouin, and the many foreigners, wandering about the deserts, and these have been commented on elsewhere.

★ ★ ★

In the medical school my main job was to organise and do my fair share of the teaching of surgery to the students, as well as sitting on various committees concerned with the curriculum and the new hospitals. In the hospitals my task was to help upgrade anything and everything, where necessary and possible, concerning the surgery of both in- and out-patients, and also to undertake postgraduate instruction; the method is the usual "what is worth doing is worth doing well" but also worth doing slowly. Nobody anywhere likes new or old brooms raising too much dust in the sweeping, and eastern peoples have a penchant for the slow approach. Sudden and drastic changes are likely to meet with lack of co-operation or opposition. *Festina lente*, says the Latin tag, "hasten slowly". Thanks to excellent anaesthesia aid given by my colleagues, Mohammed Saraj and his assistants, and not just in the theatre but before and after operation, we were doing any and all of the operations I would have done in Britain, as were my other colleagues, save for a few exceptions due to lack of complicated apparatus which will be available in the new hospitals or extensions. However, much depends on the provision of blood for possible transfusing, which can be a little constricting. There is no blood bank, and any major operation must have blood ready for possible transfusion, by hospital regulation, which means that every Uncle Abdulla and Cousin Mohammed has to turn out at the immediate relative's request, and thus to a degree plays his part in the operation. The system has its points but with no bank to draw on and the relatives, at times, somewhere out in the desert, proceedings can be more than a trifle delayed. Again, when new laboratory premises are available this will be put right.

Another of the difficulties in catching your quarry and getting him to theatre. This is a fairly easy procedure in Britain, but in Saudi and other places, a patient, having had your advice, may stomp off and consult other doctors until he gets an answer favourable to his own ideas, or just disappears to let nature take her course, as already explained. He may come back to out-patients again and then disappear, or he may be booked to come in for an operation at an exact time there and then, as writing or telephoning are "not on", he probably cannot read a letter which may well not reach him anyway, and he will not be on the telephone in his village or oasis. Just as in Britain at holiday time when a bed is left vacant—but every day is a holiday for him in this respect in Saudi—he decides not to come in for various reasons or none at all, then turns up two weeks later demanding a bed; or, again, he may come in but flee the hospital any time from shortly after arrival to just before the operation. Some are known to think twice or thrice at the operating theatre door and run, but that is rare, because with the steadying preoperative injection in him he is by that time relaxed, carefree, and ready to stay for more.

I have already explained that amputating a limb may not be acceptable on religious grounds, but the same argument does not seem to apply to the loss of tonsils, or appendix, a large piece of gut, and half the liver, over which the veil of the abdominal wall is closed—"out of sight, out of mind" is a help. Another aspect where religion impinges on procedures never entered my head until a Saudi colleague pointed it out to me. A simple operation for piles is to do a forced stretching of the closing muscles of the anus, which cures most, but like the operation for removing the piles, may leave a few patients a little weak in the control of wind, at least for a time. My colleague warned me off the stretching operation, for in prayer in the posture of bending over fully the uncontrolled noisy passage of wind would be a serious social solecism and might lead to expulsion from the mosque in retaliation; and, if misunderstood and thought to have been done in a light-hearted mood, it might mean exile from the country. In early Victorian England the punishment for such a mishap in church may well have been similar, and who knows how many Australians owe their present wide acres and millionaire status to the inadvertent release of wind on a Sunday morning by an ancestral farm worker when the sound of the organ had died away. Even today in most parts of Britain, if not all, anyone guilty of such a breach of social conduct would be put several pegs down on the social hat stand. I settled for other techniques.

★ ★ ★

Most Saudis are appreciative of attention but it is not their way to show it or express it effusively, for it is their belief that we are but the instruments of Allah who is responsible for everything; he gives, he takes away, and our thanks are due to him alone. As death, whatever its mode, is due to Allah, the death certificate, compared to the British one with its attention to statistics, is the essence of non-bureaucracy—just the late patient's name, the date of death and the doctor's signature. Many a hard-pressed British colleague would welcome it.

All the same, Arabs are very kindly, generous and interested in any event, whether an argument or a celebration, all wanting to join in. It would be more than bad manners to say, "mind your own business", or to infer that this is a matter for oneself and the other man only. Sometimes much appreciation is shown, as when I operated on the close relative of a lay high-up who, when we were changing, came to the surgeons' and anaesthetists' little sitting and changing room, and took tea with us; then we left the anxious man to go and take out the gallbladder, which, no sooner out, one of the group of my colleagues who are apt to crowd the top end of the table, took it away to show the gallstone to the relative. When I had finished and went through to the sitting room there was a burst of acclamation and much joking, tea and cakes were produced and the noise reached a pretty high level, without regard for the surgeon who needs to rest before the next operation. Just then a workman began to make a hole in the wall with one of those screeching electric drills and the decibels fairly rocketed up. One or two gave a glance at the workman, but as most Arabs seem to like noise from childhood upwards, it appeared to be much the same as a band striking up. I could no longer hear what anyone was saying, but it had clearly been a very jolly operation.

I had several times to ask for quiet in the operating theatre, reminding them that they might be waking up the patient, who does count in an operation (!), and twice I had to put everything down and command silence and direct all those assisting to do their allotted task and not everyone else's, before I would continue, It is just normal behaviour for them, and all is well meant, but it can hamper concentration at times.

A high-up lady came to see me with indigestion, accompanied by an elderly male attendant, for such ladies do not go out without some such chaperone. The old man was interested in every detail of the interrogation, interjecting comments and questions of his own, and at the end piped up that he had indigestion, too, and asked me to see to him then and there, which I did with the lady's willing agreement. I gave him a full consultation and sent him off to have the X-rays he was needing, thereby showing the lady how harmless they were by his "butting in", as we would see it. She did not see it that way at all; he was considered to be a part of the family and entitled to his say and time. Arabs are seldom stuffy.

* * *

Open heart surgery is a process whereby the blood is circulated around the body by an artificial pump and is re-oxygenated by an artificial lung, both part of the same piece of apparatus which is connected by tubes to the vessels entering and leaving the heart. This allows the heart to be stopped, then cooled to preserve its vitality, and so opened to permit essential surgery to the valves or walls; it has become a routine now in many countries. Closed heart surgery, with its limitations on what can be undertaken, had been practised in Riyadh, and in an American-run hospital at Khamis Mushait, in the Asir, a US team had been coming for a month at a time to perform open heart work. In the meantime, the authorities had been preparing everything for open heart surgery at the King Faisil Hospital in Riyadh, that successful blend of a hospital with the environment of a luxury hotel, where Saudis can get modern hospital treatment. Though primarily intended for Saudis, "the Faisil" will provide a service for anyone who cannot get elsewhere in Riyadh a particular requirement, such as radiotherapy. Cardiac surgery is also now well established at the military hospital of both Riyadh and Jeddah.

We had learnt on our arrival in September 1977, that a team of US surgeons, nurses, and technicians were coming to "the Faisil" from the cardio-vascular centre in Houston, Texas, but a further eight months went by while an operating theatre and other facilities were being completed. Then the news went round that the organiser of the project, a world famous cardio-vascular surgeon, Dr Michael de Bakey, was coming to town. I had first met Dr de Bakey some fifteen years earlier in Houston when I was a member of a surgical travelling club, paying a visit to his clinic on our way to a surgical meeting in the West Indies. He is Lebanese derived, and the Arab world are rather proud of his achievements, as they are also of the Egyptian, Mr M. H. Yacoub, one of the best cardiac surgeons in Britain.

De Bakey had the reputation of being a tense, fastidious, dynamic and skilful surgeon, difficult to serve and to satisfy, and renowned for sacking about half his interns on the spot. Dr Hisham el Roomy, one of the Saudi surgeons in Riyadh, had several years before worked in Houston as one of de Bakey's assistants, and he told me of an occasion when he was for no good reason on the receiving end of a tantrum and told to clear out. Hisham stood his ground, looked hard at his chief and said, "I've come 7,000 miles to work with you and I'm not going." He got the long stare himself for a moment, then de Bakey smiled and said, "OK, you're staying," and they got on splendidly after that.

The strain of operating, teaching, writing and research as well as the inevitable committees comes out in different ways, and to survive a job with de Bakey was said to be an achievement in itself. One wonders: this attitude may bring technical discipline, but that can also go with patience and encouragement and self-discipline, and at a moment of crisis a team will give the necessary concentration demanded by a leader. Too much rigidity caused by fear can freeze young, impressionable minds. His chief assistant at the time was Denton Cooley, also a very skilful man, but gentle and relaxed, who has come to share world fame for his exploits, and the pair of them gave much merriment to the world of surgery for the colossal row they had when, inevitably, the younger man felt that the time had come to go his own way. Everyone grows up sometime, as parents and teachers know only too well. The details are for the the surgical inner circle and have nothing to do with the fact that both men are fine surgeons, dedicated, innovators and leaders. Many American surgeons have the reputation of being painstaking but slow, with notable exceptions of whom de Bakey is particularly noted. In Houston, in one morning we saw him rattle off three operations for aneurism of the abdominal aorta, all done well, one case in a morning usually being enough for the average surgeon. When you have done a thousand cases it gets easier!

The team in Riyadh had got everything in readiness and de Bakey had arrived to check the whole set-up and to operate to put it to the test, then leave the team to carry on. I went over on the second morning, the case being similar to, but less marked than the last one I had seen him operate on in Houston fifteen years previously, congenital pulmonary stenosis in a boy. The operation in Houston was difficult, causing a high-born lady spectator on the floor of the theatre to faint. His long-time, very senior assistant who would be staying on in Riyadh to head the team was opening the chest by splitting the breast-bone down its length and then opening the outer thick membrane of the heart, the pericardium, and getting on with the attachment of the tubes to the great vessels from the artificial heart. I had changed and was on the theatre floor chatting with de Bakey during these preliminaries, and he recalled our visit to his clinic when the late Arthur Dickinson-Wright of London, renowned as much for his wit as his surgery speaking at the dinner that night given by de Bakey had cracked, in that stronghold of Texas, "Do you know how to tell if a Texan is lying? Just watch his lips and if they move he is lying."

I could see that fame and time had mellowed the famous American. He moved to the table to take over for the stilling of the heart and its opening to remove the narrowing. The television cameras were focused for the broadcast to the rest of the hospital and other cameras were clicking away, the pump was started and the heart stopped. I moved away to study the X-ray for a moment and returned to the table where the surgeons were still bent over, close at work, and obscuring a good view. De Bakey straightened, took of his gloves and moved away. It was all over. The essential detail of opening the pulmonary artery and widening the opening of the valve, all that was called for on this occasion, had taken less time than a round in the boxing ring, and I had missed it, being reminded of the famous Dempsey-Carpentier heavy-weight championship when just after the bell rang for the first round, one of the expensively-seated ring-side spectators dropped his programme and bent down to search for it, straightened up, and found that the fight was over by a knock-out. The battle here was of a different nature, the only knock-out being the star-turn who found all was well with the set-up and took the plane that night for Texas, doubtless with unmoving lips, and leaving behind him the legend that de Bakey had operated here, and that he did it well.

* * *

Criticism has been made as to why this advanced surgery should be done in Saudi, while tuberculosis, bilharzia, poliomyelitis and the like are rife and need cleaning up. This is not fair judgement. Many hundreds of patients needing heart surgery have been leaving Saudi every year for operations overseas. An act of surgery is a quick-over-and-done-with cure in most instances. Some twenty years ago only trivial surgery was done in Riyadh, and one surgeon told me that when he returned to Riyadh from overseas training about twenty years ago there were scarcely the instruments to do an appendicectomy. There has been a build-up, so that almost the whole run of operative surgery can be put through in Saudi, and it is only right that cardiac surgery which has become a routine throughout most of the western world should take its place along with all the rest. Control of the infectious diseases is a slow process but measures are being taken and the scattered population of a vast country will be gradually treated and immunised but, as was the case in the western countries, considerable resources of medical man-power and supplies are needed, as well as time. Meanwhile, treatment that can be given to those presenting with established diseases and whose lives are in jeopardy are being given the benefit of all modern aid. Neither Rome nor Riyadh were built in a day, but Riyadh is going ahead in all directions, including the care of the health of the people, much faster than did Rome.

CHAPTER XXIV

"Medicals" Saudi Style

As the oil poured out and the money in, the King and Cabinet decided on an educational programme which the country could now easily afford, of schools for all boys and a little later for girls as well. Then in 1957, four years after the accession of King Saud, the University of Riyadh was founded with courses in Islamic Religion, the arts and basic sciences and the like. Medicine was the longest course and, needing a great variety of teachers, had to wait until 1968, when the first medical school was founded in Riyadh, and in 1976 the first medical students of Riyadh graduated.

Meanwhile, doctors from anywhere, but particularly from the Muslim world and those with Arabic language, were engaged to serve all over the country, hospitals were built, and the care of the population by modern medicine went ahead. Two more medical schools followed, one in the west in Jeddah which graduated its first doctors in 1980, and the other in the east in Dammam with graduates in 1981.

In 1979, there were over 300 Saudi doctors in the country of whom eighty had graduated in Riyadh, and the rest abroad. Inevitably, numbers of the senior Saudi doctors must cease or reduce their clinical work to attend to the administration of health in government, hospitals and medical schools for, after all, it is their country and some of them must supervise the vast number of foreigners who are doing the day to day work of caring for the patients. The Saudi doctors seek advice freely from experienced foreigners.

New hospitals are being built all over the country for the public in general, or for special groups such as the Military Hospitals for members of the three branches of the services and their relatives. Each medical school has planned the last word in University Hospitals whose grounds and buildings will house the preclinical and clinical parts of the medical school. Riyadh's magnificent King Khalid Hospital and

Variety of Hospitals

1. *The King Abdul Aziz Hospital of about 100 beds which served the Teaching Hospital for male students, men and women and finally women only when the new King Khalid Hospital opened at which all the male students attended. A big expansion started, some seen in the background, but was never completed.*

2. *The Shameisi or Central Hospital, the city's emergency hospital and taking some non-acute patients. Its 600 beds were occupied by patients with a variety of diseases many rarely or no longer seen in the Western World.*

PLATE 40   299

1. *The new ophthalmic hospital of about 100 beds in Riyadh, the last word in equipment.*

2. *A hospital of 100 beds well laid out and equipped at Yenbu. The type of accommodation for staff is shown in plates 3, 4 and 5.*

1. *The front entrance to the King Khalid Teaching Hospital at Dir'iyah almost complete when this photograph was taken.*

2. *The main entrance to the King Faisil Hospital in Riyadh, reserved almost entirely for Saudis.*

PLATE 42   301

1. *Within the walls of the old medical college in Riyadh used for 13 years.*

2. *A frontal view of the King Khalid Hospital and Medical College, Riyadh.*

The King Khalid Teaching Hospital and Medical College

1. *Students in the laboratories.*

2. *An operating theatre—there are several.*

3. *One of the many lecture theatres.*

4. *Part of the library.*

5. *There are more than 600 flats for staff, all of a similar type to these, comfortably furnished and adjacent to the Hospital.*

Medical School on the fringe of the desert at Dir'iyah, near the little oasis town where the Sauds began their destiny, opened for patients and male student instruction in all medical subjects in 1982.

Most people are surprised to learn that there are lady students with three years of graduates, the first fledglings spreading their wings in 1980. Until men and women graduate they may not mix, and so in their future training the women will be at the original teaching hospital which is at the moment to be extended to more than 400 beds as their training school. I am informed in 1985 that both men and women students are having instruction at the new King Khalid Hospital.

At the time of my arrival in Riyadh the first lady students came on to the wards and we all wondered how things would go. Soon the first ever of Saudi's lady students scrubbed up and assisted me at an operation on a youth with an extensive cancer of the fibrous lining of the bone of the pelvis with a portion the size of an orange on the upper aspect of the bone and joining through the hole in the pelvic bone a further lump of tumour in the thigh the size of a grapefruit. It promised to be difficult and far from free of bleeding, but went well. The young Saudi lady, petite, gentle and quietly spoken as so many are, held her retractor, swabbed as required and stood it like a veteran. Subsequently the girls all assisted well with no signs of fainting as spectator or assistant, seeming to be made of the same stuff as their British sisters. In ward rounds, seminars and lectures they are interested and on the whole intelligent. Once inside the hospital their veils come off and they are seen by and examine men and women patients alike, who have behaved themselves sensibly and with decorum, as have the girls. None of the teaching by men instructors has been done by television as has happened elsewhere.

Men and women students are the usual mixed bag, as seen the world over, some very intelligent, going down the scale from there; some are as keen as anywhere and others display an indolence that makes one wonder how they were selected, or did they have important fathers, a consideration which may apply elsewhere to some extent, though in Saudi, where status and personal influence is fairly marked, it probably weighed at times, at least in the first years of a new medical school. The students are appreciative, expect a good lecture, like a story, and laugh at much the same things as British students. Even the girls seemed to appreciate the aged chestnuts which I had used in Oxford; at any rate they were polite enough to laugh.

Now for the big revelation, as a medical teacher, of seeing thirty or more of them together as a class. What do they look like? On the whole they are a little shorter than a similar group of British girls, and in looks they would average out about the same in figure and face. One or two in the A+ bracket might have beaten the top Italian film stars, whom many resemble in tint of complexion, for most of the women have paler complexions than the men thanks to the protection that the veil gives from the burning sun. Whatever thoughts may be entertained by anyone about the veil I believe that there are a great many Saudi women who find it a real protection against both the elements and certain types of men, and there are many Saudi men very quick on the draw, and they would be glad to preserve it for use at their chosen times, for they prize their complexions and their virginity, unlike some others elsewhere. Some of the younger women, and even the older before all has faded, need a well-disciplined set of hormones when the veils come off, and let us hope it stays that way for the sake of all concerned.

When first in the wards the girls' and boys' times overlapped, and no doubt the usual exchange of looks and perhaps a little more went on between them. Soon a complete separation was brought about, girls first in the hospital and then half an hour later the boys appeared, the girls having been rushed off in a bus, properly veiled as they left the hospital, to go to a separate college where they were lectured mainly by women, though men had to take part for lack of women staff. The girls spoke good enough English on the whole, several of them having visited Britain and some the USA. The lady surgeon in charge of the girls' instruction put three of them to examine a man who had nothing more than a small swelling of the wrist, when in came one of the physicians who, upon seeing three girls alone with a male patient, blew up and said it would not do, that the instructress must go with all the girls to a male patient. The lady asked how was it possible for her to be with ten sets of three girls when they were examining patients. At this moment in came one of the surgeons whose views were different from the physician's and said that while they were doing surgery they would examine male patients in a small group in the absence of their instructors, and what the physicians wished to do was their own concern. The age-old battle of physician and surgeon was continuing but on a different battlefield.

The attendance of the boys can be distinctly erratic. If they do not feel like attending they do not, and if they have an examination coming up they may all stay away for as much as a week at a time from ward work, to concentrate on their studies, for they have a dread of failing. In Oxford we saw exactly the same situation, when, for a time, far too much emphasis was put on incessant exams. We cured it in Oxford in the same way as in Riyadh by reducing the examinations and explaining that far more emphasis in their tests is put on the clinical work; they stayed on the wards a lot better. A mature Saudi doctor, trained elsewhere, said that he thought students were rather spoilt and lazy because they could get away with too much. They seemed at times to have apt excuses to get around us; one of the preclinical teachers told me that he had noticed that if they are in a lecture or demonstration and feel like clearing off, they say, "Excuse me, I must go and pray," and off they go to do what they please. The medical school authorities are doing all they can to keep students present and on the job, whether or not they have influential fathers. The sanction of not allowing students to sit their final examination if their attendance has been very poor is having an effect. Girl students are usually more conscientious, to the annoyance of boys, and the same applies in Saudi, and lots of the lads have not yet settled to the idea of women as doctors; but they might as well get used to the taste of it for they are here to stay, as they say, *"in sha lah"*.

Those whose lives have not been much concerned with examinations are mostly unaware of the high tension which builds up before them and the announcement of results which can effect a whole career. The incidence of cheating in all countries is much the same, and the longer the place has been at it the tighter the controls applied as a result of experience. There are always a number of examinees who would give a lot for a glance at what is in store for them, and from time to time bribes have been offered, and examiners have been known to coach on what they know of set questions to see that their students do well. Long ago in an eastern country it is said that one student who paid a visit to the printers with an "urgent" message for the type-setter, sat down on top of the type in the small press then used and walked of with the questions imprinted on his white trousers. One of the basic science teachers told some of us that two invigilators are always used, as one may be engaged in discussion by one candidate while other examinees confer about the answers; at prayer call in the afternoon in the middle of the exam, most of them rose from their seats, went to the back of the room and during the bowing and offering of prayers one of the invigilators had a very good idea that a lot of the answers were being exchanged! Another ploy is said to be to sit behind one of the best students whom you have already asked to write in large letters so that you can read his answers! The way to success is not always by the road to heaven.

★ ★ ★

One day I went on a students' outing. We were told to be ready for an 8.30 a.m. start, and moved off, as expected, about 9.30 a.m. with only some fifteen in an orange-coloured bus that could hold sixty, but with also some ten cars, since many students preferred their own impressive transport. Having gone only about a mile in the city one of the cars was held up by the police, and with customary curiosity everyone got out to investigate. A student's car had been spotted as having dark anti-glare plastic all over its windows, an accessory recently declared illegal because of the imperfect view, especially through the back window. He was asked to produce his licence which he refused to do on the sound grounds that he did not have one. As an old hand the officer was not deceived, yet all he did about it was to tell him to go and get one as soon as possible; but he must there and then remove the plastic from the back window and put the side windows down. Some twenty or thirty medical students and an assortment of clerks gathered around the police car trying charm and every blandishment to soften the legal block of cement and let us go on, but to no avail. So out came the only available pieces of metal to prise up the plastic, some car keys, and I thought we would be there half the day. My penknife helped to complete the operation a little faster and in half an hour the back window was cleared enough to satisfy the law, and on we went to cheers in the bus and the songs started. Students, as everywhere, have one to lead, and there followed a spate of Arabian songs and choruses to keep us going for a time. Then two Brits in the bus were twisted into rendering an octave or two, with "Tipperary" and "Pack up your Troubles" proving very popular.

We had imagined that our "desert" outing would take us to some distant oasis, but on the outskirts of Riyadh we turned towards a small *wadi* where a generous business man and owner of a small farm allowed the use of his villa comprising two big reception rooms, a veranda, and a concrete area for volley-ball. Some of the older ones, the clerks, got down to chess, popular in all the Arab world; most of the students quickly squatted in a circle for the inevitable card playing—not for stakes of any sort, and others set to at volley-ball. Eating is the principle exercise of all Arabian outings and very quickly two huge meat and egg rolls were thrust into my hands with the remark that it was my breakfast. I had had it three hours before, but managed one roll.

I wandered with some others under the date palms amidst which the land was being prepared for some crop by two Yemenis with mattocks, and came across the well with its pump and cistern from which the water was run into small irrigation canals all very cool and pretty in the midst of the trees. Further on was another building to which some of the students had already moved, which turned out to be a very handsome leisure house with large windows and soft suitable furnishings, all locked up, beside a well-finished, curving swimming pool with a three-inch pipe running cool water into it. The whole thing was in the stockbroker-belt style, and the water very tempting. One or two had brought bathing suits but underpants were good enough. Arab lads are very particular about not showing themselves naked. Many European lads with none of the other sex near would have stripped off if lacking bathing togs. Anyway, in they went, and I soon followed.

The Arab youths are gentle and generally not given to pushing each other around. The only body contact sports are judo, and with the shoulders at football, now played widely from infancy upwards. But here it was all suddenly different; much ducking and pushing was going on, and as new arrivals came and did not quickly get stripped they were rushed fiercely, manhandled, and hurled into the water fully clothed. One lad, a keen photographer, always immaculately turned out—on this day with cream trousers beautifully creased—and a swimmer but not a stylist, wanted none of it and shot over the surrounding wall, coming back later to take photos from the 3-metre diving board, and that was his downfall. They were up like a storming party, one snatching his camera whilst others pushed him to the edge of the board and in he went, creases and all. Another lad, the tallest and strongest, decided it was not his day for swimming but his pals had other ideas. All of them set on him and he put up a splendid fight heaving and kicking, and twice fought them off to make his point and stay dry. Charles, always well turned out, and not caring to swim without the proper garment, was also hoisted high by four lads but stayed smiling and non-resistant, and after dangling him over the water, they pulled him back, reprieved as a foreigner and possible future examiner.

The old Saudi retainer and guardian of the property did not approve of all this unorthodox camel play and turned off the inflow, opened the outflow used for irrigating and the water soon dropped by a foot. As the owner and his family and friends were coming to the villa next day I suspected that he also had doubts about the purity of the waters. Cameras were clicking away incessantly and they continued so for the rest of the outing, several students being keen members of the camera club. I turned back to the main house with lunch in view.

The meal had been prepared at the Medical Faculty restaurant and brought out in insulated boxes and served on plates a yard across covered in mounds of rice and surmounted by chunks of mutton still on the bones. We squatted in circles, the Arabs cross-legged, not an easy attitude for long without years of practice. Spoons were provided for the unhandy, the locals ignoring them in a great display of seizing some meat and gobbling away followed by a handful of rice squeezed to a ball and shoved in, or mixing them up a bit. Our Dean got full marks for skill, speed and appreciation, of the national dish. We washed hands in the bathrooms and went on to bananas and oranges in heaps. There remained, as well as the fruit-skins and bones, vast heaps of rice which I was told would go to the animals. We had another wash, and then a cardboard box was found to serve as a drum, and a young student, Bedawi, leading in everything including prayers, started Arabian rhythm on the box and the songs got going, and after a spate of traditional items everyone was called on for an individual effort, a song or dance. The Egyptian clerks did well with rather anaemic imitations of belly-dancers and the Dean wiggled a little and threatening everybody with a stick as a spear, and, with the Arab sense of equality, even the servants were brought in to do a jig. I was called on again, this time to dance, so I gave a rendering of a Maori Haka, *"turaki"*, with the full actions of the war-dance, and, it being something new to them, was rewarded with appreciative cheers, without stirring the young to retaliation. This item has now been delivered in several of the worlds' capitals on suitable occasions. They carried on while the middle-aged and older sat in the shade and drank lots of tea. The Dean and I chose to be swept back to the city in state and comfort as the afternoon wore on, in one of the students' plush American models, our duty done with a lot of fun.

At a later date on another student outing, we were due to go to the Faculty of Agriculture's farm for a rice and mutton "do" prepared on

PLATE 44   309

Activities with Students

1. *A staff outing with their families at the University Farm. My principal assistant for 5 years, Taysir Saleh (Jordanian) in the foreground looking back.*

2. *The students asked me several times to speak at their 'Cultural and Social Evenings'. My brief was 'just say anything', which called for a lot of care in another culture when telling stories.*

1. *After an evening lecture with some of the staff and students.*

2. *With some of the students at the Medical College.*

the spot, but at the last minute plans were changed and the women medicals were given the trip to the farm; whereupon, as the young men and women may not mix, it was decided we should go to Al Kharj, where we had had a previous adventure with confiscation of cameras. The trip out was longer and quieter and we were duly delivered to a public picnic spot amidst some trees with low walls forming squares built to separate the family groups. The students squatted quickly for a hand or two of cards and the expatriates strolled amongst the trees watching several other parties getting ready for a feast of mutton and rice by stripping the skin from the slaughtered sheep with ineptitude and tedium scarcely believable with a line of ancestors who had been at it since Abraham. An hour in an Antipodean slaughter house would teach them a thing or two.

Al Kharj is an extensive oasis with a good underground water supply, Riyadh getting some if its water from there. We strolled to the local swimming pool amidst the trees, with a high wall around, for men only, and watched lots of Arabs of various nations diving in and splashing about, their swimming being much like an average crowd of Britons but with fewer showing any expertise. Bathing costumes were necessary and having none I did not swim. Our meal was much the same as on the last occasion, and no sooner over than the card-playing started again. I left early in a friend's car with business in Riyadh.

There is a regulation for political reasons against gatherings but certain of these are permitted, as was a meeting under the auspices of the Cultural and Social Committee of the Faculty, which is a good title under which to allow the students and staff to have fun together instead of lectures. This particular evening's proceedings were in a large, flat-floored lecture theatre with seats for all but no stage or raised dais and no curtains. Popular characters on the staff received a mild cheer on coming in and our oldest, the late Professor Buttle, pharmacologist, and known in the war as Bottle Buttle as he is reputed to have collected about 6,000 bottles of blood before the Battle of Caen, got a splendid cheer as he ambled in, chin out and all smiles. The student compère, the one chucked into the swimming pool from the diving board, was resplendent again in a cream-coloured suit, the latest mode in well-cut Western compère wear. Students came to the microphone at ease but showing their usual slight reserve, and nearly all with an extroverted lack of self-consciousness, giving well-timed and semi-dramatic gestures to match their words. There is one great difference with Arabic students both in lectures and on social occasions in that a low hum of talking at the back seldom ceases unless the audience is really caught by special interest or amusement. Young and old respond as they do in the Western world to a good performance, a sly dig or a good joke, and they laughed easily, appreciating a witty impromptu comment from the depths of the audience. The "house" was full, with staff and students.

Firstly, three of four students gave speeches in Arabic, well delivered though mostly read. Then the Dean, Dr Fatani, gave his address, also in Arabic, informative, humorous, well-laughed at, and cheered without sycophancy. Saudis are manly and not given to oiliness of manner and snobs are rare. Part of the Muslim philosophy is that one man is as good as another, and though at times and places that might be doubted, in their mosques that is their policy; no man has a special place and any man may take the lead in the service. More students followed with speeches or poetic recitations, then came two with the Arabian lute, flute, drum and song in a good performance. The highlight was a skit about a bedouin-clothed quack doctor with appropriate wares coming on from one side, and, from the other, Dr Mahi ("ignorant"), a modern doctor complete with stethoscope and blood pressure apparatus, each trying to sell his wares to a bedouin patient. After some bad medicine from the quack and bad advice from Dr Mahi, he flees. It was good theatre, well done, fast and furious, with never a missed cue, well appreciated by the audience and would have gone down well in any British student pantomine. Then some rather feeble jokes were told and that is what the youthful audience thought of them. Two "newsreaders" dealt with "news bulletins" and got a lot of laughs, the words being unintelligible to the British but the idea clear enough.

Then, the near-80-year-old Professor Buttle was called upon with cheers and told of his Arabian linguistic misadventures and the troubles they led him into, only to be rescued by some students. Another long-staying Briton, Professor John Candlish told a story. There followed a most untrustworthy "Brains Trust" in which the students beat the staff 5-4, announced to great cheers by the judge, the Dean.

Throughout the whole performance a student photographer, or at times several of them, wandered about snapping the players and audience from far and near, while a microphonist rushed on or leapt into the middle of scenes, almost thrusting the microphone down the speaker's mouth while making his adjustments. I have never seen such stealing of the show by photographic and microphone lads. No one seemed to mind it appearing to be the usual thing, and the thieves were high in the pecking order. The medical student garb on such occasions is the same as for lectures and is always a great mixture, some wearing the long whitish thobe, some with a head-cloth, some with the head-ring as well, some with in addition a waistcoat or a formal short coat or a jazzy coat over the thobe, and some few in full western dress. They were hungry for praise and got that from most of us in full measure for they were amusing, talented and joyful, and, as a group, would have matched any comparable Western one. At one time they were keen on "taking-off" the staff but that seemed to have lapsed, evidently because of undue pomposity or sensitivity on the part of some members, which was a pity since that sort of thing gives a lot of fun and sometimes does some good. Before my final return to England staff baiting at social evenings had resumed and was as pointed as in our own medical schools.

We adjourned to the very crummy canteen to queue for cakes, biscuits, a banana and "Pepsi", after which I was lined up with a group of students for a photo only to find that all the film had run out, to much hilarity. Their future programmes might pall a little from our lack of the language but never from want of *joie de vivre* or dramatic presentation of them.

On another occasion I attended an evening in the fine assembly hall in the University Administration Buildings, identical with a modern theatre with a stage and seating for some 4-500, where prizes for the sports events throughout the year were presented and at which I had been given a day's warning to speak but given no information of what it was all about nor of who would be there. "Just say anything, it is just the students." So I took my brief accordingly and did just that, to find half the staff there as well and they did not seem too displeased with the result, but at another event of student entertainment in the same hall, in the middle of the show, a voice whispered in my ear from behind, "Would you go up and say something?" I felt I had been called upon enough without warning, because it is only too easy to put one's cultural foot in it, and declined, leaving someone else to risk it this time, and he did it well. This time the students ragged the staff and University's activities, and though I didn't understand a word I could see much humour in it. There were no complaints, skins were getting thickened by rubbing.

* * *

The Central University Library is a handsome, rectangular, domed building, well equipped, with a wide range of reference books, cool, clean, carpeted, quiet and fairly efficiently run, with good air-conditioning for reading in hot weather and hence a haven for examinees who occupy, near examination times, almost every seat and much of the floor inside and nearly all the car-parking space outside, the social instinct for everyone to do much the same thing helping to ease the grind entailed in studying books for hours on end; it all made me feel as if I was back in Oxford, with a difference. At this University for Saudis, most were in the national dress, looking like an academic army, with everyone so clean, tidy and in uniform; very different from Oxford where individuality is often expressed by sporting a grubby assortment of clothes comprising anything from anywhere—though at examinations and graduation ceremonies this would be exchanged, under compulsion, for a uniformity of academic attire suited to a cooler climate, much maligned at the time but stoutly defended later. Here, at the Library, at times of maximum pressure, even the wall space is taken up on the ground floor, while on the floor above where the books are stacked in racks with narrow passageways between, some sat on their haunches, or lay at length, or prone and leaning on their elbows, reading away, with others stretched out fast asleep between the stacks, perhaps a lack of chairs encouraging the natural national habits. Arabs from infancy are capable of sitting on their haunches for hours on end, a posture guaranteed in casual triers to send the legs to sleep in no time, while their ability to sit cross-legged serves them well but causes a lot of knee arthritis in the aged in contrast to the hips of Westerners, whose habits at work or parties of standing for hours may well help to increase the queues for hip replacements. Both cultures might be better to try chairs or Roman couches and take a chance on bedsores. Most of these were arts students and taught in Arabic, in contrast to the medicals whose courses are in English, and as I made my way past unfamiliar figures bent over their books many raised their heads to break the monotony for a moment, gazing long at the ancient western academic type. Perhaps I was some help, as I remember staring in the same way at some of my teachers at Oxford; there were no girls here, and I pondered on this for a while, wondering if the boys might not be fortunate, with no pretty faces to distract from the job in hand and fewer to hog places in the pass-lists, and only cold ambition to fire their efforts. Reality is better than dreams, as Churchill observed, and both of them may be missing something, but that is their way. The ladies were tearing into it elsewhere, similarly uninspired.

With the coming of *salat*, some of the students would go to a pile of long prayer mats in the spacious entrance hall and place them in lines, then others would rise quietly and take their places in the line of worshippers, say their prayers, make their bows by first bending at the hips, and then on their knees to the floor and head to the carpet, and so return composed and rested for another round of study. When I was upstairs amongst the shelves I noted that several did not bother to make their way down to join in, perhaps getting a black mark in consequence.

Outside in the street were some central areas of grass and a further strip on one side in front of the luxurious Equestrian Club related to the adjacent racecourse; and here, in scattered, separate circles students squatted or sat cross-legged, some with mats, equipped with tea-flasks and small glass mugs, talking away about their work—with much gossiping as well judging by the quiet laughter, while around the cars a few were a little raucous and pushing one another in the way of youth. In the evening they made a pleasant sight; this was their pub with no need for enclosure or shelter in such heat. In France, in summer, we see the table and chairs on the pavements, and in Britain the pub garden fills. Every nation needs something to go with the conversation and here it is mostly tea but sometimes coffee, though that is usually a drink for indoors. They take their tea along in an assorted variety of thermos flasks and empty the mugs frequently, for in the very hot countries everyone needs lots of liquid. Alcohol, forbidden of course, is rather more befuddling than usual, and as one goes north the wines and beer give way to the brandies and whisky while vodka seems to help to keep out the ice. These lads did not seem to be missing anything with their tea.

*   *   *

The acid test comes with the final examination, the test in medicine and surgery to see if the candidate knows, not everything, but has sufficient knowledge and its application to be able to release him on the public as not too bad a risk. The subjects in Riyadh are medicine and surgery, and paediatrics as well, which is not a bad idea in a country with a very high infantile mortality. The examination in obstetrics and gynaecology is held in the previous year when it is taught along with the specials. The final is much the same as most other places, with papers, clinical and oral. An external examiner comes for every subject taught in the medical course to help assure standards on which the Saudis are insistent, with no putting through any duds to keep up numbers. Muslim youth are well practised in memorising passages in books, starting young with the Koran, and they have no trouble in swotting up a book but have shown a weakness in the past at working hard with patients to learn the essentials of examining and assessing them. However, the authorities are insisting that this aspect must be well done, and if students are not up to standard they are failed without mercy.

Keeping to an exact timetable is a bit of a strain for all Arabs, as all the world knows, but once under way things go pleasantly. One quite good candidate turned up an hour late for his clinical, always a serious offence with many to be tested. He smiled sweetly, and said he was sorry but he was tired and had slept in. I told him he had better choose another time for that and if he did not turn up on time in the next part of the exam we would not examine him and he would fail. He did a good clinical in spite of my not very encouraging remarks and was in good time for his oral; but I was not. I slept on in my afternoon siesta having made a mess of setting the alarm, the only time in my life after sitting and examining scores of times. No one worried and I did not tell the student offender, but I hope he reads this some day. Allah is just!

In the final in 1978, out of twenty-eight sitting the exam, three failed in surgery, four in medicine, and five in paediatrics mostly the same candidates overall, some of the failures passing in the later re-sit exam. The tops were excellent, and, as ever, the lowest just scraped home after much discussion. The standard was about the same as London and Oxford with, in some of the weakest who are often poor in English as well, a trace of allowance given for slowness because the language is not their own. What Englishmen would like to do the medical course in Dutch? The elation on becoming doctors is equal to that shown anywhere else.

In my five years in Riyadh the failure rate for men has been roughly about one in ten. The women worked hard and conscientiously as ever and are equally keen to show what they are capable of when given the chance. Each year some twenty-five to thirty have sat the Finals, starting in 1980, and so far only one has failed and she passed in the re-sit later.

We were asked to stay for the graduation ceremony a few days later and it was worth it. The moment of truth had arrived and gone with the Finals' result published, and a few days later the ceremony was held in a very large "sports" hall near the new King Khalid Hospital at Dir'iyah, the building being noted for its soft roof held aloft by air pressure from within, generated by pumps outside.

There was much uncertainty for a time about the date of the ceremony, the men's and women's being confused. A notice was circulated to the effect that gowns would be available and should be collected and signed for at the Medical School, which some did, that transport would be available by bus from the University Campus in Riyadh to Dir'iyah, and that there would be a procession of all staff to their seats headed by the Vice-Rectors, Deans and Professors and so down to Lecturers, in order of Faculties. Here, the constant weakness of Middle Eastern administration ran true to form—that lack of communication—for in the event only some received the notice; no transport arrived at the stated times or later, and we had resort to our own cars, no problem with no cause for breathalysing; they did not expect us to wear a gown; no procession of staff was held; no cancellation notices for any of these were sent to us.

The staff sat *en bloc* on one side of half the hall on elevated arena-type seating, and on the other side opposite sat the proud parents, men only, a moment when I felt sorry for the proud mothers who, veiled or not, do not attend public functions. The graduates filed in in pairs wearing their gowns with the usual feature of facings in different colours indicating their faculties and degrees. This small academic army of youth who have striven to success to become the professionals of the future is always a stirring sight. They sat at one end between the crowded sides of the tiered seats of the arena, and about twenty rows on the floor, some hundreds of graduates in all, medical being only a few of them.

The centre of the hall was dominated by television cameras and the crews awaiting the arrival of the Governor of Riyadh, Prince Sittam, and the Minister of Education, Sheikh Hassan, and the Rector of the University.

After some delay we saw their entrance heralded by sudden acute activity on the television stand when the Prince entered in a cloud of perfumed smoke from incense-burners carried by servants whose duty is to walk beside them and waft the pleasing vapour about them. The dignitaries sat in the royal box in front of us and were served the traditonal small cups of coffee, and water, as required.

Proceedings opened with a reading from the Koran, followed by speeches from the Minister and the Rector; all the while American style news-photography was conducted by ruffian-looking, ill-dressed, ill-groomed photographers, breaking in incessantly with their hand-lights and their proximity, into what would have been, without their prescence, a dignified ceremony. This has become a customary feature in Saudi at the public occasions I attended, and it destroys much of the atmosphere for those present. One is all for letting the television public have their fill, but how much better to allow a period for photography and then proceed uninterrupted, with only long-distance shots during the ceremony itself. Perhaps no one cares or no one dares suggest it to the photographers.

Prince Sittam presented the certificates of the degrees, one representative from each faculty coming forward and receiving from his hand in a bundle all that faculty's degrees. In the customary Arab way, the ceremony over, the high-ups swiftly rose and departed, at which time the graduates and the rest were free to drift about the arena and we could speak with one and all, but especially to the new graduates who wore that expression I have seen so often in the streets of Oxford, of modest pride, pleasure and dignity set off by their newly-entitled garb. They are a fine lot of lads and had worked hard for it. David Wallace and I strolled about greeting them and also basked a little second-hand in the pride of having helped.

We were all stirred up by the military brass band which had been regalling us at suitable moments and now turned on excellent march music, an encouragement to step out and away, no doubt, and, reinforced by six pipers, made a spirited attack on a Scottish march which set the feet towards the door where the gowns were retrieved, and so to long tables outside strewn with cooled tins of fluid refreshment, very welcome with the summer heat drying us out.

The academic year had rolled to a close and the staff were free to go, some late that night and many next day, my own return to be in the company of Mike Ford with a little bonus for us both for having ventured this way, in the shape of a holiday by air to Jordan, and then the road to Damascus from where we flew to London. These experiences were repeated much the same for me for a total of five years.

Appendices

These appendices may concern mainly those with some medical knowledge, but others may find interest in them as well, and certainly this was considered to be the case in Saudi Arabia for the first two reports were translated into Arabic by Dr Ibrahim Bedawi and were published in full in the national newspaper, *al Riyadh*, evidently unique to students' reports.

Appendix I

| *Professor Moloney.* | *Mousa'ad al Salman.* | *Mohammed al Sobeiyal.* |

PLATE 46

The Local Healers of Qasim

The Department of Community Medicine made an annual foray with the students of the 4th (penultimate) year to study disease in the making in its natural environment, and as I have been involved in various investigations I was asked to join in as one of the supervisors, the first occasion being in February 1979, under the leadership of Dr Zohair Sebei, then Head of that Department. The two students allotted to me, Mousa'ad al Salman and Mohammed al Sobeiyal, were pleasing, co-operative, intelligent and worked well. I suggested for a project a study of the traditional healers of Qasim, the region we were heading for, some 400km north-east of Riyadh, with its three main towns of Buraydah, Unaizah and Al Rass and a vast amount of desert with scattered villages.

I stayed in a villa in Buraida with six Saudi students and one or two senior Saudis sharing in their meals, sitting on one's haunches (not for long) or cross-legged on the floor in a circle around the mutton and rice or whatever was before us, joining in their activities, except prayers, and avoiding attempts to induce me to join the faith.

Our report, "The Local Healers of Qasim", as well as being published in full in the national newspaper, *al Riyadh*, in Arabic (25.5.80 and 1.6.80) was printed in English in the collected reports of the expedition in booklet form, "Community Health in Saudi Arabia", edited by Dr Z. Sebei, 1982. The findings were very much the result of our combined effort, for the students supplied the Arabic and made access possible as Saudis and medical personnel, where a European alone would have no hope of entry or responses. My students in this and the other later investigations showed sharp intellect, good sense and lively curiosity, while my long experience supplied a measure of medical knowledge for question and comment, though the students were excellent with their own enquiries and observations. The writing was also a combination of their observations and comments being assisted by my experience, and, inevitably, their English and construction being adjusted by me. A summary of the report is presented here.

Aim—To study the practices of the local healers of Qasim, assessing their possible useful or adverse results by interview and observation and by still and moving pictures which, to our knowledge, had not previously been taken. The main headings of the study—cautery, bone-setting, bleeding, circumcision, obstetrics, herbal medicines and other practices.

Cautery—This form of therapy was in use in the Western world until about 100 years ago. Local cauterisers invited us to see them in action and to discuss their methods and allowing photography. Their strong belief and confidence in the benefits is transferred to their patients. The cauteries were primitively made in various shapes and sizes, sharp, blunt, disc-ended or a ring and most had a wooden handle (see photo) and were always applied red-hot. The sites of application for the same diseases varied greatly with different cauterisers, but one fairly constant finding was over the heel for dysentery and perhaps a few on the abdomen, and for jaundice over the ends of the ulna at the wrist and usually some over the liver, in pneumonia linear cauterisation (see photo) between the ribs (a Saudi physician telling me that he was cauterised thus for bad pleuritic pain as a child and after the application the pain was immediately removed and he could breathe easily again). For leichmaniasis of the skin a smouldering folded woollen cloth is dabbed on the lesion several times and certainly cures some, as testified by the local skin specialist at Buraida Hospital who said that it would deal with one or two lesions but with widespread disease modern medicines were essential; in sciatica scattered points along the lines of the sciatic nerve were touched, in mental disease after shaving the head the cautery was applied to the very top, while in syphilis the top and side of the head were given the full treatment (which if quite unlikely to have any curative effect would act as strong disincentives to further promiscuity) and if that did not work penicillin or terramycin were prescribed, both these antibiotics being available without prescription. The treatment seemed about right without the cautery part!

PLATE 47   321

1. *The typical black tent pitched and the carpets spread for lunch—the main meal (ghudda) for the Arabs.*

2. *In the tent awaiting the feast with the hour-long pre-prandial talk in progress.*

1. *Servants clearing away after the feast with bananas and oranges in plenty left over, which will go to the servants.*

2. *Western ladies are welcome to join in feasts and other occasions as when Mrs Vickie Martindale had finished the mutton and rice (capsa) and was on to the fruit.*

PLATE 49

323

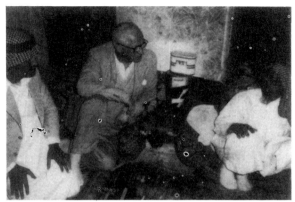

1. *An experienced cauterisor gives his views.*

2. *Umm Ahmed the 'black woman' as the locals call her is of African origin, a traditional healer of renown whose clinic of palm fronds is in the background.*

PLATE 50

1. *A variety of cauteries ready for the fire with the inevitable tea and coffee pots.*

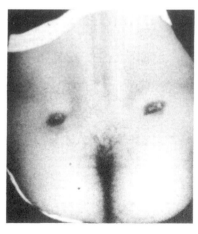

2. *Umm Ahmed applying the red hot cautery above the right buttock on a patient suffering with haemorrhoids.*

3. *The burns on the same patient after cauterisation.*

PLATE 51   325

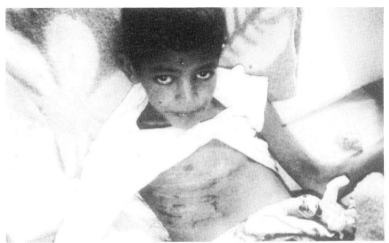

1. *A boy recently cauterised in the spaces between the ribs for pneumonia. His father proudly showed us the scars on his chest from the same treatment when he was a lad.*

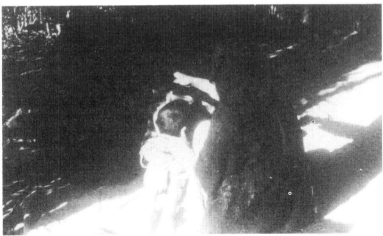

2. *Umm Ahmed treating a skin disease, leichmaniasis, on this boy on his scalp, by dabbing a smouldering roll of rags upon the lesions.*

We watched a formidable and much praised healer, Umm Achmed (Mother of Achmed—many mothers being named after their eldest sons) treat a patient with haemorrhoids. She gave the abdomen a good pummelling to be sure that there was no cause for the trouble there, which is good medicine, and then had the patient lie prone and marked, with ash from her fire for heating the cautery, two sites, one each side on the small of the back, and the calves! And then when the cautery was glowing bright red applied it to the marked sites. The patient did not move or cry out as smoke and stench rose, but as soon as it was done he adjusted his clothes and with a smile sat on his haunches beside Umm Achmed to receive further instructions. We saw another patient refuse the cautery and be sent off to the pharmacy with a prescription. That would have been my choice. Other sites for other diseases were explained to us. The burns frequently go septic and alum powder or myrrh is used but would not help much. Umm Achmed claimed great success in patients with infertility, where doctors could do nothing, by cauterising over the pubic region but if the inguinal region is burnt sterility results!

Conclusions—Some of these have been discussed earlier, but in general one can say that the cautery is still widely practised and may continue to be used in the immediate future. It has a very limited value in treatment, and is the cause of many infected wounds. We found that people go to be cauterized because they do not know of other treatment or they have no faith in other methods. With much of the population showing faith in cautery we must be careful not to disturb this belief until proper help can be given to everyone. As there is some evidence that cautery may give symptomatic relief in some diseases, notably in backache, it is worth investigating. Now that modern services are becoming available it would be better to extend these services and hope that cautery will fall into disuse.

Bone-setting—Fractures are one of the most common medical problems and can be given fairly effective treatment by bonesetters both in Qasim and in the whole of Arabia: this is particularly successful in long-bone fractures. One of the chief merits of local healers is that they do not treat severe cases of fractures into joints. We visited three bonesetters, all old, who had all learnt their skills within the family from father to son to grandson.

The first, a famous bonesetter, explained the details of his methods. He does not treat any fracture into joints, or of the pelvis, sending these patients to hospital, and in those he treats he seeks X-rays, especially in comminuted cases, but he has difficulty at times in getting the doctors to release the X-rays. In fractures of the long bones he examines the injured part by hand. We discussed this problem with the director of Buraida Hospital who said that the rules of the Ministry of Health state that X-rays may not be taken from the hospital except to go to another hospital, but one of the trauma surgeons said that the patients or relatives sometimes take them on the order of a prince. One said that the local bonesetters are doing a good job and may even repair a fracture set badly by a doctor by refracturing and resetting. Those we saw appear to be doing good work especially in fractures of the long bones.

Methods—In straightforward fractures, especially in children, the bonesetters do not always seek an X-ray, but they do try to get X-rays in cases of compound, comminuted, multiple and finger fractures. Their follow-up is good with regular home visits to study progress. If required they go to the patient's home to set the fracture, but an older man in Al Gasr said that if the patient lives far away he demonstrates his methods to the relatives who carry them out on return. The bonesetters in Buraida and Al Rass, however, go with the relatives even if they live far away, the man in Al Rass saying he has sometimes gone to Medina (450km away) and Jeddah (600km). He is very active and he hopes that doctors will come to do the work better than he does. He says that he continues to do it because of inadequate trauma service in Qasim.

Closed Fractures

(1) Preparing the splint: This is done afresh for each patient using material such as pieces of boxes or any convenient wood. The bandages and dressings may be made from old clothes or material bought in the market. The bonesetter in Buraida usually takes his material to the patient, while the man in Al Gasr said that he gave the splints to relatives but they used their own strips of cloth, though in his own village he supplied it all. He also said that he used the other limb as a splint to help reduce pain, putting a splint on it as well and binding it to the injured one. The pieces of wood are bound together at the ends by strips of cloth in ladder fashion, a method used in first-aid in the West today.

(2) Preparing the patient: The bonesetter now looks at the X-rays and palpates the region of the fracture which is being reduced by pulling on it himself or with the help of one or even two men. The man in Al Rass said that he had two special strong men for this purpose! He always aligned the limb correctly.

(3) Applying the splint: The whole splint is put around the limb; it is fixed with a bandage and a pulley arrangement is used to control the degree of tension which thus adapts it to the size of the swelling. In fractures of both femur and tibia a long piece of wood is bound to the lateral side of the limb for its whole length. The size of all splints varies with limb size and swelling. Follow up is regular unless the treatment has been by demonstration only. In fractures of the upper limb the same type of splint is used for the forearm, but for the humerus two pieces of wood only are used unless the patient is very large, when extra bandages are applied.

(4) Extra fixation of the limb, especially with femoral fractures, is done by hammering two wooden stakes into the ground on either side of the femur and tibia and fixing the leg to them. The two big toes are tied together to prevent external rotation. Bowel movements are attended to by putting pieces of cotton

wool under the buttocks; these are removed immediately after use and micturition is managed by the use of a small plastic bag.

In the case of femoral neck fracture the man at Al Rass said that he advised the patient "to go to a good hospital where a surgeon would put a nail which is better than doing it wrongly by a splint".

Humeral supracondylar fractures were discussed only with the man in Al Rass who said he treated them in a special way. With children he sees X-rays and palpates the fracture, then puts the arm into full extension on a splint for 8-10 days when, after inspection, he resplints it. He likes to leave the limb in full extension; in flexion the fragments displace easily but not in extension when the angle of the arm is best judged. He said there is no danger of adhesions at the elbow joint, which mobilizes readily in children. On removal of the splint he does not use massage or forced movements but leaves the child to its own efforts. He finds this method very successful. An orthopaedic surgeon in Riyadh said that this method has recently been reported in Egyptian medical papers where it is recommended as less likely to impair the blood supply and is better in judging the line of the bone.

In adults he does the same initially but, when the fracture has been treated by extension for 7-8 days, he changes the limb slowly into the right-angled position and maintains it there by cardboard splints. Then, after another 7-8 days, he straightens it for a time and in this way he preserves full movement by avoiding adhesions of the capsule. Novalgin is used for pain.

With regard to fractures into joints, two bonesetters said that they always send these into hospital, but the man in Al Rass said that he used traction and the splint but nothing more. He also treated a case of fracture of the spine with paraplegia in which he used traction by the lower limbs and adhesive plaster from the level of the umbilicus to the level of the coccyx; the paraplegia recovered and the fracture settled well. Clavicular fractures he treats by a figure-of-eight bandage around the shoulders, bracing them well back and tying behind.

Open Fractures (Compound)

The fracture is usually splinted in the same way but the bonesetter does not cover the wound which is left open to the air through a gap in the splint. Discharges are bathed away and the wound is bathed with myrrh or other herbal washes. It may occasionally be necessary to remove a dead piece of bone. The healing time is on average 40-60 days. The old man in Buraida said that he does not apply traction to the leg until he has cleaned and improved the wound. All the bonesetters advised a restricted diet in the form of abstaining from eggs, dates, meat and fish; they also advised abstention from sexual intercourse. The first seems unjustified and the second may be impossible to accomplish anyway.

Comminuted Fractures

The old man in Buraida said that he reduces the fractures, including the

PLATE 52   329

1. *The circumciser's kit—a razor with sharpening stone, iodine, scissors, plastic rings like a washer and a cloth.*

2. *A bone-setter splinting a fractured thigh bone.*

3. *A bone-setter instructing by demonstration to the relatives how to set a fractured leg for a patient many kilometers away. He would only attend personally in his neighbourhood.*

patella, saying that many patients come to him having been advised by a doctor to have the patella removed, but he has splinted the fractures which have healed. He seemed to have no idea of the late consequences, though these may have been in the mind of the man in Al Rass who said that he never treats any comminuted fractures but sends them all to hospital. The Buraida man said that he had a fair chance of success with these fractures but that sometimes a piece of bone comes out even in closed fractures.

The bonesetters said that doctors always chose the simplest way out and even advised amputation in some cases but the patients would come to the bonesetters and they would save the limb. They therefore thought that if the doctors failed in the treatment of their patients they should seek the help and experience of the bonesetters and that they (the bonesetters) should not be neglected by the health authorities or by the doctors in the hospitals.

Conclusions—Bonesetters give good value knowing their limitations and using X-rays when they can. They should be encouraged and permitted to use or see X-rays of their patients.

Circumcision

In Saudi Arabia circumcision is done for all the male population as a religious and traditional practice, being performed either by a doctor or by a local healer, though the percentage of operations done by doctors is increasing. In towns such as Unaisa usually just one or two people do it, but among the bedouin of Qasim any male adult—even the father—may do it. Female circumcision is not done in this region. The local circumciser told us that the only possible instance of which he had heard occurred nearly fifty year ago when a religious man in the area was said to have done it to his daughter.

In Unaisa we visited a man, ibn Monissier, who had been circumcising for thirty years and who showed us his materials and methods. He usually circumcises between the ages of five months and five years, sometimes earlier or later, though he prefers to do it as early as possible to get quick healing, even eight days after birth. The materials used are only a sharp razor, different sized plastic rings, scissors, a hone, cotton wool and some antiseptic.

The child sits on a stool in front of the operator with his father holding his arms from behind. The operator starts by applying some antiseptic (Dettol or iodine), then passes the foreskin through a hole in the plastic ring and, pulling firmly on the foreskin, distracts the child's attention while making a quick cut which the child may not be aware of. Any residual portions may be trimmed away with scissors. After applying iodine he wraps the cut around with cotton wool. In other parts of Qasim the healers use a plastic string or a rubber strip (sometimes cut from an inner tube) to tie around the foreskin beyond the glans penis for safety, and cut distal to it, then dress it in the same way. Healing usually occurs in a few days. Sometimes local medicaments are applied to the wound and even fire ash is used, especially amongst the bedouin. If there is bleeding which the local healer cannot control he usually sends the patient to a hospital immediately. Other complications are adhesions, stricture and infection. Dr F. Jawwad, a general practitioner in Unaisa, told us that she receives about 5-7 cases of complicated circumcisions per month—especially from the bedouin. The local healer there said that he might get one case of troublesome bleeding in a thousand which he had to send to hospital, but we felt sure that he keeps no records.

Discussion and Conclusions

The use of an antiseptic indicates that the healers are aware of the danger of infection. The use of a ring or string gives good protection to the glans penis but a doctor in Al Rass told us that he had had to deal with several cases of injury to the tip of the penis. As there is no preliminary freeing of adhesions they do persist at times. Complications, which are greater amongst the bedouin because of their lack of skill and ignorance of antisepsis, are sent to hospital. On the whole the local circumcisers do good work with a low complication rate; as the population at large has great faith in this, it is best to encourage this work by them and even help them with some instruction in asepsis and the best means of avoiding complications. Their results are likely to be better than the few which every young doctor as an intern has to do. Encouraging the bedouin to take their male children to the local circumciser could well be a useful solution.

Bleeding

Bleeding is still one of the native medical practices in Qasim, but is used to a very limited extent and much less than cautery. Few of the local healers use bleeding; most gave it up long ago. In Unaisa the local healer, ibn Monissier bleeds occasionally but only for headache, sunstroke and some cases of hypertension and diabetes which have already been diagnosed in hospital. His usual method is to produce congestion of the veins of the head by encircling the neck with the guttra (the Arab head-dress) and twisting it, then making a quick cut of forehead vein with a razor and letting the blood flow until 1-2 teacups (60-120ml) are filled. In Al Rass, a local healer told us that he practises bleeding from forehead veins in hypertension and asthma. In severe pneumonia he gets the patient to curl up the tongue and cuts one of the small lingual veins, but in less severe cases he does it from a vein on the dorsum of the hand, collecting up to 10 teacupfuls (600ml) in a bowl. We were told that bleeding is more common amongst the bedouin; one bedouin healer in Khusaiba uses bleeding from the dorsum of the hand in cases of pneumonia.

Discussion and Conclusions

Bleeding was widely used in the Western world until about 100 years ago on much the same theory as that of the local healers who alleged that in some diseases, the blood is bad and the body should get rid of it, and "when the black blood is run off and a lighter-coloured blood appears he stops the bleeding by pressure" (Western medicine would regard that theory as nonsense). Dr M. Kamal, a surgeon in Unaisa, told us that he had heard of two cases who were bled to death. We believe that bleeding has rare uses in modern medicine, giving no benefit but causing other troubles such as anaemia when much blood is lost. Our conclusion is that it is a practice which is disappearing.

Obstetrics

The practice of obstetrics in Qasim is carried out by mothers, grandmothers, wise old women, nurse-midwives, and in hospital. Though the number of hospital deliveries is increasing most babies are delivered at home from where they are moved to hospital if complications arise such as:

(1) Obstructed labour: In a survey done by Dr Najma, an obstetrician in Buraida, of ninty-three cases of obstructed labour in one year only four were booked cases, the rest admitted as emergencies.

(2) Infections: Puerperal sepsis arising from lack of antisepsis and asepsis; and neonatal infections, including tetanus as a result of using infected materials, e.g. a kitchen knife to cut the umbilical cord.

(3) Retained placenta: The placenta may be left for a few days in the uterus.

(4) Postpartum haemorrhage.

Umm Achmed told us about her practice in obstetrics, saying that she never does a vaginal examination and never pulls the baby out in delivery. To remove the placenta she uses successive gentle pulls on the cord while the uterus is gently squeezed by the other hand. She diagnoses breech presentation by palpation and deals with it by raising the patient's legs over her back and then shakes her vigorously, claiming that this method delivers a breech baby! The use of this technique by bedouin healers was confirmed by Dr Jawwad, of Unaisa. Umm Achmed claimed also that she does external cephalic version in transverse lie during labour with success! Dr Jawwad also told us that some greasy material is sometimes used vaginally to ease the passage of the baby. In postpartum haemorrhage Umm Achmed does cauterization in two places—just above the anterior superior iliac spine and just below the medial malleolus, using the right side if the baby is male and the left if female, a subtle slant of professionalism not likely to be adopted by Eastern or Western doctors. Cautery is never used in obstructed labour for fear it might harm the baby.

On visiting the local hospitals to ask about the local midwifery, it was found that most deliveries are admitted as emergencies, many with complications.

Discussion and Conclusions

Placental delivery, if done as Umm Achmed described to us, is similar to modern medical practice. In breech deliveries it is difficult to judge her success rate and doubtful if shaking makes any difference, while version of a transverse lie with a patient in labour and without an anaesthetic must be seldom possible. If she tries it, however, complications are likely. In any attempt to abolish the practice of midwifery by local women we must consider the available services and to what extent they can cope with the demands of the population, at the same time remembering that spontaneous deliveries at home cannot be prevented. Therefore a better service must be provided for them but in the meantime acknowledge the usefulness of local practices to which many of the people turn as traditional. Even so, any patients with complications should be encouraged to use the hospitals as quickly as possible and early education along that line might be a good start.

Some Other Practices

Some aspects of acute retention of urine and its management by the patient are reminiscent of former practices in Europe. One of the urologists in Buraida Hospital told us that patients with dysuria and even acute retention acquire a catheter, perhaps by buying it at a local pharmacy, and then pass it on themselves until they are finally admitted with heavily infected urine and pyelonephritis. In one instance the patient passed a length of straw along his own urethra.

The doctor also told us that otitis media was frequently treated by the bedouin by putting powdered henna in the ear, and it is frequently treated by cautery. Wounds and ulcers are treated at times by creams bought at a pharmacy and sometimes toothpaste is used for this purpose. Umm Achmed said that she used penicillin powder for infected wounds.

The dermatologist in Buraida told us of the frequency of dermal leishmaniasis, saying that he treated up to eighty cases a month, and that he was well aware of the uses of heat and cold in its treatment and he believed that the treatment of a localized area of the disease by dabbing with a smouldering cloth could produce cures but if the disease were widespread it could not. The bedouin use hot camel dung wrapped in a cloth and dabbed on the areas as a convenient form of heat.

Umm Achmed treated anaemia in an orthodox way be sending the patient to the pharmacy with a prescription she could just manage to write though she preferred one of her children to write it for her. This produced a bottle of a familiar formula containing all the vitamins and minerals including iron to keep various deficiency diseases in check.

Umm Achmed treated eczema by heating a powder from India; she got this from the *souk* and put the affected area over the smoke and held the smoke in by folds of the clothes. This immediately stopped the itching and the treatment was repeated for forty days. The patient dieted for the duration of this treatment. The details of the restricted diet sounded very similar to the diet that doctors use in such cases. She emphasized that if the patients lapse from the diet the disease is likely to recur.

Medicines Used by Healers in Qasim

Many types of medicaments are commonly prescribed by the local healers, including locally grown herbs, foreign herbs and other substances both metallic and organic. For our study we were able to collect samples of some local medicines with a description of some of their uses as stated by both the people and the local healers. Dr Abdullah al Sheikh, a botanist in the Faculty of Science, who was a member of the group at Qasim, helped us in putting the proper scientific names to some of our samples. To make a proper evaluation of these local medicines an extensive study would have to be made; this would include finding their proper names and the active substances in each, comparing their uses by the local healers with those in orthodox medicine as set out in the pharmacopoeia, and trying to discover any new uses. All we were able to do for this study, however, was to collect samples and find their proper names and any uses told to us by the local healers.

We also noted a new trend by the healers; this was the prescription of some types of modern medicines for their patients, and we were able to collect some data about that by visiting the local pharmacies. The healer prescribes the medicine as would a doctor and the patient buys it from the local herb and spice *souk* or from a pharmacy. Most medicines are taken orally—usually with hot drinks—and some are applied locally. Their Arabic names and large numbers make citing them here pointless.

Modern Drugs

Many modern drugs are prescribed by local healers; these include analgesics, multi-vitamins and minerals and sometimes antibiotics. Umm Achmed gave instructions in front of us on the use of penicillin injections to a man for his wife who had a skin disease, telling him to give one injection each day for eight days. A 100-year-old healer in Eneiza used different analgesics and antihistaminic ointments such as Algesan and Algipan. On a visit to the local pharmacies in Buraida we found that each of them receive about three prescriptions a day from local healers, sometimes with no definite medicine named but with a sentence such as, "a medicine for kidney infections". Umm Achmed also uses penicillin powder over wounds and she prescribes purgatives on prescription.

Discussion

A full investigation and evaluation of these herbs should be made, along the lines suggested in the introduction. They are used over a broad spectrum for a variety of symptoms with no accurate delineation of the use of each. Most of them are used mainly for wounds and gastrointestinal problems, being applied in various combinations, and are chiefly used to treat symptoms with no specific drugs for defined diseases. We imagine that the local healers blindly prescribe most modern drugs, as there is no scientific background for their prescribing.

Conclusion

The use of local medicines cannot be abolished unless it is proved that they are harmful, and, in case they are or if they have some beneficial effect of which we are unaware, a proper investigation of them should be made. The use of modern medicines by the healers indicates their willingness to take advantage of modern treatments and it is our impression that they might easily be influenced, if young, to use the simpler and safer modern medicines in their

PLATE 53 335

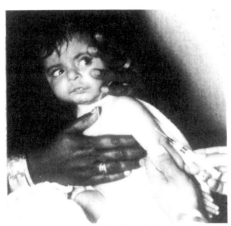

1. *and* **2.** *Physicians were conducting investigations and giving inoculations as well. The small child's reaction to a needle is as suspicious as a western's one.*

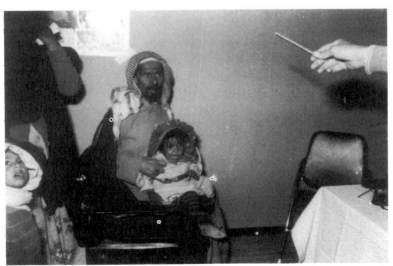

3. *Fathers, as well as mothers, are particularly good in their concern for their children. An eyesight test in progress, intended for the child and not the father!*

practice. Doctors and nurses might be able to co-operate with them by instruction in simple modern medicines while adequate medical services are being built up, in the form of primary health care throughout the nation. Young relatives of local healers who are likely to assist and later take over the practices might also be given a little training in a similar way, and should be informed of the seriousness of delay in sending complicated cases to hospital. The correct usage of medicines in the home and in first aid might be included in health education programmes in schools and on television and radio.

Appendix II

Shams Ghandoura   *Khalid Shaibani*   *Mohammed Bazarbashi*   *Professor Moloney*

PLATE 54

The Way of Life of some Villagers of Jizan and its relation to their Diseases

The second expedition was in February 1981, under the leadership of Dr Mohammed Shawky as Head of the Department of Community Medicine, when the students allotted to me were Mohammed Shawky Bazarbashi and Khalid Mohammed al Shaibani, and joining in a little later, Shams Ghandoura, all being highly competent. We were due to go into the malaria and schistosomiasis infested south-west corner of Saudi to Jizan where several other diseases are endemic, and I suggested that we study the way of life and the living conditions of some of the villagers and its relation to their diseases in some of the villages 40km away and some further at the foot of the mountains. This time we were housed in bungalows used by the engineers while they had constructed the new hospital of nearly 500 beds halfway between Jizan and Abu 'Arish. On the occasion of the visit to Qasim I was the only one of European stock in the party, but this time Dr John Simms, a Canadian from Ottawa, teaching Primary Care in the University, came along and we shared a villa and had almost exclusive use of an excellent swimming pool made by the hospital constructors. Again the approach to the investigation was the same with me making out a questionnaire and instructing the students in the approach and helping with interpretations and writing, the students asking all the questions and adding some extra ones of their own. We obtained a lot of information on hygiene, standards of living, and the relative values in life of a sample of the population.

Children were interviewed in three schools, and the teachers there, if belonging to the district. As well we went to the *souk* where I offered free consultations which attracted many who were then agreeable to be interviewed by the student members, this proving to be a highly successful combination for extracting information.

1. *Children at the ice-cream wagon beside the sweet shop. The litter on the street is characteristic of so many villages. Towns are being cleaned up.*

2. *An 'osha' type house with the school in the distance and in the foreground the vector and villain of hydatid disease.*

3. *On the same wall of branches is the source of much tuberculosis and other fevers.*

PLATE 56   339

1. *Looking down from the school at some rather scruffy nearby housing.*

2. *The village flour mill, run on diesel oil, was in the building on the right and beside it I gave free examinations to the populace whilst my students asked their questions.*

3. *Quieter questioning of the pupil's in the school by Khalid in front, and behind Shawky examined the pupils by having them lie down on three desks placed end to end.*

The Houses—The houses are almost of the same style, also the organisation of the streets and the *souk* and public buildings such as the schools, though the latter varied in structure. Many of the houses are in the form of huts *(osha)* made of wooden bases with straw roofs and plaited ropes of reeds hanging from a pole at the apex to hold down the layer beneath (see photo), while inside the walls are covered over by a mixture of soil and cow dung, which dries hard, making the shape of the ceiling inside the same as the outside. From the apex of the domed roofs of many of the huts where formerly there projected the attractive finishing touch of a thin pole there now sprouted TV aerials, while TV sets stand in the doorways of various of the huts or can be seen inside through the open door with the housewife enjoying the programmes as she does her duties outdoors.

Living conditions and their effect on health—We studied the number of persons living in one room and it is clear that crowding is a feature of their lives and this can well play a part in the transmission of infection. In addition, the houses are very small and most of them full of flies and often dirty, and the flies can be seen settling on the eyes and mouths of the infants and little children.

In larger families the huts are divided into two parts by a curtain and some more prosperous families build one or two rooms beside the hut. The floors are not cemented, which adds to their general state of dirt. In the hot weather the father and sons sleep outside in the open while the rest of the family sleep inside. Sleeping in the open would result in greater exposure to mosquito bites with its dangers. An idea of the degree of crowding in these houses can be gleaned from tables we made showing 40% had four, five or six persons in a room, while 9% had eight or nine to a room.

With inadequate washing facilities and no good clean toilets, it is common for the people to micturate and defaecate in the open, near casual water, which adds to the high incidence of flies about their faces. There were no windows, and the doors, usually two to a hut, had no mosquito netting and were kept open all the time with more flies and mosquitos inside than out in some houses.

The nutritional state of the villagers—The people, especially the young ones, have a characteristic build, many being thin and short, which we thought at first was entirely due to malnutrition, but as teenage comes on they put on weight, and then the majority seemed to be well enough covered and moderately healthy.

The nutritional state was studied in thirty children aged ten to fifteen randomly sent to us from the classes at schools, and a further study was made in two older age groups, one in adults fifteen to forty, and the other above forty. In those aged ten to fifteen more than half were thin, some markedly so and to study this apparently poor state of physique we investigated the type of food, their work and the amount of exercise of each group.

The daily diet of the older age group, those over forty, is a little different again, the older having first pick it would appear, and might help to explain the difference in the contour between the old and the younger groups.

There appears to be a definite deficiency for many of the children in meat, milk, cheese, vegetables and fruit, which may be partly responsible for the slim build of many, and this is aggravated by the chronic infections which are prevalent in many of them in this area. Their immunity against infection might well be better if their diets were not deficient.

With regard to the second group—young adult to middle age—there appear to be deficiencies in eggs, vegetables and fruit.

Milk is consumed more by the older people than the young, an unexpected finding. Besides the three main meals a day, eating between meals is a bad habit and major problem, and contributes to the consumption of sugar-containing sweets, juice and beverages and is one of the most important causes for the rising low density lipoprotein in the blood. The introduction of these sugary beverages has contributed a lot to these bad habits, to the extent that such people take in a least one to two "Pepsis" or the equivalent every day and in the hot weather several more. Another example of this was our survey of chewing gum and sweet-eating in the villages which showed that in children of all grades about 66% eat sweets and chew gum frequently, while in the older age group only 15% chew gum and 9% eat sweets.

One school had a shop of its own just outside the gate but sold only stationery and soft drinks, mostly of a high sugar content.

An ice-cream waggon of the usual sort travels about the villages with its tinkling bell and its following of excited laughing children and sweets could be easily found in the village stores.

*The filling of leisure time—*We noticed that a lot of young boys and younger adults were just lying on a bed during the day time, and we thought that they were supposed to be engaged in some sort of work at that time. Evidently only very few of the school children help their fathers at any form of work. Games and diversions were rarely practised by the older age group in whom TV and listening to the radio were the common way of passing the time. We got the impression of their passing empty days with no work and depending on their sons to bring home the money to keep going while they lay about shunning exertion.

Football is the chief game in these communities and we found in our study that it is played by 76% of children and young adults.

The schools had an area for football within the school grounds or just outside, as well as facilities for *volley-ball* or *net-ball,* though these appeared to be less used than the football area. At one school we were told that a 45-minute session of football was given to each class each week. One small boy with a large malarial spleen, and ulcerated face and a haemoglobin of 7gm appeared to be taking part; hospital was arranged for him instead. A strong

PLATE 57

1. *Enjoying a break in lessons and amused at the foreigner in their midst. These schoolboys show a variety of features including dark African whose parents were slaves prior to 1963.*

2. *Khalid and another student with a group of schoolboys.*

3. *Shawky presenting the results of the investigation to the rest of his class in the Medical College.*

impression was the ease with which village children can find a flat area anywhere for football or other games, free of traffic and in easy reach at any time, in contrast to the lack of facilities in the towns where children must take to the streets to play games with a heavy mortality and morbidity from motor traffic.

Other games and diversions are mostly not very popular but 25% of the children played such games as *dominoes, cards* and *keram*. *Swimming* in constructed pools is not available but some of the children and young adults do make a point of swimming whenever there is flood water, which presents the problem of parasitic infestations, especially schistosomiasis. Although this could be treated by praziquantal in one dose, reinfection is highly likely if they persist in swimming in casual water. There is *some organisation into club-like groups* in the villages for playing football and for arranging matches against other villages.

Reading and *writing* is found to a restricted extent in the groups of school children and educated young adults, but even so reading has a very restricted role as the availability of a variety of subjects does not exist, and *newspapers* and *magazines* arrive in the villages two to three days late.

TV and *radio* seem to fill most of the leisure time of the women and older men. Radios run on batteries and TV sets run on generator units have been used by many for some time, but we learnt that as soon as main electricity arrives at a village the sale of TV sets proceeds rapidly.

Motor cars are now numerous in and around the villages as another sign of modernity and even more so are the many *motor cycles* seen in this region compared to other areas of Saudi Arabia, many being of the very light variety, a pointer to the adaptation of a poorer community to the modern need for longer hauls to find work and diversion. As in other parts of Saudi and much of the world these modern trends have taken over completely from the camel, horse and donkey.

Smoking habits—We were surprised by the figures we obtained and it would seem that there will likely be quite a lot of lung cancer in this district in the future.

Age groups
Over 40:   20% smoke more than ten cigarettes a day.
25-40:   24% smoke more than twenty cigarettes a day.
Another 24% smoke *shisha* where a wet tobacco with other substances is used and the smoke is filtered through water in the bottle.
15-25:   36% smoke more than ten cigarettes a day and 30% smoke *shisha.*
Under 15: 10% smoke more than three cigarettes a day and 12% use *shisha.*

This excessive use of tobacco by all age groups would seem to point to the need to provide other forms of diversion to pass the time rather than indulgence of dangerous levels of smoking.

Shamma, also known as "orange" by some of the local people, is a local mixture for chewing and sucking, and is mainly used by the older age groups, though some school children take it, and in some instances whole families, men, women and the children take it. Women use it as much as men, in general, and this will be referred to later. We first learnt about it by one of the children in one of the schools producing some and showing us how it is used. Evidently it is officially forbidden at school but is used there by a number of the children. *Shamma* is in the form of a pale powder with a faint yellowish tint consisting of tobacco and *dagdagah,* a highly abrasive material containing carbonate of lime and ash according to taste. We learnt that Dr Jamil Salem, a Dental Surgeon in Jizan Central Hospital, knew a lot about it and we paid him a visit when he told us that he knew of it both in Jizan and in Yemen where he had spent a year and where he saw many cases of carcinoma of the mouth which he attributed to *shamma.* He said that in his opinion *shamma* is the cause of carcinoma of the mouth in this southern part of the Arabian Peninsula and not *gat.* He said that he had not seen any cases of cancer where *gat* had been used over a long period, and all the patients with carcinoma of the mouth he had seen had been taking *shamma* for many years. The teeth are stained yellowish or brown with it and the crowns of the teeth are worn down by the abrasive substance, in some instances almost flat, and at the same time the teeth frequently show marked periodontitis and may be loosened and may come out spontaneously. The carcinomas occur characteristically in the fold between the cheek and the gum, where the *shamma* is stored in the mouth and sucked, but when first taken it is chewed and during this time the teeth are damaged and during the storage period the irritants are responsible for the production of carcinoma. In edentulous patients the *shamma* is stored between the tongue and the gum in the front of the mouth and this is where the carcinomas occur in these patients.

The contrast in numbers between cancer of the mouth and all the rest in Jizan is marked, with twenty-two in the mouth alone. The exact composition of the constituents of *shamma* is being investigated in the Faculty of Pharmacy in view of its carcinogenic properties and its destructive action on teeth. Dr Salem also made available to us the details of the age, sex, and site of lesions in his patients. They are the basis of his thesis:

There is a sex ratio of twelve female to ten male, ages ranging from thirty-eight to eighty with an average of fifty-two, and fifteen of the lesions on the left where most of them prefer to chew it on the left side and three on the right with four unstated. Dr Salem told us that in his opinion the floor of the mouth is affected only when some of the teeth are deficient.

From our questioning it would appear that *shamma* is used much more in the older age groups (35%) while only 3% of the school children and young adults admitted to using it, but as the school authorities prohibit it, it is very difficult to get an accurate figure.

In a monograph by Drs Zahran, Jamjoom and Eed at the King Abdul Aziz University in Jeddah, on "Surgery of Advanced Cancer in Head and Neck" they say that *gat* and *shamma* are predisposing factors to cancer of mouth, and that *gat* is more dangerous than *shamma*. But we believe that *shamma* may be the predisposing factor and not *gat*.

Also in that research they reached the conclusion that males are affected more than females contrary to Dr Salem's findings.

Gat, a leaf from a tree in Yemen, which produces euphoria and fantasies, especially sexual ones, is prohibited by the Saudi Government, with severe penalties for those traffickers discovered, but it is well known to be brought across the border and from general talk it would appear to be about in some quantity. However, it is impossible to get people to admit to using it and we obtained no figures about this problem. *Gat* stains the mouth greenish and also causes flabbiness of the buccinator muscle due to the big wads of the leaves they store in the buccal vestibule. Dr Salem was definite in his opinion that *shamma* is a carcinogen but that *gat* is not and said that during his dental practice for a year in Yemen where *gat* is extensively used and is not forbidden by law, he saw no cases of carcinoma of the mouth in patients using *gat* alone but where *shamma* was used alone he saw several cases of buccal carcinoma.

Conclusions and Recommendation—The houses should be replaced by modern structures with air-conditioning, insect-proof netting, and good washing and toilet systems. The authorities have already in action various units, one of which we saw, for spraying the breeding grounds of mosquitoes around the areas should be drained. As has been seen in the cities, when good facilities for pleasant hygienic living are provided the people soon learn to use them and are glad of them.

Nutrition—In spite of the presence of motor cars, motor cycles and sprouting TV aerials there is clearly much poverty about. Fruit and vegetables do not reach the villages regularly. The staple diet is rice and bread, with small additions, and an increase of proteins and fat would help them a lot, especially as many of them are living in symbiosis, feeding as well as themselves the organisms of malaria, schistosomiasis and tuberculosis. They need help with better supplies of meat, fish as well as fresh vegetables and fruit.

The filling of leisure time—For older men and women conversation used to be the principal way of passing the time, but like much of the rest of the world, first *radio* and now *TV* have come to fill many of their hours. There is no doubt about the people's own priority about TV for they will often buy a set before, or instead of, other important and useful electrical goods such as refrigerators and washing machines, and with such priority given to TV and radio there appears to be much leisure time to fill and clearly they bring enjoyment and interest to their otherwise rather dull lives.

Sport for the young is mainly *football* with an official game in school hours once a week, and the larger villages having a flat area for a football ground, but in the smaller villages any site will do.

As the only places for *swimming* in many of the rural areas are casual water and temporary streams, the dangers of schistosomiasis is increased, so the young men of the small towns and surrounding villages would be greatly helped by *providing proper swimming pools* with filtration processes, in a land where heat and sunshine make bathing and swimming most attractive pastimes. In the towns, thousands of private pools are in use but the poor of both towns and countryside have no such facilities, with occasional exceptions, and proper pools for both would be excellent for health and pleasure.

Gat and Shamma—Though *gat*, the leaf of a plant, is forbidden in Saudi Arabia on account of its stimulant properties, *shamma* is freely available. With the finding of its carcinogenic properties known for the mouth, and possible dangerous effects from absorption to other parts of the body from its high tobacco content, its use should be fully examined. Perhaps *shamma* is more dangerous than *gat* and such a possibility should be looked into widely. Perhaps the ancient chewing gum of Yemen, *liban bikhur,* or even the Western variety, favourite to Americans, might be encouraged as much safer. If villagers knew of the dangers from chewing *shamma* they might well abandon it for the other varieties, and here, education by radio and TV might help.

Smoking—Our analysis clearly shows that cigarette smoking levels are high in the villages, with a quarter of the twenty-five to forty age group smoking more than twenty cigarettes a day, a level known to be productive of carcinoma of the lung, and with 10% of those aged under fifteen already smoking more than three cigarettes a day and others using *shisha*, the smoking habit is being ingrained early. The problem and its solution is world wide and calls for no further comment here.

Sickle-Cells and Saudi Lady Students in the Hasa

The third expedition in which I joined was in the winter of 1982, this time with the lady students, when my duty was not to make a separate study with one or two students, but to help as a general supervisor, my white hair being considered appropriate for the duties of chaperone, while at the same time supervising the girls' work and advising on any medical matters beyond their experience (and mine also at times). This I believe, is the first occasion on which a British-New Zealand "Caucasian" variety of non-Muslim has taken part in such work with Saudi ladies; and it is more appropriate that I report on the general activities of the group and the medical investigations as a whole.

The venue for study was some villages around al Hofuf which is the town on the inland side of the oilfields, being much used by Americans in their early searches for oil and for surveys of the whole eastern region, and is still an important centre. At one time, it was the capital of the Hasa, the eastern province, having now grown to a population of 150,000 to 200,000 with many satellite villages around it. Large numbers of the men both in the town and in the surrounding villages make the daily or weekly trip of 160 kilometres to Dhahran or Damman for some duty in the oil industry. al Hofuf lies in the midst of a large oasis with abundant water—to breed the mosquitoes of malaria.

The hospital has 500 beds, being one of five of similar build in various Saudi cities, but with only about 400 of its beds occupied, we were all lodged in the spare rooms, the lady students in a separate group. We all had a room each and a bed and metal wardrobe but that was all, there were no curtains but as the weather was warm, even though this was the heart of winter, I used my blanket to cover the window at night and a sheet only for myself.

The Medical School in Riyadh had sent over, as always in these expeditions, a very large truck complete with mattresses, bedding, and all the medical apparatus and equipment for the various tests that would be done on the unsuspecting locals. In consequence, there were numbers of drivers, not only of the truck but also for the cars, and a large bus to take the girls and staff each day to the various villages. I usually spent a little time with the drivers and part of that evening sat amongst them as we watched the television, drinking rounds of tea and Arabic coffee, and talking away while they took photos of each other, a popular hobby these days.

The next day, Friday, and so the equivalent of our Sunday, I spent in the morning looking at the hospital, which was identical with the one we had seen in Jizan the year before, and talked with numbers of the staff, almost all

1. *Entering the caves at al Hofuf, the Saudi lady students in their 'shailas', the black overall outer garment.*

2. *Taking coffee in the evening with the drivers, a strain on my feeble Arabic as they had no English. The characteristic small cups for the 'white' Arabian coffee are seen, and the feet with the soles turned in.*

the nurses and more than half the doctors being Chinese from Taiwan. The medical administration was interesting; too many Saudi doctors have to sacrifice a measure of their clinical skill and time to run the hospitals and here I found that the medical administrator was only two years out of medical school but clearly doing a good job, in spite of difficulties from his inexperience. He was an Arab, a graduate of Damascus, originating from the Hadramaut in Yemen, a good looking, moustached young man wearing European clothing and a tie. The Saudi lay administrator of the hospital, Ibrahim, was a good example of what is needed in Saudi for this purpose, having a BSc in biology and chemistry then spending four years in Georgia, USA, getting a degree in hospital administration. He had worked for two years at the Shameisi Hospital in Riyadh, being responsible for various improvements there. Such capable and well-trained men are invaluable in sparing the medically qualified from administrative work. There was a splendid view from the roof of the hospital of the whole of the Hofuf region which from time immemorial has been a wet part of Saudi, the reason for the city developing over this large palm-covered area.

One of the obstetricians and gynaecologists from the Medical Faculty in Riyadh, Dr Abdul Rahman Mishari, a native of al Hofuf, came to join the expedition to act as host, and did much to arrange entertainment for the whole party. Late that morning students and staff went off in the bus and cars a few kilometres to the famous caves of Hofuf, which are cracks in the limestone hills leading to caverns, much used at one time by the people of Hofuf in the heat of the summer, being always moderately cool within. There was a good deal of photography, care being taken to avoid any direct pictures of the Saudi ladies' faces.

We went on thence to the farm of one of Dr Mishari's brothers, one of the old type Arab farms of palm trees with *alfalfa* (lucerne) growing between them; also there were small fields of lemon trees, and in amongst them all the irrigation channels, V-shaped and mostly of concrete, for which this district is famous. All about this region can be seen very large channels—big enough to be called streams—with walls of concrete elevated above the surface of the ground and from them are distributed the smaller channels in all directions. This farm was not meant to be highly productive but was for pleasure and to keep an interest in the land. In one walled compound were twelve cows and a bull and, for fun, Dr Mishari pulled off his red head-cloth and started waving it at the bull, but Arab bulls seem to be much the same as others and started to perform in traditional fashion with much pawing of the ground, enraged looks and bellowing, and we thought it better to clear off before medical attention was called for the medicals.

Lunch was the traditional mutton and rice *(capsa)*, followed by fruit, in carpeted tents pitched on the farm land, but we were soon driven off the territory by a plague of flies due to the recent dunging of the whole area.

Although men and women doctors mix freely with the lady students in our duties as teachers, here were other men about, drivers and farm workers, and so all the ladies had their lunch separately, and as well they were given the use of the swimming bath, the chuff chuff of its pump sounding very pleasant on this fine afternoon; the water of this district all comes up rather warm so heating arrangements are not necessary. In the ordinary way all the activities of the ladies are ignored—no questions are asked—but a little Egyptian boy who was allowed to bathe with them as a youngster said that one of the girls had fallen in with her clothes on, smiles amongst the Saudis present being permitted.

The next day we went off to a village where the girls were working in a school on their different tasks and were already accustomed to their duties, a certain amount of rotation of their duties being made for their experience. I joined them in the school, whether as the first non-Muslim male entering such a girls' school I do not know, perhaps so, but no one seemed to mind. The schoolgirls were ever the same—dashing about, lots of interest in everything, eyes peeping round every corner, then screaming as they dashed away. I watched first of all the eye testing; they were all excellent patients, taking instructions well and behaving sensibly, being examined first for general eyesight, and I was told by the eye specialist Dr Shahazad, that in too many of them it was not as good as it should be.

All of them, without exception, had trachoma in varying degrees—mainly slight, and on top of the trachoma comes, in some, a secondary infection with fiercer organisms; there is no question but that all these children should be treated regularly with eye drops to keep the trachoma at bay or there will be, inevitably, a certain amount of blindness resulting from it. Their heights, weights and size of heads were measured and a body check made on a mattress on the floor. On the whole, in this particular school, they were well-nourished but a little dirty in appearance in contrast to a later school where the parents were more prosperous and the children better dressed and cared for.

I wandered over to the dispensary where I saw the action for a little while, the Egyptian doctor there saying that he saw upwards of 100 to 200 patients a day—some of them, of course, come just for repeated medicines, some for consultations, very brief, for he had little time to examine many of them in detail, and if there was anything he felt needed serious treatment it meant a letter to the hospital—seemingly very much like the British National Health Service.

In all the schools and health centres students were taking blood for the investigation, particularly, of sickle-cell anaemia or the sickle-cell trait. Preliminary examinations were being made by the haematologist in the party, but other tests were on blood sent to Riyadh.

Sickle-cell anaemia is an interesting form of blood disease and much about it is still debatable. It occurs in areas where there is, or has been, malaria for generations. The particular defect of the blood can, rarely, occur in any country, but malaria causes a concentration of population with this particular trait. It is thought to come about this way. There is not just one type of haemoglobin; there are many types, and there are two similar diseases that affect the haemoglobin inside the red cells of the blood. One is the sickle-cell trait, and anaemia may be associated with it, where the haemoglobins are said to be abnormal, and another variety called thalassaemia where the haemoglobins are joined up wrongly—it is a subtle difference for the experts, but that is the gist of it. The normal red cell has the shape of a solid wheel indented (concave) on both sides, and in various blood diseases it takes on all sorts of curious shapes. In sickle-cell anaemia the abnormal haemoglobins concentrate and cause the cell to shrivel into various shapes some of them being like a sickle—hence the name.

Its relation to malaria is this, that in the ordinary way when the mosquito bites it squirts the plasmodium (organism causing malaria) into the bloodstream which then enters the red cells. Different varieties of plasmodium cause a disruption of the red cells at varying times thus liberating the haemoglobin which in turn causes the fever, perhaps daily or every other day. In people who have the abnormal concentrated haemoglobins the plasmodium cannot penetrate the red cells and so these people tend to survive better in malarial infested districts, but the concentrated haemoglobin does not carry oxygen so well putting these people at risk if they suffer any oxygen lack even for a very short time as in operations under general anaesthesia, in shock from accidents and in some illnesses. They may also become anaemic and develop pains in the abdomen and bones and the head, and have other features from abnormal clotting, but on the whole they survived malaria just that much better in malarial districts over the centuries, and so where malaria exists or once existed populations show sickle-cell features (trait) of the blood, but only a restricted number will be anaemic or have other symptoms. But those with the trait are in danger in the conditions explained above.

As well as testing their blood, their physical features were assessed such as height, weight, size of head, using a tape around it, and the shape of the head is noted, for in sickle-cell subjects the forehead often bulges forward in a big curve.

During the mornings two or three of the students at a time would knock at the doors of the houses, only the wife and children being home, explaining the health purpose of the visit, and being admitted to the house where they would quickly assess the surroundings—how many fridges, or TV sets, and the general condition. In this climate all had fridges, some of them two, and all seemed to have television no matter what the state of the rest of the house. After questioning the mother about the living conditions and the family health, they would lead her and the children to the health centre where the weighing and measuring and blood taking was done. The next day if they tried another lot of houses in the same village they would often find that the doors would be slammed in their faces—a new experience for these girls—as the mothers did not want their children pricked and bled.

During the activities in the health centres a little before noon small boys, released from school, usually carrying on their backs school bags half as big as themselves, would come wandering over to see what was going on; first poking their heads round the doors, then getting bolder and coming right in and standing in the midst of the activity with eyes of wonderment, and, when shooed away by one of the male servants, would appear at another door, eyes and nose first then gradually creeping in until shooed away again, and so the process went on until they started to feel it was time for their lunch and disappeared.

It was decided to take blood from some of the boys to get a balance of results and Dr al Aska and I had made arrangements with one school about this and when returning the next day, we were giving a lift to one of the Saudi girl students, having in the car as well one of the lady doctors helping us with the investigations. In the end we decided to take the girl student with us as an extra pair of hands to complete the job. Samira, the Saudi girl, went in and seemed to be well enough received, the only objections being from one large boy—perhaps twelve or thirteen—who was rather rude to her, saying he was not going to be examined by a young woman. Shortly afterwards while he was having blood taken he went down in a faint being the only to do so, and he was out for a little while; the masters were rather concerned, but he soon came round and was a little less proud from then on.

I noticed that several masters came along to ask me about their complaints and to have their urine tested to see if there was any sugar present, which task I was allotted, but I also noticed that they cast frequent glances at the pretty Saudi lady who was working with us.

That evening, after supper, we all assembled to be told the arrangements for the next day, when we were to leave later in the afternoon; a visit had been arranged by Dr Mishari through another friend of his, to a small farm and garden with a swimming pool. There was great argument with the girls—some of them said they did not want to go at all and others said they wanted the morning to pack and tidy up. I think one hour would have served very well for those purposes, and their supervisor said: "What you really want is to sleep in as it is the weekend, is not that it?" The boys and girls are all adept at sleeping. They did not want to go shopping, they had bought their presents for home and they did not want to go to the swimming pool. In the end practically all of them did go to the pool the following day.

That night, at a meeting reviewing the activities, the girls were asked for their opinion about the trip and a colossal row broke out between two of the medical staff—a man and a woman. They went at it ding-dong in front of all the girls, who were rather upset by it. Fists were shaken in faces in a real confrontation—I thought there might even be blows and tried to calm things down, but short of pushing them away had not much hope of cooling it. It faded out with long distance shots from the door. The girls had drifted off upset. We went back to our rooms and half an hour later I went along to the room where the supplies were kept and here were the two Arabs, not Saudis, still at it, and how long they continued that night I do not know—I had had enough and crept away to bed.

The little farm we went to next day was very attractive, with palm trees that were well cared for; greens of all sorts grew between them, and then some of the ordinary types of vegetables—onions, lettuce, cabbage, cauliflower, and tomatoes, were all growing very well. The girls went through into the house and then to the swimming pool, the walls of which were some ten yards away from us, and there we sat about outside drinking Arabian coffee, then tea—the owner and his two sons who had very kindly come, the five drivers and one or two doctors. The girls had gone into the house past us, pulling their veils close to their faces, and before long there were shrieks of delight from the bath-house, which was beside us, and all the time in the Saudi way, we took no notice whatsoever of what the women were doing; no comments of any sort were made about this and then, a little later when they had dried off and gone through to the sitting-room, handclapping in unison started up, but again no notice of any of this was taken. We ate many dates, the flies being tiresome, attracted by the many date stones lying about. The chuff chuff of the pumps went on; the girls came out and passed by us to their bus and then we happened to notice that they were now in the bus, and it was time for all of us to go our ways.

The group of girls were more or less what one might expect of any group of thirty or forty; some of them had the average normal responses; three or four were rather sophisticated and had travelled a lot and would not sit with the others, as either they found them such bad company or they could not tolerate some of their attitudes; on the other hand three or four were very religious, remained veiled all the time and were called by one of the non-Saudi staff "the robbers" as they wore facepieces—just the eyes showing.

Everyone gathered their belongings and we gradually made our way to the airport. I was nearly the last to enter the plane and it was pleasing to see all the girls sitting on one side—scarcely one veiled as they had been in the airport, smiling and excited, ready for home to tell their parents about the great adventures they had had in the past fortnight.

As I left the aircraft in Riyadh, a cultured young Saudi had noticed that I had spoken to some of the girls as I passed out of the aircraft and he said to me "Saudi ladies are very beautiful?" I told him I thought very much so, and felt at the same time it was better to explain to him how it was that they were unveiled and how I came to be speaking with them, for one does not in the ordinary way speak to a Saudi lady at all in such circumstances. They collected their bags and went on their way having been met or taken by car to their homes or hostel. For me it had been something quite out of the ordinary and rather delightful and I will never experience the like again.

BIBLIOGRAPHY

ADLINGTON, RICHARD, Lawrence of Arabia. Collins, London, 1955.

ARMSTRONG, H. C., Lord of Arabia. Arthur Barker, London, 1934.

BIDWELL, ROBIN, Travellers in Arabia. Hamlyn Group Ltd., London, 1976.

BOYCE, R., The Story of Islam. Religious Educational Press, Oxford, 1975.

BULLARD, SIR READER, Britain and the Middle East. Hutchinson's, London, 1951.

CAMPBELL, D., Arabian Medicine and its Influence in the Middle Ages. Kegan Paul, Trench, Trubier & Co., London, 1926.

DAWOOD, N. J., Translation of the Koran. Penguin Books, London, 1974. (Used for the quotations from the Koran.)

de GAURY, GERALD, Feisal: King of Saudi Arabia. Arthur Barker, London 1966.

DOUGHTY, CHARLES M., Travels in Arabia Deserta. Cambridge University Press, 1888.

ENCYCLOPEDIA AMERICANA, Concerning the number seven, p.609. Americana Corporation, New York, 1971.

GARNET, DAVID, The Essential T. E. Lawrence. J. Cape, London, 1951.
The Letters of T. E. Lawrence. J. Cape, London, 1938.

HOLDEN, D. & JOHNS R., The House of Saud. Sidgwick and Jackson, London, 1981.

HOWARTH, DAVID, The Desert King, a Life of Ibn Saud. W. Collins, London, 1964.

KAY, SHIRLEY, Travels in Saudi Arabia. R. Ingrams editor, S.A. Nat. Hist. Soc., 1979.

KIRK, G. E., A Short History of the Middle East. Methuen & Co., London, 1948.

LACEY, ROBERT, The Kingdom. Hutchinson & Co. Ltd., London, 1981.

LACKNER, HELEN, A House Built on Sand. Ithaca Press, London, 1978.

LAQUER, WALTER, Confrontation. Abacus, London, 1974.

LAWRENCE, A. W. (Ed.), T. E. Lawrence and his Friends, J. Cape, London, 1954.

LAWRENCE, T. E., Seven Pillars of Wisdom: A Triumph. J. Cape, London, 1935.
Some original letters in Jesus College, Oxford.
LESLIE, SHANE, Marks Sykes; His Life and Letters. Cassel & Co., London, 1923.
LUKE, SIR HARRY, Ceremonies at Holy Places. Faith Press, London 1972.
MONTGOMERY, HUGH, Solitary in the Ranks. Constable, London, 1977.
MORLEY, S., A Talent to Amuse. Heinemann, London, 1969.
MORTON, H. V., In the Steps of the Master. R. Cowan Ltd., London, 1934.
NEWMAN, E. W. P., The Middle East. Geoffrey Bles, London, 1926.
NIEBUR, CARSTEN, Travels Through Arabia. Copenhagen, 1772.
          English Translation published T. Vernon, London.
NUTTING, A., Lawrence of Arabia, The Man and the Motive. Hollis and Carter, 1961.
PHILBY, H. ST.B., Arabian Days. Robert Hale, London, 1948.
PUGH, W. A., Riyadh, History and Guide. Publ. by author, 1969.
SHAW, T. E., (Translation), The Odyssey of Homer. Oxford University Press, N.Y., 1940.
SEBAI, Z. A. Ed. Community Health in Saudi Arabia. University of Riyadh, 1982.
STEGNER, W., Discovery. MEP Library of Congress Cat. No. 74 148026.
STORRS, SIR RONALD, Orientations. Nicholson and Watson, London (def. ed.), 1943.
THESIGER, WILFRED, Arabian Sands. Longmans, London, 1959.
THOMAS, LOWELL, With Lawrence in Arabia. Hutchinson & Co., London, 1959.
WINSTONE, H. W. F., Captain Shakespear: A Portrait. J. Cape, London, 1976.

The information about the siege of the Grand Mosque in Mecca comes entirely from the reports in one of the two excellent Saudi newspapers printed in English, the *Arab News,* from the first reports on 30th November, 1979, until the details given before and after the executions on 10th and 11th January, 1980.

Index

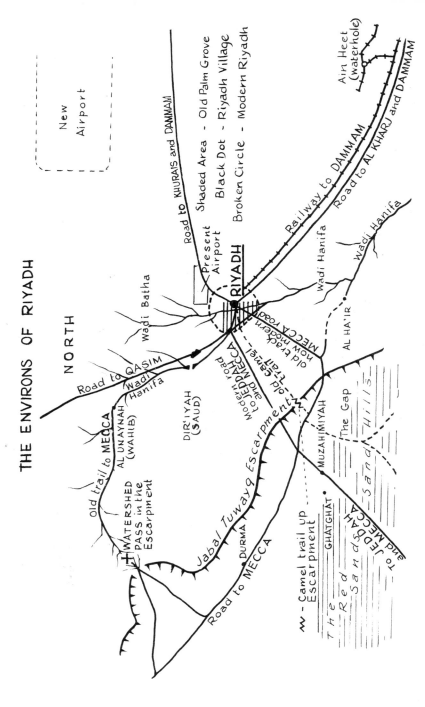

THE ENVIRONS OF RIYADH

NORTH

New Airport

Road to KHURAIS and DAMMAM

Shaded Area - Old Palm Grove
Black Dot - Riyadh Village
Broken Circle - Modern Riyadh

Present Airport

RIYADH

Wadi Batha

Railway to DAMMAM

Road to AL KHARJ and DAMMAM

Ain Heet (waterhole)

Wadi Hanifa

Wadi Hanifa

Road to QASIM

Wadi Hanifa

old track now modern MECCA road

camel and train

Wadi Hanifa

AL HA'IR

DIR'IYAH (SAUD)

DAMMECCA
modern road to MECCA

Old trail to MECCA

AL UNAYNAH (WAHIB)

WATERSHED PASS in the Escarpment

Jabal Tuwayg Escarpment

MUZAHIMIYAH

The Gap

Red Sand Hills

Road to MECCA

DURMA

Camel trail up Escarpment

GHATGHAT

to JEDDA HAJC and MECCA

The Red Sandsea

~ - Camel trail up Escarpment